In this book Hanna Scolnicov examines space as an icon of the problem of woman. Through her historical and comparative study, Scolnicov reveals the changing conventions of the theatrical space as faithful expressions of the changing attitudes to woman and her sexuality. The theatrical space has shifted accordingly from the front of the palace, to the street, the piazza, and then, progressively, into the drawing-room, the kitchen, the bedroom, narrowing down the scope and infringing on the privacy of intimate relations. Some contemporary playwrights have gone further, deconstructing the familiar naturalistic room to form a non-mimetic interior. From this unusual vantage point, Scolnicov looks at plays by a wide range of authors, including, among others, Aeschylus, Aristophanes, Plautus, Shakespeare, Jonson, Molière, Ibsen, Chekhov and Pinter, relating them to contemporary pictorial and architectural evidence.

The book will be of interest to scholars and students of theatre and theatre history, comparative literature and women's studies.

# Woman's theatrical space

# Woman's theatrical space

HANNA SCOLNICOV

CAMBRIDGE
UNIVERSITY PRESS

PUBLISHED BY THE PRESS SYNDICATE OF THE UNIVERSITY OF CAMBRIDGE
The Pitt Building, Trumpington Street, Cambridge, United Kingdom

CAMBRIDGE UNIVERSITY PRESS
The Edinburgh Building, Cambridge CB2 2RU, UK
40 West 20th Street, New York NY 10011–4211, USA
477 Williamstown Road, Port Melbourne, VIC 3207, Australia
Ruiz de Alarcón 13, 28014 Madrid, Spain
Dock House, The Waterfront, Cape Town 8001, South Africa

http://www.cambridge.org

First published 1994
First paperback edition 2004

*A catalogue record for this book is available from the British Library*

*Library of Congress cataloguing in publication data*

Scolnicov, Hanna. Woman's Theatrical Space
Hanna Scolnicov.
p. cm.
Includes bibliographical references and index.
ISBN 0 521 39467 8 (hardback)
1. Women in the theater. 2. Theater – Stage-setting and scenery.
3. Space and time in literature. 4. Sex role in literature.
5. European drama – History and criticism. I. Title.
PN1590.W64S36 1994
792'.082 – dc20 93-29417 CIP

ISBN 0 521 39467 8 hardback
ISBN 0 521 61608 5 paperback

To my best friend, Shmuel

Allegories are things that Relate to Moral Virtues. Moral Virtues do not Exist; they are Allegories & dissimulations. But Time & Space are Real Beings, a Male & a Female. Time is a Man, Space is a Woman, and her Masculine Portion is Death.

William Blake, 'The Vision of the Last Judgment'

# Contents

# Illustrations

# Preface

This book grew out of a paper, 'Theatre space, theatrical space and the theatrical space without', presented at the 1985 London conference on the theatrical space and published in *Themes in Drama* 9: *The Theatrical Space* (Cambridge University Press, 1987). To James Redmond, organizer of the conference and editor of the series, must go my first thanks for his generosity, encouragement and interest.

That paper was the original nucleus of the book, and in it I attempted to make some basic distinctions and coin some terms necessary for the discussion of spatial structure in the theatre. Also, I tried to convey my excitement about finding an alternative, and to my mind powerful, approach to the analysis of drama, replacing the traditional analyses in terms of plot, character, theme and so on.

As the idea took shape, I discovered that the analysis of the theatrical space reveals not only the general ideology of the play, but, more specifically, its attitude to the place of woman in society. It suddenly became evident that woman is so closely associated with space that almost any articulation of space on stage or in the play is directly expressive of her position, her life style, her personality. In other words, I did not start my investigation from a feminist position: that position was forced on me by my material.

Looking at familiar plays from a woman's point of view made my work on the book simultaneously a voyage into myself, an examination of my own place as a woman in family, home and society at large. In this sense, although this book is devoted to masterpieces of dramatic art, it is also a very personal book.

My greatest debt is obviously to the members of my family, my three children who have, in their different ways, taken an active interest in the development of my book, and above all my husband, who supported my work from first to last and, in the process, became something of a feminist himself.

Many friends and colleagues made my 1988/9 sabbatical year in Cambridge a fruitful and enjoyable experience. Foremost is Peter Holland whose good advice and kindness helped me through many a difficult moment. Clare Hall provided the warm atmosphere and the intellectual stimulation necessary for developing one's ideas. With my friends there, chiefly Barbara and Bill Rosen, Sanae Asahara, Philip King and Tom Lundskaer-Nielsen, I discussed different aspects of the work, always receiving honest and constructive criticism.

Chapter 5 is based on a paper, 'The woman in the window: A theatrical icon', written for the 22nd International Conference at the Centre d'Études Supérieures de la Renaissance in Tours and published in *Spectacle & Image*, ed. by André Lascombes (Leiden, E. J. Brill, 1993). My thanks to André Lascombes, who also organized the conference, for permission to use material from the paper. Jean Chothia, of the Department of English at Cambridge, offered helpful criticism and suggestions.

Sarah Stanton, of Cambridge University Press, deserves a special word of thanks for seeing through and encouraging this project from its beginning with unfailing patience and optimism. I acknowledge with gratitude the thoughtful comments of the anonymous Reader. Victoria Cooper saw this work through the press at its last and exhausting stages.

Last but not least, I am indebted to my students in Israel, at The Hebrew University of Jerusalem and at Tel-Aviv University, on whom I have tried out many of my interpretations. From my work with them, I became convinced that the analysis of the theatrical space is a readily understood and easily applicable technique.

I am grateful to the following for their kind permission to reproduce objects from their collections: William Francis Warden Fund, Courtesy of the Museum of Fine Arts, Boston (Figs. 1a, 1b); The Trustees of the British Museum (Figs. 2, 3, 4, 6, 9, 11); The Blacker-Wood Library, McGill University, Montréal (Fig. 13); Drottningholms teatermuseum, Stockholm (Fig. 14); Munch-museet, Oslo (Fig. 18). Fig. 8 is reproduced by permission of the Musei Vaticani; Fig. 17 is reproduced by permission of the Universitetsbiblioteket, Oslo.

## Chapter 1

# Woman's theatrical space

The momentous move from the outdoor theatre of classical times to the indoor auditorium in the Renaissance and after has been echoed by the evolution of the theatrical space. The scene has shifted from the open air, the front of the palace, the street, the piazza, into the state-room, the parlor, the kitchen, the bedroom, narrowing down the scope and infringing on the privacy of intimate relations. Some contemporary playwrights have gone further, deconstructing the familiar naturalistic room to form a non-mimetic interior or abstracting space altogether. This book is an interpretation of both the perceptual and conceptual configurations of the theatrical space as defined by the play and executed on stage in performance.

Seen from a feminist point of view, the articulation of the theatrical space is an expression of woman's position in society. Her relative confinement in traditional societies to the seclusion of her home puts the onus of the action on the man, thus making him into an active agent of time, and her into an element of space. The Odysseus story is archetypal: while Penelope waits at home, freezing time by unraveling each day's work, Odysseus wends his way home, moving from one adventure to the next. The central thesis of this book is that the changing spatial conventions of the theatre are faithful expressions of the growing awareness of the specificity of gender differences and the changing attitudes to woman and her sexuality.

My discussion is limited to those plays and theatrical traditions in which the question of woman is paramount. I shall be tracing one particular line of development from classical to Renaissance theatre, and from there to naturalistic and modern drama. The medieval theatre represents an exemplary 'alternative' tradition, meriting a separate, extensive treatment of its multifarious forms and genres. The absence of the theatre building in the Middle Ages highlights the problematic relationship between the space of the theatre and everyday space. There has been some excellent research into this specialized topic both in English and French, most notably perhaps by Elie Konigson.[1] For these reasons, there will be here no separate treatment of the medieval theatre.

Replacing traditional analyses in terms of plot and character, the investigation of the theatrical space leads directly to an understanding of the particular philosophical framework and *Weltanschauung* expressed by the play. In order to analyze plays from this uncommon angle (rather than track the causality of the chain of events or psychologize the characters), it is necessary to make a few basic distinctions and develop an appropriate terminology.

The first distinction is that between *theatre space* and *the theatrical space*. Theatre space is an architectural concept. The given theatre space is the shell or the hulk within which each performance creates its own theatrical space. The performance may take advantage of an existing space such as a hillside or a public square; or make use of a converted building such as a church or a hangar; or take place in a specialized architectural space such as an open-air theatre or a closed auditorium. All these are fixed spaces, the dimensions and parts of which have been predetermined by the chosen site of the production or by an architect.

Unlike the theatre space, the theatrical space is created anew by every production. Every performance defines its own boundaries in relation to its own space–time structure. It is only within these circumscribed limits that its inner logic can function. These boundaries are set up by each production within a given theatre space. The theatrical space is an autonomous space which does not have to submit to natural laws. Liberated from the universal co-ordinates, the theatrical space stands apart from the everyday space that surrounds it and in which the spectators and even the architectural space of the theatre itself belong. The theatrical space is an organized space, qualitatively different from everyday space, much in the same way that the sacred space, as shown by Ernst Cassirer and Mircea Eliade, is qualitatively different and cut off from profane space.[2]

The autonomous nature of the circumscribed theatrical space is especially apparent when the magical or supernatural achieve a certain reality and naturalness within its boundaries. The medieval stage employed theatrical illusion to represent biblical miracles. Unfettered by natural time, space and causality, the plays were free to roam between Paradise, earth and Hell, the Creation of the world and the Last Judgement.

The self-conscious and even self-proclamatory shrinking of space in Shakespeare's *Henry V* is well known: the chorus asks the audience to use its imagination to traverse the Channel from England to France and to visualize the clash of two mighty armies within the 'wooden O'. In Michel de Ghelderode's *La Mort du Docteur Faust* (1925), there is a partition across the stage: on the left-hand side of the stage is a twentieth-century street, from which characters enter the right-hand side of the stage, to find themselves in Doctor Faust's sixteenth-century study.[3] In fact, it is the miraculous aspect of theatre, its freedom from physical restraints, that has traditionally been one of the sources of its special attraction. It is only in the naturalistic theatre that the theatrical space tries to fool the audience into believing that it is essentially analogous to everyday space.

The theatrical space is a composite creation of the play, *mise-en-scène*, acting, choreography, scenery, lighting, etc., as well as the given theatre space. Together, these elements form the theatrical space in which the action of the play unfolds. The play-text has a unique, privileged position in pre-determining the spatial parameters of all productions. But it must already have taken into account the other components: the theatre in which the play is to be performed for the first time or the general features of contemporary theatre buildings, their potential and their limitations, existing theatre conventions and how these may be stretched or circumvented, the available technology and acting style. In a sense, then, the play-text itself is already to a certain extent a collaborative effort reflecting the theatrical means at the disposal of the playwright. The production will fill out and enrich the spatial conception of the play, but only the performance, each particular performance, will actualize the theatrical space of the piece.

The theatrical space of a performance is organized, heightened and symbolic; it is structured rather than arbitrary, calculated to be expressive and meaningful. The economy of the work of art dictates that every element be subordinated, in some degree, to the total effect or design, and this is true even of the most random-looking naturalistic play. It is this symbolic aspect of the constructed space that creates the qualitative difference between it and the contiguous everyday space.

A further distinction, central to my whole argument, is the distinction between *the theatrical space within* and *the theatrical space without*. The theatrical space within is the space on stage within our field of vision, the space in which the actors perform in front of our eyes. Along with the visible theatrical space, the play may also define spaces which, although crucial to the plot, are to remain unseen in the actual production. These are off-stage spaces, from which the characters are supposed to enter or to which they exit. Even though such spaces are not shown on stage, events of great moment may take place in them. Any such space implied by the play but not constituting part of the spectacle, i.e. not realized on stage, I shall call a theatrical space without.

Although in stage directions a character goes 'in' when he exits the stage and comes 'out' when he enters it, it suits better the nature of my argument to call the on-stage 'within' and the off-stage 'without'. This antithetical pair of terms is useful in suggesting that the theatrical space, whether seen or unseen, forms a continuum which is quite distinct from the theatre space. The within and the without are ontologically on a par, the reality of the one depending on the reality of the other. These terms are indifferent to the specific values assigned by different plays to the on-stage and off-stage spaces. Although co-extensive with the theatrical space within and without, the on-stage and off-stage spaces carry different connotations. They refer primarily to the stage – which is not a universal feature of all theatres – and to the actual space within which the performance takes place. By contrast, the theatrical spaces within and without refer to the universe created initially by the play and realized in performance.

Theatrical spaces without may be either close at hand, as for example an adjacent room behind a door, or far-off, as an overseas country to which a character may travel. In the Greek theatre, messengers were used in order to inform the audience of events that took place in the theatrical spaces without. These messengers or attendants, as they are indifferently called in the translations, are in fact of two different types. The one was the *angelos*, the other the *exangelos*, or the messenger who told news from a distance as opposed to the messenger who brought out what was happening in the house or behind the scenes.[4] These nameless messengers are no more than dramatic functions that stress the distinction between the two types of background theatrical spaces without. A further distinction, conventionalized in the Roman theatre, was that between the two side-entrances, the one leading to the relatively close centre of town, the other to the far-off countryside or to the harbour from which the traveller arrives. These differently distanced spaces, organized relatively to each other, create a conceptual perspective that focuses the spectator's attention on the theatrical space within.

The theatrical space without is not defined in merely negative terms, as that space which is not visible on stage. Nor is it identical with the audience's everyday space. The space without is perceived as an extension and an extrapolation of the visible space. A character who leaves the stage is presumed to be going to some other theatrical space, not to the actor's dressing-room. A climactic event, such as a murder, may take place in this unseen place, and the agonized cries of the murdered man may reach the audience, thus providing an aural, if not a visual, perception of the theatrical space without.

The theatrical space without is carefully delimited by the play itself. The unseen space can be described in the dialogue or related in some other way to the visible theatrical space, e.g. through a connecting door. But the definition of the theatrical space without may also rely on the audience's general knowledge to supplement the sketchy information: the disruption of the studies of Hamlet and Horatio at Wittenberg and the return of Laertes to the University of Paris unleash cultural and theological associations pertinent to the central themes of the play.

The relation between the theatrical space within and the theatrical space without is close to, though not identical with, the similar distinction between *perceived space* and *conceived space*.[5] This set of terms is useful where a less structuralist and more phenomenological approach to the plays is required. For the audience, the theatrical space within is a perceived space, directly apprehended by the senses, mainly by sight, on stage. The theatrical space without, although no less credible, is mainly a conceived space, not seen on stage but imagined to extend beyond the limits of the perceived space. The reality of the conceived space is assured by some sort of continuity of action with the perceived space, such as entrances and exits, and references to events outside or to the travelling of characters between the two spaces. But the two distinctions are not totally overlapping: a theatrical space without, though not seen, may also be perceived, as when sounds issuing from that space give it immediate reality or even define it further by moving across it.

Roughly analogous categories are suggested by Michael Issacharoff, who distinguishes between architectural, scenographic and dramatic spaces, and then between what is shown and what is not shown to the public, i.e. the scenic and the extra-scenic, or the visible and the invisible spaces.[6] His architectural and scenographic spaces parallel what I prefer to call theatre space and theatrical space, whereas the dramatic space is similar to what I see as the parameters of the theatrical space predetermined by the play. In general, Issacharoff seems to me to compartmentalize the spaces created by the building, by the scenography and by the play, while the terminology I use emphasizes the interpenetration and mutual influence of the disparate elements that combine to create the particular composite space of the performance.

Issacharoff's semiotic approach leads him to differentiate further between mimetic and diegetic spaces. The first is transmitted without mediation, the second is mediated by the dialogue.[7] On the face of it, this distinction is parallel to my own between the theatrical space within and the theatrical space without. The theatrical space within is directly perceived on stage, whereas the theatrical space without is, in the typical case, verbally referred to in the dialogue. But Issacharoff's distinction involves him in the problem of what he himself sees as an intermediary case: that of a character on stage speaking of the perceptible, referring to the setting, the furniture or the props. It would seem that here the on-stage space is at once both mimetic and diegetic. These terms are thus unhelpful in making the central distinction between the visible and the non-visible theatrical spaces, between the space realized on stage and that imagined as extending off-stage.

The antithesis between mimetic and diegetic is the theatrical equivalent of the narratological dichotomy between telling and showing.[8] But the perception of what is being shown on stage, in the theatrical space within, is sensuous and direct also when bolstered with words. Even in the absence of a visible setting, when the characters point at or refer to non-existent objects on stage, the theatrical effect is to conjure up those elements or the positions they are supposed to occupy, so that their relative placing creates a continuous, perceived space. The phenomenological approach that views the theatrical experience as a totality which is created through the interplay of word, gesture, choreography, scenery, lighting, etc., seems to provide a more cogent terminology for the analysis of the various manifestations of space in the theatre than the semiotic approach that separates between the messages conveyed by the different 'languages'.

The division of the theatrical space into a within and a without, a visible space and a non-visible space, in itself constitutes an inherent elementary structure and a basic tension that demand to be interpreted by the playwright. The opposition between the seen and unseen spaces is most readily interpreted in terms of the everyday opposition between outdoors and indoors. In the open-air theatre of classical times, the *skene* at the back of the stage was often seen as representing the front of a house. The shut-off theatrical space nearby was understood to be the inside of the house. The action took place in the outlying, visible area in front of the *skene*, which took up its meaning as a specific outdoors in contradistinction to the indoors behind the *skene* wall.

Following the advent of the indoor theatre, the polarity of within/without as outdoors/indoors is reversed. In drawing-room drama, the theatrical space within, in which the action unfolds, represents an interior, while the nearby theatrical space without, behind the scenery, is the outdoors from which the characters enter the house.

I shall be focusing on those forms of theatre in which the spatial relations of within and without are conventionally paired, directly or conversely, with the outdoors and the indoors. The most demonstrative examples will be drawn from classical theatre on the one hand and nineteenth-century realistic theatre on the other hand, where the unity of place guarantees the fixity of these relations, often directing our attention to their problematic nature. My other examples will include both plays that accept one of these scenic conventions as well as plays which move from one locale to another. Although some of the latter plays are not so singularly devoted to the question of the home, they too explore, in varying degrees, its significance in theatrical terms, scenically and thematically, in the characterization as in the plot.

The structural division of space into the interior and the exterior of the house carries with it social and cultural implications. Gender roles are spatially defined in relation to the inside and the outside of the house. Traditionally, it is the woman who makes the house into a home, her home, while the world of commerce, war, travel, the world outside, is a man's world. As Simone de Beauvoir noted, 'man is but mildly interested in his immediate surroundings because he can find self-expression in projects'; whereas for woman, the house is the centre of the world, 'reality is concentrated inside the house, while outer space seems to collapse'.[9] From the spatial point of view, the world of man and the world of woman meet on the threshold. Thus, the very shape a play gives its theatrical space is indicative of

6

its views on the nature of the relationship between the sexes and on the position of woman in society.

'Women', wrote Virginia Woolf, 'have sat indoors all these millions of years, so that by this time the very walls are permeated by their creative force.'[10] The near-identification of the woman with her house is so old that it is part of our linguistic heritage in the Indo-European languages, built into the very words we use. In *Le Vocabulaire des institutions indo-européennes*, Émile Benveniste pointed out that the Greek word for legitimate wife, *dámar*, is derived from two roots, *\*dam-* (Latin *domus*), house, and *\*-ar*, to order or arrange, hence 'she who administers the house'. The woman is the dame in charge of the *domus*, the mistress of the house.[11]

As to the house itself, Benveniste distinguishes between two different aspects of *domus*: house as family residence and house as building. It seems that the original force of the word was exclusively social and that the material sense was grafted on as a consequence of contamination between two homophonic roots.[12] In English, these two senses are easily distinguishable as home and house.

Benveniste derives a whole phenomenology of doors, of opening and closing one's door to someone or showing someone the door, that defines the physical and emotional limits of the house. The door becomes the symbol of either separation or communication (depending on whether it is closed or opened) between the circumscribed and secure space of the house and the hostile and alien world outside. This symbolism assumes mythical and religious dimensions, as evidenced by Eliade's description of the primordial fear of the outside as a 'chaotic space, peopled with demons and phantoms'. De Beauvoir sees the home in similar terms, as a 'refuge, retreat, grotto, womb' that 'gives shelter from outside danger'.[13]

The opposition between outdoors and indoors is often invested in the theatre with these atavistic values, interpreted dramatically as the fragile security of the home separated only by a door from the menacing outside. Seeing the within and the without in terms of the outdoors and the indoors immediately transforms the theatrical space into a gender-charged environment, naturally fitted for acting out the drama of man and woman. The question of the theatrical space thus becomes the question of woman.

Traditionally, the house has been associated with woman's social place, but it can also be seen to stand for her body and her sexuality. Thus, for example, it was a commonplace in the Renaissance that 'the best way for a woman to keep a good name was for her never to leave her house'. The virtue of chastity was assured by the woman being closed off, immured in her house, while the open door and the open mouth were taken to signify sexual incontinence.[14] In the theatre, the contrast between interior and exterior space, between house and outside, is eroticized, and the seemingly innocent plot aimed at gaining access into the house takes on almost explicit sexual overtones of penetration. The doors and windows of the house, as

7

ways of entrance and of communication, assume in this context a heightened significance as bodily orifices.

From the male point of view, the action is directed at entering female space. Conversely, from the woman's point of view, and especially in modern times, the problem is how to escape the restrictive space of her house. Woman's emancipation finds its theatrical expression in an actual, physical act of leaving the house. The representation of the theatrical space within as the outdoors, the male space, lends itself naturally to a plot the goal of which is man's conquest of the house. Reversing the scene so that it represents the female indoors tends to change the drift of the action in the opposite direction, to woman's struggle to sever her bonds and abandon the house.

The articulation of the theatrical space within as the outside or the inside of a house is widespread but by no means universal, and not all plays deal with the problematics of house and home. But, in the many instances in which the question of woman is addressed directly or indirectly, the ideological positions of the society and of the playwright shape the contours of the theatrical space. Thus, the abstract conception of woman's place in society finds concrete expression in the spatial relations materialized on stage, whether realistically represented by scenery or merely indicated by word and gesture.

The interaction of house and gender yields a variety of relations between woman, man and house. In broad strokes, woman is seen in relation to her house as its mistress, prisoner or escapee. Man meets woman on the threshold, or when he succeeds in entering her house (elopement sometimes follows), or, in more recent drama, when he makes the house his own, usurping woman's space. The house itself begins as a household, chiefly a productive economic unit; it progresses into the bourgeois home as a family dwelling; it breaks apart with the final obliteration of the house as a unique female space. The original household is gradually pared down, losing one by one its various functions. Many of its wider economic aspects are taken out, to become middle–class male occupations. Now what remains as the core of the bourgeois home is the relationship between husband and wife; hence the central place of sexuality. But this sexuality is repressed and hidden behind a façade of gentility. In contemporary times, sexuality is open but it becomes dissociated from home and family, thus emptying the house of its last residual content.

In the following chapters I show how the analysis of the theatrical space directly reveals the changing conceptions of woman's position in the family and in society. I start in chapter 2 on Greek tragedy with the basic opposition between the indoors and the outdoors and woman's place by the hearth, as mistress of the house, and demonstrate how the plot of the *Agamemnon*, the first domestic tragedy, derives from the articulation of the theatrical space itself. Chapter 3 considers the comic

8

effect, in Aristophanes, of women's attempt to reverse gender roles, usurping men's outdoor space. Doors played a crucial role in Greek tragedy and comedy, but by the time of Roman comedy they became a facile convention. Chapter 4 examines the games played by Plautus' male protagonists with the stage doors in their attempts to circumvent the obstacles presented by the scenic and social conventions of woman's place indoors.

On the Renaissance stage, the door as the unique type of aperture to the house is supplemented by the window. Chapter 5 looks at the theatrical fortunes of the archetypal figure of the woman in the window as both seductress and prisoner. Chapter 6 deals with Molière's representation of the height of patriarchalism and its demise in man's futile attempt to keep the woman a prisoner in her house and achieve total control over her.

In Ibsen's drawing-room dramas, analyzed in chapter 7, the move indoors, into woman's own territory, turns out to be disappointing: the expected intimacy is replaced by a growing alienation of the woman from her house, leading her in one case to abandon her home, in another to sexual frustration and despair. Chekhov's leading female characters refuse to accept their roles as homemakers, preferring their own independence and self-fulfilment, even at the cost of the dissolution of home and family. Chapter 8 investigates the shifting prism of theatrical spaces in Chekhov's plays, in itself an expression of the disintegration of the home.

From the wreckage of the home, Pinter salvages the basic notion of the room as a place of refuge, in which the woman still tends the stove, providing food and warmth. Chapter 9 investigates Pinter's theatrical spaces, non-mimetic yet hyper-realistic rooms. Chapter 10 deals with the experimental theatre of Beckett and Handke. Beckett's theatrical spaces are seen as abstract, symbolic and metaphysical. On this level of abstraction, the question of gender and its direct spatial expression are of no interest. Rejecting mimesis, Handke constructs in his theatre a solipsistic world. With him the theatrical space has reached a critical stage which is paralleled by the contemporary feminist crisis, the unresolved tension between woman, man and home. Some contemporary women playwrights return to more mimetic spaces in order to uncover the kernel of the problem: the place of the child. The Coda glances briefly at this present-day shift from the woman's space to the child's space.

## Chapter 2

# Indoors and outdoors

The introduction of the *skene* building at the back of the acting area was of paramount importance to the development of the Greek theatre. The self-enclosed circle of theatre separated the performance from the audience, in the same way that the sacred space of ritual was set apart from its surroundings. The *orchestra* with its central altar commemorated these primitive origins of the theatre. But the frontality or linearity of the *skene* introduced a differentiation within the theatrical space itself. Not only did its façade form a backdrop to the action on stage and provide the actors with a convenient entrance door, but it also served as a visual barrier, separating the space in front from the space behind.[1]

The articulation of the theatrical space in the *Agamemnon* seems to have been created in response to this novel development in theatre design. Already Flickinger showed the influence of the changing physical conditions of the theatre of Dionysus, discovered in Dörpfeld's excavations, on the localization of dramatic action. In the earlier plays of Aeschylus, in the absence of a backdrop, 'the scene is laid in the open countryside with not a house in sight and with no scenic accessories except an altar, tomb, or rock'.[2]

Many classical scholars, from Wilamowitz to Oliver Taplin, believe that 'the *skene* was an innovation of the last ten years or less of Aeschylus' life'.[3] The scholarly controversy over the introduction of the *skene* building, which involves the dating of Aeschylus' plays, highlights its unique and incontrovertible role in the *Oresteia* as a whole, and especially in the *Agamemnon*. If indeed the *skene* had just made its appearance in the theatre, then Aeschylus' use of it in the *Agamemnon* is truly revolutionary, attesting to an almost instantaneous recognition of the theatrical potential of the new architectural element. By attributing a particular meaning to what was in reality the outside wall of the dressing room, Aeschylus drew it in 'as part of the world of the play itself'.[4]

The dramatic genius of Aeschylus is revealed in the assigning of a simple, almost natural, meaning to the neutral façade of the stage building at the back of the stage, making it into the front of Agamemnon's palace. The use of the *skene* as a house-front was to harden into a convention carried over from the Greek theatre to Rome, and from the Roman theatre into the Renaissance. But this should not blind us to the brilliance and originality of the initial conception. The interpretation of the *skene* as a scenic element within a particular production is also a first step in the development of scenery as an independent theatrical element. Within the framework of the original performance of the *Agamemnon*, the convenient stage door was transformed into the palace gate and the stage itself was thereby defined as the area in front of the palace. The off-stage too was given a meaning: the interior of the *skene*-building became the inside of the palace, and the *parodoi* led, on the one side, to the sea-shore, and from there to far-off Troy, and, on the other side, into town. The new feature in theatre building was turned into a theatrical asset by incorporating it into the very structure of the play itself. Furthermore, the organization of the theatrical space served as a source of inspiration for the dramatic structure.

The palace is primarily a representative home, and the myth of Agamemnon, Clytemnestra and Aegisthus is interpreted as a domestic tragedy, elevated to an exemplary status through the stature of the contestants and the importance of the religious and ethical issues which form the core of the drama.

In order to communicate with the outside world, Clytemnestra must issue from her home, with which she is closely associated. While Agamemnon was fighting the war in Troy, she remained at home, in charge of the household. For ten years she waited, while he travelled the world. The insistence on the distances covered by the fire-signals announcing his triumph in Troy emphasizes the extent of his travels, underlining his dynamic character as opposed to her stationary position. To his temporal activity she opposes her spatial dimension.

The returned hero now seeks admittance into the house. The meeting between husband and wife takes place out of doors, in front of the house, as dictated by the structure of the *skene*. Taplin stresses the function of the *skene* as threshold:

> The *threshold* demarks the frontier of the house ... the doorway in and out of the palace has an important place within the play.[5]

The *Agamemnon* focuses on the threshold, making this architectural feature into the central issue of the play, in terms of both plot and theme. The house front is seen as the border-line between the outdoors and the indoors, two worlds which are defined not only spatially but also conceptually, as *oikos* and *polis*, the woman's realm and man's world.

The notion of the household, *oikos*, is central to Greek culture, especially in contrast to the public affairs of the *polis*, dealt with in the open air of the *agora*. The privacy of the *oikos* is represented in the *Agamemnon* by the almost impenetrable façade of the palace, with its central door.

The architecture of stage backed by *skene* carves up theatrical space into a seen space and an unseen one. Interpreted in the *Agamemnon* as the outdoors and the indoors, the public domain and the private quarters, the man's world and the woman's sanctuary, this spatial conception of Aeschylus came to dominate the theatre, pre-determining the dramatic structure of many other tragedies.

In *The Use of Pleasure*, Michel Foucault analyzes Xenophon's *Oeconomicus* as a treatise on married life in classical Greece.[6] Gender differences are equated with social and economic differences: the young bride should be instructed in the economics of housekeeping so as to allow her husband to engage in truly male activities in the fields or in the *agora*.[7] Seen from the vantage point of Foucault's discussion of sexuality, the function of the *skene* in the classical theatre assumes even greater importance. The dichotomy of the theatrical space brings about its sexualization: as the front of the *oikos*, the *skene* wall divides the theatrical space into a male and a female space in social and economic as well as sexual terms. The façade of the house thus marks the barrier between the genders and it is only on the threshold that man and woman can meet.

For Xenophon, the house is primarily a shelter, *stegos*. The shelter, in Foucault's words, 'gives [the family] its spatial organization'; by contrast, the descendants 'provide the family with its temporal dimension'.[8] The idea of a shelter is understood in spatial terms, opposing the outside to the inside, and these, in turn, assume symbolic values as the spaces of men and women, respectively. Thus the *oikos* differs from the modern home not only as a social, economic and religious institution, but also as a conceptual space.

The Greek house is a shelter because it is a closed, impenetrable space, enjoying complete privacy. The modern abode often opens up onto the street with wide glass windows, and modern telecommunication systems break down the isolation of the home by maintaining a free flow of news in and out of the house. For the Greeks, space was not homogeneous: they perceived the space of the *oikos* as qualitatively different from outdoor space.[9]

These sharply contrasted qualities of outdoors and indoors were carried over into the theatre when Aeschylus assigned to the *skene* the representative role of house front. The liminality of the threshold became the focus of his theatre, with the conflict of the genders intensified and magnified around the question of crossing that threshold. The whole action of the *Agamemnon* revolves around the question of how, and on what terms, Agamemnon will be allowed to enter his palace, as well as if, and how, he will ever exit again. First there is the question of the manner in which the returning war-hero will be re-admitted home, then the anxiety over what will happen in the privacy of that home, and finally, the public repercussions of what has taken place indoors.

In naturalistic drama, as in modern everyday life, entrances and exits are neutral, functional, unceremonial acts, in themselves normally devoid of any special

13

significance. Not so in the *Agamemnon*, where crossing the threshold is a monumental 'life-crisis ritual' for the hero, and takes on the ritualistic pace and character of a *rite de passage*. Conversely, van Gennep saw the *rite de passage* as 'often accompanied by a parallel passage in space, a geographical movement from one place to another', taking the form of 'a mere opening of doors or the literal crossing of a threshold which separates two distinct areas'.[10]

The dichotomy between home and outdoors, female and male spaces, is further enriched through their religious overtones. Jean-Pierre Vernant discusses the differentiation between the interior and the outside world in terms of the antithesis between Hestia and Hermes, the gods celebrated in the Homeric 'Hymn to Hestia' as dwelling together in friendship 'in the glorious houses of men who live on the earth's surface'.[11] In his essay on 'The religious expression of space and movement in ancient Greece', Vernant sees the pair of gods as embodying these abstractions. The central hearth of the *oikos* is dedicated to Hestia, while Hermes is the messenger god, a constant traveller, the personification of movement and impermanence.

Hermes is also the protector of the threshold, present at front doors and gateways. Hestia is his counterpart who resides inside the house. Her important symbolic role derives from antiquity, from the rounded hearth which marked the centre of the *megaron*, the Mycenaean dwelling. The hearth denoted the navel which ties the house to the earth. It was 'the symbol and pledge of fixity, immutability, and permanence ... For the poets and philosophers, Hestia, the node and starting point of the orientation and arrangement of human space, could be identified with the earth, immobile at the centre of the cosmos'.[12]

In making the stage wall represent the outside of the home, Aeschylus was enriching his minimalist theatre with some of the oldest archetypes of the collective subconscious.

Hestia and Hermes, hearth and home *versus* threshold and travel, also personify the female and male principles. Vernant stresses the sexual compartmentalization of the spatial division:

> In Greek, the domestic sphere, the enclosed space that is roofed over (protected), has a feminine connotation; the exterior, the open air, a masculine one.[13]

The sexual attributions are so deeply embedded in the spatial conception of the *oikos* that the act of marriage, in which the woman must abandon her home to join her husband, is viewed as an act of defiance against the virginal Hestia. The association of Woman with Hestia is evidenced in her duty of tending the fire as in her culinary activities.

Hestia, the hearth, is the very heart of the house. For Homer, the cruelest touch he can add to intensify the horror of Agamemnon's murder on the day he returned home is that he was killed at his own hearth (*Odyssey*, 3.234). When the hearth is viewed as Hestia's altar, the murder assumes sacrificial overtones.

The anthropological researches of Foucault and Vernant illuminate the nature of the strong bond between woman and her home in Greek culture and it is this bond that is carried over to the theatre when the *skene* comes to represent the *oikos*. Accordingly, an analysis of the theatrical space of the *Agamemnon* reveals the play's basic assumptions about women and their place in society.

The *Agamemnon* is a play about the murder of Agamemnon, but this central event of the play takes place off-stage, out of the sight of the audience. In terms of the plot, the murder forms the climax, but the playwright relegates it to the theatrical space without. The murder takes place inside the house, i.e. behind the *skene*. But the audience is made fully aware of this invisible incident, primarily because it is audible: from indoors issue Agamemnon's two death cries which indicate the moment of the murder. W. B. Stanford points out that these are the first death cries in Greek tragedy and that

> We who encounter them first in cold print must make a great effort of imagination to realize what they would have sounded like when uttered with all the emotional power of a dedicated actor's voice in the theatre of Dionysos ... almost as if, in the Watchman's words, the House had been given a voice.[14]

The unseen dramatic moment serves as the hinge around which the action revolves. It is extended through premonition on the one hand and recapitulation on the other. From Agamemnon's fateful entrance into the palace and up to his piercing cries, the tension is built up through the stratagem of Cassandra's prophetic foreknowledge. She seems to react to the house sensuously, 'keen scented as a hound' (l. 1093), sensing that the floor of the house is 'swimming with blood' (l. 1092), and envisaging the unsavoury feast of Thyestes. In her clairvoyance she sees the things to come:

> Ah, fell woman, so thou wilt do this deed? Thy husband, the partner of thy bed, when thou hast cheered him with the bath, wilt thou – how shall I tell the end? Aye, soon it will be done. Now this hand, now that, she stretches forth! ... What apparition's this? Is it a net of death?
>
> (lines 1107–15)[15]

Stanford has an interesting gloss on Cassandra's description, 'Now this hand, now that', which he translates as 'hand reaching out from hand': the movement described is like that of a fisherman when he draws in a net.[16] It is characteristic of the prophetess' vision that things seem to surface and come into focus only a step

*Fig. 1a The murder of Agamemnon, Attic red-figure calyx-krater by the Dokimasia Painter, 470–460 BC; William Francis Warden Fund. Courtesy, Museum of Fine Arts, Boston*

at a time, so that it is natural for Cassandra to provide this precise account of Clytemnestra's movements even before she has perceived the net in which the Queen will envelop her husband (see Fig. 1a).

Cassandra's prophecy leads up to her resigned entrance into the palace which, to her, appears as 'a charnel house'. The smell of death apparent to her over-keen senses is interpreted by the chorus as 'the savour of victims at the hearth' (l. 1310). Here as elsewhere the differentiation between the sacrifice of thanksgiving on the hearth/altar and the murder is deliberately obfuscated. It is through this stratagem

*Fig. 1b The murder of Aegisthus, Dokimasia painter; William Francis Warden Fund. Courtesy, Museum of Fine Arts, Boston*

that Aeschylus achieves his central aesthetic aim of juxtaposing the murder of Agamemnon with the sacrifice of Iphigenia, a theme I will return to later.

Cassandra's anticipation is matched by Clytemnestra's validation, at the other end of the climactic event, and after the chorus has expressed its doubt about what has actually taken place indoors, 'For surmise differs from assurance' (line 1369). Now the doors are thrown open, revealing the tableau of the dead bodies with the murderess towering above them, unrepentant. Her description of the manner of Agamemnon's death matches Cassandra's prophetic insight:

Thus have I wrought the deed – deny it I will not. Round him, like as to catch a haul of fish, I cast a net impassable – a fatal wealth of rope – so that he should neither escape nor ward off doom. Twice I smote him, and with two groans his limbs relaxed. Once he had fallen, I dealt him yet a third stroke to grace my prayer to the infernal Zeus … Fallen thus, he gasped away his life, and as he breathed forth quick spurts of blood, he smote me with dark drops of ensanguined dew.

(lines 1381–90)

The neat symmetry of Cassandra's premonition and Clytemnestra's recapitulation directs our attention to the crucial dramatic moment, both framing and replicating it. The unseen event thus assumes much greater importance than if it were experienced directly. But from the very beginning, from the watchman's initial veiled hints of a family secret lurking behind the closed palace doors and the chorus' recollection of the unsanctified sacrifice, everything in the play moves forward to the moment of the murder or looks back to it.[17]

The question of how Agamemnon will step down from his chariot and enter his palace slows down the pace of events so as to increase our expectation of what will happen to him inside. The suspense is further drawn out through the stratagem of Cassandra's initial refusal to enter and her delivery of the prophecy discussed above. The briefness of the moment is contrasted with the dragging out of time in the almost ritual, preparatory steps.

The focus of everything that happens on-stage is off-stage, like an invisible perspective vanishing-point perceived through the multiplicity of sight-lines leading towards it. The most crucial event of the play, its turning point, takes place in the theatrical space without, although in proximity, and in an almost negligible length of time.

For the last, pathetic movement of the tragedy the consequences must be drawn out. The bodies are revealed, presumably on the *ekkyklema*, if there was one. According to Pollux writing in the 2nd century,

> The *ekkyklema* is a high platform on posts, on which stands a throne. It shows the dreadful things done indoors, behind the skene. The word for this operation is ἐκκυκλεῖν (i.e. to wheel out).[18]

Despite the lack of any external evidence, Peter Arnott feels confident that the use of the *ekkyklema* can be presumed in the *Agamemnon* on purely dramatic grounds.[19] The tableau of the dead bodies, accompanied by Clytemnestra, wheeled out through the *skene* doors can be understood as a way of overcoming the impenetrability of the indoors. The *ekkyklema* provides a view of the moment after, the *fait accompli*, the tragic scene to be studied and contemplated.

18

In contrast to its reserved, off-stage treatment in the play, the murder of Agamemnon was tackled in the visual arts head-on. This scene is depicted on bronze shield-bands, terracotta plaques and vases, so that art historians can speak of an evolving iconography of the scene. The different examples assembled by A. J. N. W. Prag reveal the essential, repeated elements of the story:[20] the fateful triangle, the co-operation between Clytemnestra and Aegisthus in the bloody act, the helpless posture and the diminished stature of their victim (Agamemnon appears smaller than his assailants due to his bent knees). Significantly, it is always the moment of the overpowering of the legendary hero, celebrating his triumph over Troy, by a mere woman, aided by her lover, that is chosen as the most dramatic and demonstrative, an ironic exemplum of the extremes of human pride and frailty, of love and hatred.

Perhaps the most interesting rendering of the scene appears on a calyx-krater by the Dokimasia Painter (Fig. 1a), probably antedating the play by only about ten years.[21] Here, then, is a visual image of the murder of Agamemnon which is almost contemporaneous with the play and can thus both supplement and correct the images conjured by the play in our minds: here we can see what the net enveloping Agamemnon was supposed to look like.[22] Also, although the net does not appear in the earlier depictions of the scene collected by Prag, its appearance here attests to its iconological nature and shows that it was not an Aeschylean invention.

As in Aeschylus, where the *Agamemnon* constitutes merely one movement within the larger structure of the *Oresteia*, so also on the calyx-krater, the murder is depicted as an incident within the wider framework of the family saga. The Dokimasia Painter chose a structure that juxtaposes two different phases of the action, one of which is the direct outcome of the other: the murder of Agamemnon on one side of the vase is balanced on the other side by the scene of Orestes' revenge (Fig. 1b). Clytemnestra appears on both sides, trying here to instigate, there to prevent, the murder.

In addition to the pictorial parallel, the two scenes are also related as cause and effect, murder and its bloody revenge. The artistic treatment on the calyx-krater has much in common with the playwright's rendering of the different phases of the action within the framework of a trilogy of plays as separate yet interdependent. Both combine the principle of causality with a structural symmetry, thus achieving a heightened aesthetic effect. Revenge presumes an ethical causality: the murder of Aegisthus is the direct consequence of the murder of Agamemnon, it is the story of the murderer turned victim. The movement from the *Agamemnon* to the *Choephori* parallels the movement from one face of the vase to the other. The overall artistic design keeps the two phases apart, thus enabling us to observe the sameness of the basic pattern. In both artistic mediums a balance is achieved between the dynamic and static, the temporal and the spatial.

The close structural parallels with the visual conception serve to accentuate the glaring differences in the treatment of the well-known story. Aeschylus seems to have swerved from the accepted iconology, re-shaping the traditional material. The most significant change he introduced is the reversal of the relative roles of Clytemnestra and Aegisthus, making her the murderess and him a mere accomplice. In this he deviated not only from the pictorial iconography used by the Dokimasia Painter,[23] but also, even more importantly, from Homer's written codification of the story in the *Odyssey* (3.194, 232, 307). The role-reversal is indicative of the playwright's recognition of the explosive power of centring the action around the woman and making her the active agent of revenge. His antagonists in the play are not Agamemnon and Aegisthus but Agamemnon and Clytemnestra or rather Clytemnestra and Agamemnon. Although the play is named after the epic hero, it is Clytemnestra who is given the most lines and is the dominant character.

It is in his circumspect treatment of the murder itself that Aeschylus displays his originality. The murder takes place not within the sight of the audience but within their hearing, momentarily transforming them from spectators to auditors. The audience experiences the heightened moment without actually witnessing it. Aeschylus makes the supremely dramatic moment of the murder take place off-scene, in the theatrical space without, within the palace, so that what the artists depicted visually is here only suggested and left to the audience's imagination to recreate. The spectators are allowed to see only the aftermath, the consequences of that moment, the dead bodies of Agamemnon and Cassandra brought out on the *ekkyklema*.

The comparison of the play with its visual forerunners serves to underline the way in which it skirts the crucial scene while focusing on it. This effect is accomplished through the stratagems discussed earlier, such as Cassandra's premonitions, Clytemnestra's vauntings and Agamemnon's own death cries, all of which depend on the spatial conception which allows the event to take place close at hand, yet out of sight.

The principles of ethical and aesthetic symmetry and causality not only bind together the separate plays which form the trilogy, but are also mirrored in the *Agamemnon* itself, in the backward-looking glance cast towards the antecedents of the events depicted in the play. Clytemnestra's motive for killing her husband is to avenge her daughter. The sacrificial overtones of her crime, which she alludes to as a sacrifice on the central hearth (line 1057), link it directly with that other dubious offering, the sacrifice of Iphigenia. While Agamemnon's death takes place within the duration of the play, Iphigenia's death takes us back ten years, to the beginning of the war against Troy, the victory over which is celebrated in the opening of the play.

Although the conflict in the play is of a domestic nature, it is intimately connected with the fortunes of the great war. Agamemnon sacrificed his daughter in Aulis for the sake of the war, in order to pacify Artemis who had sent opposing winds which prevented his fleet from sailing. Thus, from the start, success in war is paid for by the sacrifice of a loved one. On the stage, the division of the theatrical space into a without and a within, a private and a public domain, facilitates the symbolic depiction of the conflicting claims of *oikos* and *polis*.

In sacrificing Iphigenia, Agamemnon has sacrificed the happiness of his family for the public benefit. According to Sarah Humphreys, 'Tragedy is private life "raised" to the political level'.[24] Like Iphigenia, all the lives lost in the war have been private sacrifices for the public cause. The sacrifice of the daughter serves as an exemplum of the sacrifice of all the warriors. The chorus speaks of the many loved ones who have returned home in urns (line 436) or have been buried in Ilian land (line 455), and of the growing, whispered resentment that they have fallen 'for another's wife' (line 448). In other words, the apparent public cause for which they have been sacrificed turns out to be someone else's private cause – Menelaus' wish to regain his wife. Thus, a dialectic of public and private causes is established: Helen's adultery brought about the war, and this in turn has brought about Clytemnestra's adultery. In recounting the story, the chorus implies its moral judgement of Agamemnon:

> So then he hardened his heart to sacrifice his daughter that he might prosper
> a war waged to avenge a woman, and as an offering for the voyaging of a fleet!
> (lines 223–6)

The play does not accept the myth, Calchas' prophecy, Iphigenia's sacrifice or indeed the Trojan war, at face value, but probes into the religious and ethical dilemmas and the manner in which they were resolved by the protagonists.

Although preceding the events dramatized in the play, the story of Iphigenia is of supreme importance to the play. In Swinburne's words,

> The hinge of the *Oresteia* from first to last is the sacrifice at Aulis. From the
> immolation of Iphigenia springs the wrath of Clytemnestra.[25]

Not only does her sacrifice begin the chain of events which is concluded with her father's murder, but also it provides an opposing emotional pole to that event, establishing a kind of equilibrium of horror with the final tableau on the *ekkyklema*.

The story of Iphigenia is introduced early on in the play, in the *parodos*. Though only a short narrative-inset of some twenty lines, it is highlighted through its own intrinsic beauty, through the poignant quality of its lyricism:

> Her supplications, her cries of 'Father', and her virgin life, the commanders
> in their eagerness for war reckoned as naught. Her father, after a prayer, bade

his ministers lay hold of her as, enwrapped in her robes, she lay fallen forward, and with stout heart to raise her, as it were a kid, high above the altar; and with a guard upon her lovely mouth, the bit's strong and stifling might, to stay a cry that had been a curse on his house.

Then, as she shed to earth her saffron robe, she smote each of her sacrificers with a glance from her eyes beseeching pity, and showing as in a picture, fain to speak; for oft had she sung where men were met at her father's hospitable board, and with her virgin voice had been wont lovingly to do honour to her loved father's prayer for blessing at the third libation.

(lines 227–47)

Writing on the expression of emotion in Greek tragedy, Stanford singles out the Iphigenia passage for its emotional impact, which is 'as powerful as any scene in Greek tragedy'. If the aim of tragedy is to arouse pity and fear, then this passage certainly accomplishes that aim. The particular density of the passage is achieved through the compression of three major tragic themes: the death of a virgin, the parent compelled to kill his child and the contrast between present disaster and past happiness.[26]

The poet employs bold, sharp effects. He contrasts the young girl's pleas for mercy with the commanders' inhumane refusal to respond. He shows her 'as in a picture' (l. 240), self-consciously painting with words. The famous picture is very vivid: Iphigenia is lifted by the soldiers high up and carried face downward, as if she were a kid, to the altar. But unlike the kid, she is a young woman whose mouth must be tied to stifle the curse, and the pity for her is increased through her attractiveness. She is carried by the men, wrapped up in her robes. Deprived even of the ability to speak, it is her eyes that beg pity as 'she shed[s] to earth her saffron robe'. Stanford suggests that in a last effort to soften the hard hearts of the men around her, Iphigenia 'lets her robe fall to the ground and stands before them totally naked, hoping that the sheer helplessness and innocence of her dying body will move them to pity', though he notes that many have contested this interpretation on the grounds that 'complete disrobement of this kind is unparalleled in Greek literature'.[27]

The erotic touches of the scene are enhanced through the particular choice of word for 'virgin'. Stanford points out that *ataurotos*, literally 'unbulled', evokes the bull as a symbol of male violence, thus colouring the sacrifice of the virgin with the sexual overtones of rape.

The death of Iphigenia is linked with the death of Agamemnon in many subtle ways. Iphigenia's disrobement before the sacrifice is paralleled by Agamemnon's undressing for his bath. The saffron colour of her robe is probably meant to be the colour of blood, thus 'anticipating the blood-coloured tapestries on which Agamemnon will walk to his death',[28] and the blood-stains on Clytemnestra after the murder. The deaths are also linked by the inner pattern of hunter turned hunted and sacrificer turned sacrificed which Vidal-Naquet discerns in the *Oresteia*.[29]

The subtlety and refinement of Aeschylus' treatment may be contrasted with two extant vase-paintings. The sacrifice of Iphigenia which appears on a contemporary Etrusco-Campanian neck-amphora (Fig. 2), showing the prone girl being carried to the altar, is executed very crudely. Much more satisfying aesthetically is the work of the Timiades Painter on a Tyrrhenian amphora on view in the British Museum, which depicts the analogous sacrifice of Polyxena (Fig. 3). The painting captures the moment of hoisting the girl up high above the burning altar and slitting her throat. The abstracted, ornamental human figures on the vase parallel the nameless 'ministers' who lift Iphigenia 'with stout heart' in the Chorus' description. Although it is difficult to compare a picture with a play, it is possible to see how naive and detached the treatment of the Polyxena story appears in comparison to Aeschylus' word-painting. The uniform and indistinguishable faces on the vase fail to convey any emotion or individuality. Despite the similarity in the narrative treatment of the episode, Aeschylus has succeeded in charging his account with emotion, making us feel pity for the innocent victim and forcing us to consider the religious and moral issues.

Unlike the murder of Agamemnon, which takes place within the palace while the audience is watching the play, Iphigenia's sacrifice is an event of the past and of a far-off place – Aulis. Her part of the story lies beyond the plot, but it is so important to the plot that Aeschylus made it stand out poetically. It is a story which contrasts the private lives of women (wife, daughter) with the public career of men. That this was the playwright's general intent can be concluded from his approach to the subject-matter gleaned from the *Odyssey*.

The plot of the *Agamemnon* is based on the story at the fringe of the great epic. For Homer, the Agamemnon story serves as a structural parallel with his main plot. Agamemnon's return home to the unfaithful Clytemnestra is contrasted with Odysseus' return to the unyielding Penelope, and Telemachus' search for his father is compared to Orestes' revenge.[30] The parallel between the two women is spelled out by the soul of Agamemnon, speaking to a fellow inmate in Hades, after hearing of Penelope's famous stratagem for keeping her suitors at bay:

> How good was proved the heart that is in blameless Penelope, Ikarios' daughter, and how well she remembered Odysseus, her wedded husband. Thereby the fame of her virtue shall never die away ... Not so did the daughter of Tyndreos fashion her evil deeds, when she killed her wedded lord, and a song of loathing will be hers among men, to make evil the reputation of womankind, even for one whose acts are virtuous.
>
> (24.195 ff.)[31]

*Fig. 2 The sacrifice of Iphigenia, Etrusco-Campanian neck-amphora, 465–450 BC; British Museum*

The Argive family serves as a foil to that from Ithaca, the nature of the familial bonds between husband, wife and son being compared and contrasted with each other, and the central issue which comes into focus is the question of constancy and faithfulness.

Aeschylus chose to foreground the domestic and private aspects of the Agamemnon story, moving the Trojan war into the background. This perspective is imposed from the start, with the poetic emphasis on the moment of victory over Troy relayed to the audience in 'real time', with the speed of light, but experienced

*Fig. 3 The sacrifice of Polyxena, Tyrrhenian amphora by the Timiades Painter, 565–550 BC; British Museum*

from the other end, from home. It is further accentuated through the visual image of the entrance of Agamemnon on a chariot laden with war spoils, which stops in front of his house. From *skene* to house front to the boundary between female and male domains to the threshold between Hestia and Hermes to the dangerous divide between private life and public career – this is how Aeschylus transformed the novelty of a stage-wall into a meaningful theatrical space, setting a norm and creating a useful scenic language of antitheses: indoors and outdoors, female and male, *oikos* and *polis*.

The great prevalence of the house or palace front as the background of Greek tragedy has often enough been commented on, but the convention established goes beyond a mere attribution of meaning to the *skene*. Later tragedians accepted the

Aeschylean conception of the stage as natural and used it over and over again, making the most of its symbolic spatial relations. I shall illustrate this derivative usage with two examples.

In *King Oedipus*, the *skene* represents the palace from which Oedipus was taken as a new-born baby, and to which he returned as an adult. Jocasta is the lady of the house, both mother and wife to the murderer of her husband Laius. The house becomes the image of the womb from which Oedipus was cast out and to which he incestuously returned. Fleeing from his adoptive home, his destiny leads him back to the house in which he was born and from which, after unknowingly committing his heinous sins, he must again be exiled. In Sophocles' dramatization of the Oedipus myth, the house becomes the focus of the action, and the hero's quest for his identity becomes a quest for the home which defines his identity. The poles of the action are his craving for home and his expulsion from it. And home is defined by the woman who lives there, with her double identity as mother and as wife.

The *oikos* enfolds the family secrets until they pollute the whole *polis*. It is only then that the private matter becomes public knowledge. From this point on, what takes place indoors, in the near theatrical space without, becomes a public concern. As Oedipus' self-blinding and Jocasta's suicide occur inside the palace, it is necessary for an attendant to come out and report what has happened. Then the doors are opened for the *ekkyklema* to display its burden of horror. Like the attendant, this piece of machinery, this 'thing wheeled out' is a conventionalized mechanism for revealing what has gone on in the near-by theatrical space without, by physically pushing the without into the within.[32]

The theatrical space without of the play is not confined to that which lies behind the *skene* doors. Characters arrive from far off, from Delphi or Corinth, through the *parodoi* or side-entrances. The action that unfolds in the foreground is given depth by the two differently distanced planes which form its background. The relative positioning of these two planes is provided by the two messengers, the *angelos* and the *exangelos*, the one bringing news from afar and the other telling what happened inside.[33]

While the action of the play is limited to one place, there are many references to other places. Taken together, these places form a virtual geography around Thebes. The action depends, to a large extent, on reports of characters who have travelled to Thebes from one of these peripheral places. Creon comes back from Delphi with an oracle, the *angelos* arrives from Corinth with his news of the death of Polybus, and the Shepherd is summoned from Mount Cithaeron, where he has been grazing his flocks. Oedipus' own voyage from Corinth to Thebes antedates the events of the play, but is also recounted. This wider geographical area accommodates the various events that are excluded from the concentrated plot which unfolds in the visible theatrical space. Seen from this angle, it is the theatrical space without that guarantees the unity of place in the theatrical space within and, along with it, also the unities of time and action.

The theatrical space without contains all the necessary points of reference: Mount Cithaeron, the crossroads, and Corinth, which together define the world of the characters. As a baby, Oedipus was transported from Thebes, via the mountain, to Corinth; as an adult, he traced his way back. The *angelos* too has travelled between these two cities. It is almost natural that the fatal meeting should have taken place at the crossroads, between Thebes and Corinth. Another important point of reference is the Oracle at Delphi: Laius, Oedipus, Creon, all have consulted it. The theatrical space without is thus in constant interaction with the theatrical space within, intruding upon its sense of security, preserving the memory of things past, destabilizing the tenuous equilibrium of the space within.

In *Medea*, it is the woman who is the protagonist, much as if Clytemnestra had been the heroine of *Agamemnon*.[34] Euripides portrays his heroine being banished from her home. She is a foreigner and has been jilted by her beloved and father of her children, Jason, for whom she had betrayed her own home. Before she leaves, she exacts her awful revenge by destroying the home from which she is being expelled, killing the young wife Creusa as well as her own children.

The audience hears Medea's piercing cries from the house before it is allowed to set eyes on her. The chorus pointedly asks the Nurse to 'go inside and bring her / Out of the house' (lines 180–1).[35] The many scattered references to the house reveal the self-consciousness with which Euripides handles the by-now conventional interpretation of the *skene* as the front of a house or palace.

Medea expresses the loneliness and helplessness she experiences as a woman and a stranger to the city. Her personal plight is thus extended to encompass the wider feminist complaint:

> Of all things which are living and can form a judgement
> We women are the most unfortunate creatures.
> ...
> A man, when he's tired of the company in his home,
> Goes out of the house and puts an end to his boredom.
> ...
> What they say of us is that we have a peaceful time
> Living at home, while they do the fighting in war.
>
> (lines 230–49)

Unlike the male, who can divert himself with other women or go out to fight in the wars, all woman is left with is her home and her husband. Medea, moreover, is well aware of her precarious status as a stranger in Corinth: 'I, without a city, am alone' (line 255). Her predicament is thus seen in terms of being excluded from both *oikos* and *polis*.

That woman is closely associated with her home has become a cliché over the ages. But this bond is especially powerful in Greek tragedy, due to woman's atavistic association with the hearth and its deity. The channelling of this primeval strength from the religious into the theatrical sphere lies behind the explosive confrontations of the genders on scene. The most renowned of epic heroes, the mighty figures of mythology, find their antagonists at home, in their own wives. The very nature of the theatrical space eschews the battle field, placing the events on the threshold, at the meeting point of *oikos* and *polis*, private and public, woman and man.

*Chapter 3*

# Reversing gender roles

Seated in the Theatre of Dionysus, at the foot of the Acropolis, watching Aristophanes' new play, *Lysistrata* (first production 411 BC), the Athenian audience could not have failed to grasp the intricate web of spatial–geographical and cultural–historical connections between the constructed theatrical space of the play and the actual theatre space. Traditionally, classical scholars have tried to elucidate the political moment, 'the very darkest period of the Peloponnesian War',[1] recreating for their readers the background of events needed to appreciate the fantastical comic solution offered by the wily protagonist. But beyond the relevant political associations there is a further rich contextual fabric of life in Athens embedded in the very structure of the theatrical space of the play.

The ground-plan of the Acropolis is often appended to discussions of the play, but it is used merely to tidy-up Aristophanes' place-name throwing or as a realistically oriented aid to the understanding of the mock-military manoeuvres. However, in order to appreciate the play in performance we must try to visualize those maps in elevation, remembering that the ruins of today were functional buildings, housing important institutions. Many of them were brand new edifices, expressing the self-confidence of Athens after the defeat of the Persians. The Periclean spate of building between 449 BC and the outbreak of the Peloponnesian War in 431 included the grand entrance gates of the Propylaea, as well as the three temples of Athena, all of them alluded to in the *Lysistrata*: the Parthenon, sacred to Athena Parthenos, i.e. the virgin, the temple of Athena Nike, or Victory, and the temple consecrated to Athena Polias, the guardian of the *polis*, known as the Erechtheion.[2]

These places together with other named sites, all easily accessible referents in real everyday space, form the constitutive elements of the theatrical space of the play. The latter is artificially constructed from a variety of chosen elements and lacks both the continuity and fullness of natural space, in accordance with the selective character of all mimetic art. Thus, despite their partial overlapping, the two spaces cannot be viewed as identical, and although the theatrical space is made up of verifiable geographical locations, these lose their concreteness, becoming part

29

of a conceptual theatrical system. To appreciate their meaning in this system, these locations need to be put within a cultural and social, rather than a geographical context. Only by this devious method can we hope to approximate the un-mediated (and un-premeditated) response of the original audience to the play.

The theatrical space of the play, built from elements with real referents in everyday space, affords an alternative space, in which new, wild, perhaps improbable ideas can be experimented with, dangerous, fantastic, anarchic, farcical, surrealistic ideas.

Aristophanes achieves his special articulation of theatrical space in the *Lysistrata* by changing the by now conventional attribution of meaning to the *skene* doors as house doors. He makes the central double doors of the *skene* represent the Propylaea, the grand entrance portals leading to the Acropolis; the *skene* wall becomes then part of the Acropolis walls; and the theatrical space without, enclosed behind the *skene*, out of the viewers' sight, is transformed into the Acropolis itself. This becomes evident when Lysistrata explains that the noise heard indicates that the older women have just seized the Acropolis (line 241) and that she will now enter the citadel and help the women inside to bar the doors.

The Acropolis, the upper-city, is the fortified citadel and the holy precinct, *temenos*, of Athens. The Athenians called it simply *polis*.[3] By fortifying themselves inside the Acropolis, the women have exchanged *oikos* for *polis*, thus publicly proclaiming the reversal of male and female roles.[4] By changing the conventional designation of the *skene* doors from house-doors to Propylaea, Aristophanes hit on a direct, spatial means of expressing the change in the relation between the genders.

The whole action of the play is dependent on this preliminary decision to make the stage represent the area in front of the Propylaea, literally 'in front of the gates'. This is a crucial decision in a play about women. Instead of being tied to their own private front door, the female protagonists of this play gather in front of the entrance to the Acropolis. Their daring is underlined in the comic opening scene by the gradual arrival from all over Greece of women who have abandoned their homes, rallying to the call of Lysistrata. By choosing to meet in this particular spot, the women indicate their intention to seize the stronghold of political, i.e. male, power and further their own goals. The scene of the storming of the Acropolis by the women must have sent a shudder down the spine of the audience sitting so close to the real citadel.

The bold transformation of the stage convention from 'in front of home' to 'in front of the Acropolis' is a direct expression of the women's rebellion which forms the guiding-line of the plot. The spatial conception itself also provides the basis for the various incidents which constitute the plot, e.g. the women's occupation of the Acropolis and the men's siege of it, or Myrrhine's public seduction of her husband.

*Fig. 4 Theseus overcomes Andromache, Queen of Amazons, dinos from Agrigento, Classical period; British Museum*

The courage and ingenuity displayed by the women in the dramatic action are matched by the theatrical iconoclasm of their creator.

For the Athenian citizens, the significance of capturing the Acropolis would be related to their growing awareness, as the play progressed, of the women assuming the characteristics of Amazons, the ancient mythical warrior-women, who had attempted to capture the Athenian citadel in by-gone days. The Male Chorus draws a direct, derogatory parallel:

> Well a woman sticks on horseback: look around you, see, behold,
> Where on Micon's living frescoes fight the Amazons of old!
> Shall we let these wailful women, O my brothers, do the same?
>
> (lines 677–9)[5]

The Amazons' reputation for skillful horsemanship, recorded in famous wall-friezes and in countless vase-paintings, is here cleverly drawn into the bawdy joke. The scholiast on this passage connects the mounted Amazons with the paintings in the Stoa Poikile, or Painted Porch, one of whose subjects was the battle between the Amazons and the Athenians before the Acropolis.[6] But it might just as well refer to Micon's earlier frescoes[7] in the Theseum, the sanctuary built to house the bones of Theseus. That legendary hero had raped an Amazon and then repelled the Amazons' retaliatory attack on the Acropolis. The defeat of the Amazons by the 'aggressively misogynistic' Theseus was counted by the Athenians as one of the founding acts of their civilization,[8] and was, therefore, a central artistic theme (Fig. 4).

The same scene was also commemorated on the Acropolis itself. The visitor

*Fig. 5 Athenian and Amazon, marble copy of group from the Shield of Athena Parthenos;*
*Piraeus Museum*

passing through the Propylaea would be facing the western façade of the Parthenon.
On the metopes below the west pediment he could view the battle of the Amazons
and Athenians for the Acropolis. Another Amazonomachy was depicted in relief on
the shield of Phidias' statue of Athena which stood in the Parthenon.[9] The patron
goddess of Athens and her temple are thus associated with the city's legendary
triumph over the female warriors who had long ago threatened to capture the
Athenian citadel (Fig. 5).

That pseudo-historical battle, alluded to in the reference to Micon's frescoes,
and very much in evidence in the artistic conception of the Parthenon, surely served
Aristophanes as an antecedent to his own intrigue. The original audience could not
have failed to notice where the idea for the women's assault on the Acropolis was
taken from. Modern commentators, such as Leo Strauss and Jeffrey Henderson,
have noted the various references to the Amazon myth, but have not offered a
sustained interpretation of the plot as a latter-day Amazonomachy. Nicole Loraux
comes closest to appreciating the Amazonic model but does not pick up this scent,
wandering off instead to the dead trail of interpreting the women's actions as a
regression to their pre-marital status, when no male intermediate stood between the
girl and the city.[10]

The uprising of the Hellenic women takes on the frightening aspect of a new
Amazonomachy, as the liberated housewives assume the threatening aspect of

*Fig. 6 Achilles and Penthesilea, black-figure neck-amphora by Exekias, 545–530 BC; British Museum*

female soldiers. The different episodes offer opportunities for the women to exhibit their Amazon-like features. Two of them, Lampito and Myrrhine, are even named after Amazons.[11]

Recalling the Amazons evokes an age-old fear of women at the very heart of Athenian culture. Froma Zeitlin has diagnosed this anxiety as an 'Amazon complex'.[12] The sheer quantity of the visual depictions of Amazons, and the prevalent iconography of the woman defeated by a male hero, sinking to her knees or dead, indicates the centrality of this fear to Greek civilization (Fig. 6). The vagueness of the myth and its uncertain origins only make it even more unsettling and disturbing. This is especially true for the Athenian audience for whom the overcoming of the Amazons by the legendary Theseus served as the official foundation myth of their city.[13]

Imitating the Amazons in rejecting and reversing their traditional roles as wives and home-makers, Lysistrata and her followers raise the spectre of female rebellion, of a return to the archaic threat of the strong, independent, indomitable women. Aristophanes manipulates audience response by casting his own Amazonomachy in comic form, thus dissolving the fear in laughter. Kenneth Dover suggests that 'to the Athenians of Aristophanes' time the presentation of women conferring, conspiring and forcing a change of policy on the city is as great a flight of imaginative humour as the presentation of birds building a city and forcing the gods to surrender'.[14] But surely the male ego, whether fifth-century Athenian or modern, is far more threatened by women than by birds, and the idea of women controlling public affairs is not as fantastical as the idea of birds building a city.

Both the menace and its comic antidote remain ambiguously intertwined, leaving even some modern readers uneasy about the seriousness of the threat posed by the rebellious women: Are they really able to fight? And what about their claim that their handling of household affairs has prepared them for taking over the affairs of state? Could they really want to control the state treasure? Is this all part of a preposterous joke, a fantasy on the scale of Cloud-Cuckoo-Land, or should this comedy be taken more seriously? These questions become pressing in the light of Aristophanes' significant departure from the mythical precedent: whereas the Amazons were defeated by Theseus, Lysistrata's forces win the day, dictating the terms for peace and achieving reconciliation (embodied in the allegorical figure of the beautiful girl Diallage) between Athens and Sparta.

Aristophanes' audience must have shared the anxiety exhibited by the male characters of the play in the face of the female threat to the established order of things, and, therefore, to the male ego. This effect, one of Lysistrata's prime objectives, was created by a male playwright writing for an all-male cast. It is also intriguing – though unproductive – to speculate about whether the performance was conducted in front of an all-male audience. A. E. Haigh, still the best source for the relevant evidence, believes that 'if considered without prejudice', there were no restrictions on the attendance of women and children. Later scholars sift the same material, each reading it in the light of his own preconceptions.[15] The evidence seems to me too fragmentary and insubstantial for any definite conclusion. But even before a mixed audience, the dialectics of gender are at work here on all levels: in the dramatic structure of the play as a whole and in its parts, notably the *agon* between the two choruses, in the relationship between performance and audience, and especially in the intricacies of male actor impersonating a woman who decides to act in a manly manner.

Cross-gender dressing is taken a step further in the *Ecclesiazusae*, where Praxagora and the other women steal out of their homes at dawn dressed in their husbands' clothes in order to usurp the men's vote in the Assembly. Praxagora's husband, on the other hand, finds nothing to put on but her clothes. In the *Thesmophoriazusae*, Mnesilochus, whose female disguise makes him into a parody of Pentheus in the *Bacchae*, is forced to 'strip naked' before a 'female' audience. These examples of theatrical interplay of genders show a surprising range of variations in contrast to the more limited Elizabethan convention of boy-actor impersonating the girl-disguised-as-boy.

Despite the solidly male view-point – whether of the playwright, the actors, or the audience – the *Lysistrata* is no doubt the most feminist of Aristophanes' plays. The class-consciousness of the women is raised by Lysistrata, a born leader, to such a pitch, that they overcome their national differences forming a pan-Hellenic union devoted to the furthering of their goals as women. Conducted as a veritable revolution, their uprising has two main components: a general sex-strike all over Hellas and the seizing of the Acropolis. The strategic importance of this last move is augmented by the control of the state-treasure stored in the Parthenon, a military move meant to prevent Athens from carrying on the war.

The extreme militancy of the female cause is expressed in Lysistrata's provocative transformation of the Homeric adage 'War is the care and the business of men' (line 519) into 'War is the care and the business of women' (line 538). This quotation is taken from Hector's rebuke of his wife Andromache, who tried to dissuade him from fighting Achilles:

> Go into your house and see to your tasks, the loom and the distaff, and bid your handmaidens do their work; but war is the care and the business of men, and especially mine, of all men that dwell in Ilios.
>
> (*Iliad* 6.490–3)[16]

Lysistrata's clever substitution of a single word signals a total cultural upheaval.

Aristophanes perceives the nature of the obstacles standing in the way of an activist like Lysistrata to achieve such an upheaval:

> 'Tis hard, you know, for women to get out.
> One has to mind her husband: one, to rouse
> Her servant: one, to put the child to sleep:
> One, has to wash him: one, to give him pap.
>
> (lines 16–19)

This comical apology by Calonice invokes one of the strongest arguments used by modern feminists to explain the lack of female class-consciousness and class-struggle: women's strength and determination is sapped by their many pressing social commitments and biological obligations, which prevent them from taking stock of their condition and from uniting to take steps towards changing their enslavement to home and family.

Lysistrata tries to unite the women in order to create a female power that will save Hellas from internal wars. Lacking in self-confidence, having a poor self-image, the women's first reaction to Lysistrata's astounding declaration is timid:

> What can we women do? What brilliant scheme
> Can we, poor souls, accomplish? We who sit
> Trimmed and bedizened in our saffron silks,
> Our cambric robes, and little finical shoes.
>
> (lines 42–5)

Lysistrata picks up these apparent signs of feminine ineptitude and weakness turning them into the very powerful weapons the women will wield in their struggle. Extreme coquetry is to be practiced until the men are brought to their knees. They should be sexually provoked until they submit and agree to make peace.

Generations of readers have focused on the women's sex-strike and on its powerful effect on the men, overlooking the centrality of the treatment of female sexuality in the play. After all, it is the women who take the initiative, motivated by the sexual abstinence forced on them by their husbands being away at war, and the men are put on the defensive, at a loss to find a proper response. The reversal of the traditional passive and active roles in society must have been much more shocking to the sensibilities of the original audience than to us, although it still functions successfully as the stock-in-trade of many conventional comedies.

The women are portrayed throughout as having strong sexual desires of their own, and this is the cause of their initial rejection of Lysistrata's plan as well as the later spate of desertions. Lysistrata is exasperated with the weakness of their support:

> O women! women! Our frail, frail sex!
> No wonder tragedies are made from us,
> Always the same: nothing but loves and cradles.
>
> (lines 137–9)

Eventually the women harden themselves to the urgings of loves and cradles and disperse to their homes to carry out the public master-plan in the privacy of their homes.

The female need for sexual gratification, a great discovery in twentieth-century literature and psychology, is treated by Aristophanes in quite a nonchalant manner, with jokes about women's craving for the phallus or its substitute, the 'eight-inch toy' or 'leathern consolation' (lines 109–10).[17] Female sexuality is brought to the fore and problematized.

The plan is for the women to retaliate for their lack of sexual satisfaction imposed upon them by the absence of their men, by denying the men any such satisfaction in their turn. As has often been noted, the motives of female pacifism as presented in the play are limited to the sexual domain, and there is no mention of the women's grievances as mothers or wives afraid for the lives of their beloved.[18] The strategy of a sex-strike is eminently suited to the complaint it aims at redressing.

The most intimate and private of human activities is drawn out for public discussion with the convening of the women in front of the Propylaea. And their public decision is going to influence their private behaviours in the secrecy of their homes. But the public discussion is not confined to the theatrical space of the play;

36

the performance, taking place in the everyday space of the theatre, moves it into the public domain, forcing the audience to confront the question of gender roles. This public perspective is adhered to throughout the play.

Aristophanes engineers the entrance of his two choruses, of old men and old women, so as to create a spectacular clash between male and female contingents. Here then is yet another example of how the austere minimalism of the Greek theatre was used to advantage to create a striking effect. The old men enter stumbling under the weight of firewood with which they intend to burn down the citadel gates. They also carry a pot of lighted cinders for igniting the wood and keep blowing on them to keep the fire alive, the blowing forming a refrain to their song. After they have broken in, they mean to smoke out the women.

Not to be outdone, the chorus of women now enters carrying pitchers full of water. A war of words in *stychomythia*, an *agon* between the genders, now ensues,[19] replacing the actual test of water against fire. However, unlike fire, water can be used safely in the theatre, so that the women can score their point by dousing the men with the cold water in their pitchers.

The conflict between the men and the women is carried out by the two choruses on several levels: verbal, physical, symbolic and archetypal. The dramatic war of words is theatricalized through the action, the men's threat to burn down the Propylaea in order to force an entry into the Acropolis and the women's actual or merely mimed pouring of water over the startled men. The props called for by the action – the heavy logs, the brazier full of smouldering cinders, the water jugs – contribute to the vividness of the spectacle. Beyond both the verbal and the physical confrontations between the choruses stands the symbolic elemental opposition between fire and water which Aristophanes weaves into his text. Although fire bears the more aggressive image, it is water that will win over fire, quenching it. Fire and water stand for the archetypes of gender in the erotic innuendo: the men carry fire and the women cool down their zeal or lust by drenching them with cold water. The women seem to be enjoying themselves when they taunt and humiliate the dripping-wet men: 'Watered, perhaps you'll bloom again' (line 384),[20] thus driving home the realization that the old men's failure to overcome the women is an indication of their impotence. The war of the sexes is given theatrical presence through the interplay of prop, action and word.

Having captured the Acropolis, the women guard the state-treasure stowed in the back-chamber of the Parthenon, the temple of the warrior Goddess. They bar the entrance to the holy precinct, refusing admittance to the men. When the Probulos or Magistrate tries to crash the gates with crowbars, he is surprised by Lysistrata who opens them from within, to offer her free advice that persuasion will get him further than force. His pitiful attempt at gate-crashing points to the wide range of possible attitudes to the opening and shutting of stage doors.

The sex-strike which is the guiding theme of the action is directly expressed in the theatrical space by the resistance of the doors. Aristophanes sets up the double doors of the *skene* as the Propylaea. The action defines them further as the gates of the female precinct being stormed by angry males. Finally, they come to represent symbolically the vaginal orifice:[21] the forceful entrance attempted by the Magistrate is akin to rape, the alternative being suggested by Lysistrata's own willing opening of the doors from within. The door is the threshold which the male attempts to penetrate. Theatrical space itself is eroticized, every movement within its framework assuming sexual overtones.

Jeffrey Henderson, in his otherwise wonderful treatment of obscene language in Old Comedy, seems to miss totally the theatrical dimension of the dialogue, arguing that

> Although the physical action must have been fast-paced and colorful, it is primarily in his verbal pyrotechnics that the genius of Aristophanes... resides.[22]

He demonstrates the metaphoric use of words like 'door', 'gate' and 'fire', but misses their embodiment as scenic elements around which the action of the play revolves.

The closed doors, the attempts to break in forcefully, the women's insistence that the men gain admittance only if they agree to peace talks – all these transform the theatrical space into a blown-up public image of the sex-strike practiced by each of the women on her own husband in the privacy of her home. On the personal, marital level, the refusal of penetration is staged much later in the play, in the farcical scene between Myrrhine and her husband Cinesias, whose sexual excitation is all too visible. Lysistrata instructs Myrrhine to arouse her husband even further and lead him on without yielding to him. She is to act the perfect tease. This scene is so powerful because the couple act out 'the basic drama of the sexes, but without the usual climax'.[23]

Myrrhine refuses to go home with Cinesias until he supports the conclusion of the war. He therefore asks to make love to her on the spot. Seeming to acquiesce, Myrrhine keeps finding fault with the arrangements and, solicitous of her husband's comfort, rushes off time and again to fetch the missing articles: a couch, a mattress, a cushion, a blanket, and even a scent-flask. In front of our eyes she assembles the bed with all its covers on which she is to lie with Cinesias. The bed stands on its own, in the open, in front of the *skene*. The mere suggestion of having sexual relations *al fresco* may be an added allusion to the Amazon-like nature of the rebellious women, for it was believed that Amazons mated outdoors,[24] and it should not be forgotten that Myrrhine is the name of a legendary Amazon.

Fussing around her husband with excessive care and affection, Myrrhine builds up his passion, then leaves him summarily because he will not vouch to vote for the peace treaty. This very funny and fantastical scene serves two contradictory and complementary purposes: first, it exemplifies how the sex-strike is carried out in the privacy of each home, and second, by assembling the love-couch in public, it shows that the most private of human relations will not be put back into its intimate surroundings until the public issue of making peace is resolved. Myrrhine does not 'turn(s) the acropolis into a bedroom' as Foley would have it. On the contrary, the theatrical point of this scene is the fantastical and ludicrous transference of the privacy of her bedroom into the open (in front of the Propylaea, not inside the Acropolis). It is not that 'the distinction between acropolis and home collapses',[25] but rather that Myrrhine's act stresses this distinction only the more. The out-of-place bed is the image of the reversal of the public and the private domains and the disruption of the home. Aristophanes makes a virtue of necessity, creating an outlandish bedroom scene in front of the Acropolis gates in a theatre space that cannot accommodate indoor scenes.

The interrupted love-scene marks the turning point in the fortunes of the female revolution, a change predicted by the oracle: it shows that the vaunted superior strength of the male sexual drive makes the men more vulnerable to abstinence. It is a source of weakness which the women can cleverly manipulate to their own advantage. This is evidenced by the comically exaggerated erections with which the delegates to the peace negotiations arrive on stage.

The women's defiance in moving out of doors to seize the control of public affairs, traditionally a male prerogative, brings about, even if only temporarily, a reversal of male-female roles. When the Magistrate objects to the female insurrection, he is punished by being dressed up as a woman. His humiliation is complete when he is fitted out with a spindle and a basket of wool and told to 'sit humbly at home, munching beans, while you card wool and comb' (lines 536–7).[26] Now war has become the business of women, who alone can be trusted with the affairs of state after the men have botched them altogether, and it is the men who should take up spinning, the traditional female occupation, and stay in the *oikos*. The Magistrate's punishment is thus a necessary concomitant to the neat reversal of Hector's patriarchal views in his admonishment of his wife.

## Chapter 4

# The comedy of doors

On the question of the number of doors in the *skene* there is agreement only as to the beginning and end situations: originally there was one double door, and by the time of Plautus there must have been three doors.[1] Dover reconstructs the staging of such plays as *Peace* or *Ecclesiazusae* (*Women in Parliament*) using a multiple-door *skene*, but concedes that it is possible to work out the staging using one door only.[2] More than one house may be required, but, if the houses do not need to be there simultaneously, a single door can be made to represent the several houses. In the absence of either archeological evidence or contemporary documents, scholars can only fall back on the internal evidence of the plays themselves.[3]

The multiplication of doors in New Comedy allows for a more intricate plot, in which characters living in different households interact. Also, it contains a comic potential in the breach of discretion involved in entering a house other than your own.

The elongated stage comes to be defined as a street in front of three houses.[4] The side entrances of the stage become conceptually and visually integrated as marking a segment of that street and as leading on the audience's right to the market place and harbour, and on their left to the country. These accepted attributions had developed from the actual topography of the Theatre of Dionysus in Athens, where the *parodoi* would seem to be leading, on the spectator's right, to the harbour of the Piraeus and the market place, and, on his left, into open country. In an unroofed theatre, in broad daylight, such geographical relations would be much more evident than in a closed modern auditorium, where the spectator loses his sense of orientation. This natural geographical layout was conventionalized when Athens became the imaginary scene of plays which were performed in other towns.[5]

Vitruvius codified the two side-entrances as leading the one *a foro* and the other *a peregre*, i.e. from the market and from abroad, respectively.[6] This might suggest that the entrances became spatially redefined as leading the one to a closer the other to a further removed perimeter. Thereby the whole spatial organization would become more regularized, with the theatrical space without articulated in three separate planes: the house, the city and the out-lying country. The result would be a perspective view of the ensemble, akin to that achieved in some Roman frescoes which create a feeling of depth through the portrayal of a number of receding planes.

The greater flexibility offered by the multiple-door *skene* did not interfere with the Classical conception, according to which the stage represents the outside of a house and the doorstep is the meeting place of the genders. New Comedy appropriates this theatrical framework, re-interpreting it within contemporary culture, making it into a leading comic theme and trying to manoeuvre around its imposed limitations. In its adherence to and manipulation of this stage convention, New Comedy follows Greek tragedy closely, without exhibiting any awareness of the imaginative, anarchic experimentation of Aristophanes with the *skene*.

Stage conventions, dramatic decorum and social propriety, all meet in New Comedy around the *frons scenae* of the Roman theatre. The social code for the conduct of women in public restricted the dramatic situations possible in the given outdoor convention:

> With a few exceptions ... the only women with recognised citizen status who appear on the stage are either married or widowed; as young, unmarried citizen girls appeared in public only at festivals, dramatic realism denied them a major role in comedies whose action was imagined to take place in public.[7]

The *meretrix* was so popular a character in the Roman theatre not least because she could be more readily portrayed outdoors, not being bound by the decorum of matrons. In contrast to the women confined to their homes, the male characters are free to come and go, travelling, engaging in business or litigation. These gender-determined distinctions thus endow the standard scenery with symbolic meaning and turn it into a structural matrix rich in potential dramatic situations.

In Plautine comedy, the house-façade which blocks the inside from view is used to advantage, serving as a safe haven for tricks and tricksters and arousing the curiosity of the audience as to what is going on behind the closed doors. The *Miles Gloriosus* (*The Braggart Soldier*) and the *Amphitryo* will serve as illustrations of the game established between doors and duplicity.

In the *Miles Gloriosus* (*c.* 204 BC), Plautus creates a farcical situation which is wholly dependent on the proximity of two stage doors representing two neighbouring houses. The heroine Philocomasium is made to pose as her own twin, using the secret passageway Palaestrio has opened between the two adjacent houses in order to move quickly from the one to the other, to await the alternating entrances of the slave Sceledrus. The latter firmly believes that 'There's no way of getting from this house to that except through this door.'[8]

The kidnapped heroine who belongs to neither of the houses is allowed to display her wit in leading the slave to believe that she is both herself and a twin sister. This masquerade is dependent on the theatrical façade-convention onto which is added the dramatic invention of the secret passageway between the two houses. In actual terms, all the actor playing Philocomasium is required to do is to leave the stage through one door, walk a few paces across the dressing-room, and enter again through the other door. The simplicity of the technique does not of course diminish from its theatrical effectiveness.

If in the *Miles Gloriosus* Plautus made one character appear as two, for the central comic invention of the *Amphitryo* (*c.* 195 BC)[9] he employed the inverse stratagem, two characters appearing as one. Jupiter assumes the likeness of Alcmena's husband Amphitryo in order to make love to this irreproachably virtuous woman, while his son Mercury takes on the likeness of Amphitryo's servant Sosia. Plautus' doubling of characters was imitated so often that it became generic, and Sosia's name became, in French and other Latin languages, a general noun designating any double or impersonator. The supernatural status of the two gods is used in the play as a cover-up for some of the cruder aspects of the farce. This phantasm is something the audience must take on trust if they are to enjoy the comedy of errors that ensues. The improbable dramatic situation becomes plausible within the constricting stage convention.

Mercury, speaking as Prologue, introduces the listeners to the disguising-trick, and even takes the trouble to teach them how they can tell the one from the other by watching out for the feather in Mercury's bonnet and the little gold tassel in Jupiter's. In a modern production, the problem may be how to make the supposed doubles look alike, but in the Roman theatre, where the actors wore masks, the difficulty was apparently how to tell them apart. Moving deftly between his person as actor and his two personae as Mercury and as Mercury-disguised-as-Sosia, he reminds us that the whole question of identity and assumed identity is of the essence of theatre and especially of comedy. As actor, he points to the stage-building and declares it to be Amphitryo's house, expanding its meaning by supplying information about the inmates of the house. Under his magic wand, the theatre space is transformed into a theatrical space.

In this comedy, Plautus restricts himself to one door only. The house in this play is Alcmena's house, in which she awaits her husband, the commander of the Theban army, who is away at war. In his absence, Jupiter has usurped his place by pretending to be the visiting husband. Thus, the basic situation is reminiscent of the *Agamemnon*, where Aegisthus has taken the place of the hero at home. Here the domesticity of the situation is extended through Alcmena's pregnancy. The story of her double pregnancy, to both the real and the fake Amphitryos, has all the makings of an Italian *novella*, but the theatrical medium seems to clash with the theme, preventing us from observing Alcmena and her two husbands. The whole drama becomes focused on the door-step, where the faithful wife can appear to welcome her husband or part from him, and to which the men take turns in arriving.

The inviolability of wife and home, which is emblematized in the convention of *skene* as house front, is both breached and respected in this comedy. The heroine's virtue remains intact, yet her illicit lover enjoys complete freedom of access thanks to his clever disguise. He has no difficulty in making his way into that citadel of chastity which is Alcmena's home. What is nothing short of rape is therefore accomplished without resort to violence.

Although there is only one house in this play, diversity is assured through the doubling of the characters. There are two husbands and two servants, and even the one and only Alcmena is, though unwittingly, given a dual personality as both true and untrue. Her good name is only saved by the revelation that she was tricked by Jupiter's impersonation of her husband. The untying of the impossible knot is achieved through the birth of twins – only thus can both rightful husband and divine lecher achieve their goals without blemishing Alcmena's reputation as an ideal wife.

The nurse Bromia issues out of the house to inform the audience as well as Amphitryo of what has taken place inside. She recounts how Alcmena has given birth to twins, while thunder and lightning, Jupiter's own attributes, struck the house. Like the intimate scenes of love, Alcmena's *accouchement* also takes place out of the sight of the audience, in the theatrical space without.

The *frons scenae*, a given scenic impediment, is directly responsible for the particular dramatic shape Plautus gives to the mythical story. The play can be seen as a naughty bedroom-farce in which a lover tricks the husband, usurping his place. But of necessity, this is a bedroom-farce minus the bedroom. As the house-door closes on the loving couple, the audience is left with Mercury pretending to be Sosia guarding the door. It should be remembered that Mercury is the Roman equivalent of Hermes, the god whose statue protected the entrance to the *oikos*, and whose figure characterized the male principle of travel and movement as opposed to Hestia, the female goddess of the hearth.[10]

The interior of the house is closely associated with Alcmena, the alluring lover, faithful wife and expectant mother. The two types of (unseen) scenes that take place in it, in the course of the play, are sexual communion and childbirth. The woman's association with the house is thus sharply limited to an erotic one, as the house becomes the place of insemination and parturition. In terms of the theatrical space, the house is clearly used as a spatial metaphor for the womb, and entering it is penetration or even violation. Because two Amphitryos rather than one have been allowed in, the structurally satisfying aesthetic ending is achieved with the birth of two babies, bringing to fruition and completion the two separate gestations.

44

The theatrical convention of the feminine indoors and the masculine outdoors was imitated in the Renaissance, in the contemporary sense of imitation as emulation of a classical model of excellence. In *The Comedy of Errors* (*c.* 1594), his only direct imitation of Roman comedy, Shakespeare combined the two comical principles of the Roman stage, the multiplication of doors and the doubling of characters. He increased the number of houses he found in his source play, Plautus' *Menaechmi*, from two to three, and doubled the number of twins, in order to expand the farcical potential of the plot. Thus, his variations on his sources reinforce the Roman character of his comedy.

The three house fronts on stage belong to the wife, the courtesan and the mother of the protagonist. Each of the houses is closely identified with one of the women and defined by her dramatic function, and all three reflect different aspects of the hero's relations with women. Shakespeare has here provided three houses and three women for the three aspects of woman which Plautus condensed into the single house and the single person of Alcmena.

While critics are agreed on the scenic necessity of these three houses at the back of the stage, it is not at all clear how they were represented in Shakespeare's own time. Some maintain that, as the play may have been written for performance at Gray's Inn, the houses should be envisaged in the Humanist Terence tradition we find in fifteenth-century illustrations of play-texts: a conventionalized arcade overhung with curtains (Fig. 7).[11] Such a view is, however, irreconcilable with the internal evidence of the play, for how could Antipholus complain of the door being locked on him and ask for a crow-bar in order to force it open when faced with fabric hangings? Though the Elizabethan theatre was of a symbolic rather than a realistic nature, its use of props was real enough. Also one should bear in mind that the question of the houses should not be tackled apart from that of the street entrances leading, true to Roman tradition, *a foro* and *a peregre*, which the play also requires. The apparent incongruence between the classical requirements of the play and the available theatre spaces of Shakespeare's time cannot be resolved for lack of evidence. One must therefore fall back on the text, which happily defines its own spatial requirements and makes the most of it in theatrical terms.

The day-long action centres round the midday meal. The *epitasis* or climax of the plot occurs when Antipholus returns home for lunch and finds the door locked while his wife is lunching with his identical twin brother. Structurally, this forms the very middle of the play. Lunch thus assumes a central position in terms of time, plot and overall design. This is reinforced by the enormous build-up leading to the lunch. When the local Dromio mistakenly urges the visiting Antipholus to hurry home for lunch, his speech conveys the atmosphere of a comfortable household with both a pig and a capon being roasted for dinner and Adriana impatiently awaiting her husband. The verve and wit of Dromio's description generously

*Fig. 7 Illustration to the Comedies of Terence; J. Trechsel, Lyon, 1493*

compensate for our inability to see what is going on inside the house, behind its façade. The poetry makes virtue of necessity, turning the theatrical limitation into its source of strength.

While Dromio's master has been at 'the mart', his mistress has presided over the elaborate preparations of the mouth-watering meal. These conventional sex-roles are part and parcel of the outdoors/indoors tradition to which Shakespeare here adheres. When Adriana and Luciana 'enter' the stage[12], by exiting from the house, they debate the relative positions of men and women. To present their point of view they must come out of the hidden interior of the house and converse out of doors. This stretches the convention and shows its rigidity. Significantly, their conversation takes off from the present concern about the tardy husband to the broader issue of the relative liberty of men and women, the double standard of morality. 'Why should their liberty than ours be more?' protests Adriana; to which Luciana retorts: 'Because their business still lies out o'door' (2.1.10–11). Thus, the terms of the discussion derive from the very structure of the theatrical space in which it is set.

The climactic scene is carefully prepared and executed. When Adriana finally has her way with her husband's look-alike, she sets the scene to come by directing Dromio to keep the gate (2.2.209), play the porter (line 214) and prevent any disturbance to their dinner (line 213), and by leading her supposed husband to dine with her 'above' (line 210). As the door shuts behind them, in come the legitimate husband and his guests, bargaining for more hospitality than they are to find. For the farcical scene which follows, Shakespeare collated Plautus' *Amphitryo* with the *Menaechmi*.

The greatest comical scene of the play is totally indebted to the conventional assumption of an interior behind the visible façade of the house. This is a very daring scene, for here the secret of the errors is constantly in danger of being revealed by the door being forcefully broken open or by one of the twins spotting the other. Should that happen, the play would come to an abrupt end. In lining his characters on both sides of the door, Shakespeare is exhibiting theatrical brinkmanship. Whereas up to this point the farce has depended on quick, alternating entrances and exits of the two pairs of twins, a game of permutations, now its scope has been dangerously narrowed to the one central door, on the strength of which the immediate future of the audience's pleasure hangs.

It is difficult to know how the locked-door scene was meant to be staged. But it is clear, in any case, that the two pairs of masters and servants are ranged on the wrong sides of the impenetrable door, the visitors having usurped the place of the locals indoors. The dialogue conveys the spatial relationship of within and without not only through the references to door, porter and street, but also, more directly, by Antipholus of Ephesus' inquiry 'Who talks within there?' (3.1.38). Modern editors have liberally sprinkled the interchange with the stage direction 'within'. The Folio stage direction 'Enter Adriana' (following line 61) means that she is visible to the audience, presumably appearing above, i.e. on the gallery, but neither seeing her husband nor being seen by him.[13] The special effect of the scene depends on the conversation being conducted between those characters we can see in the theatrical space within and those we can only hear from the theatrical space without.

The two other doors required by the play offer alternative kinds of solace and refuge to the hungry and weary husband. The ensemble of the three doors reinforce, by their physical presence on stage, the archetypal male-phantasm of woman as wife, prostitute and mother. Thus, the conventional three-door façade with side-wing entrances, the legacy of the Roman stage, itself derived from the Greek model, becomes part of the deep structure of the play itself, an expression of its views of the human personality and sexual relations.

## Chapter 5

# The woman in the window

Plautus' *Amphitryo* inspired the imagination of many comedy writers, from Molière to Giraudoux. The deceit, duplicity and clever resolution seem to have crystallized into essential comic features which offered themselves for further exploration. Plautus may have canonized the myth, but even before him, the Amphitryo story must have been regarded as both funny and intriguing, built as it is around an inner core of moral ambiguity. Already in the fourth century BC, an Italian vase-painter depicted a different version of the story. Assteas, the probable Master of the Alcmena vase, pictured Zeus carrying a ladder over his head towards his beloved's window, while his son Hermes lights his way with a lamp (Fig. 8).[1] Clearly predating Plautus' play, this *phlyakes* vase illustrates a scene from some lost mythical burlesque. In Plautus, Jupiter, the divine lecher, gains access in a less adventurous manner, by simply impersonating the absent Amphitryo, thus exonerating Alcmena. Assteas' version is naughtier, making Alcmena into a willing accomplice, and the father of gods into a lascivious, low-comedy character.

Alcmena appears on the vase in profile, elaborately coiffured and adorned with jewellery. Her head is framed by a window which appears on its own, with no reference to any architectural structure. The ladder carried by Zeus will enable him to reach Alcmena through her window. This accentuates the importance of the window as a necessary element in the development of the plot.

For his 'incidental' vase-painting Assteas extracted in visual terms the essential features of an old literary and theatrical *cliché*. The typological nature of this dramatic situation is underlined by the appearance, on another vase, probably by the same painter, of a scene which takes the action a step further. Here the lover is seen climbing up the ladder to the window and apparently offering the woman some gifts he has brought her; the slave who accompanies him again provides lighting, this time with a torch held up high (Fig. 9).[2]

There is no evidence of windows being used on the ancient stages, although some commentators have suggested the use of a window in addition to a door or doors for the staging of the scene in *Ecclesiazusae* in which a young girl and three old hags quarrel over a young man.[3] However, on the Renaissance stage, windows assume

49

*Fig. 8 Zeus and Alcmena, phlyakes vase by Assteas, fourth century BC; Vatican Museum*

increased importance not only for their theatrical functionality but also as integral parts of the contemporary scenic design.

The typical Renaissance *décor* offers a conventionalized outdoor scene. The characters can enter from the side-streets or from the houses up front, and the action takes place out of doors, in the street or piazza. The window opens up new possibilities for the theatre, extending rather than disrupting its conventions. It helps in circumventing some of the difficulty posed by the scenic house-front which bars from view the inside of the house. The presentation of the indoors on stage is a relatively late development, intimately tied with the emergence of the roofed theatre building.

The basic notion of a street with house-fronts was elaborated in the Renaissance

*Fig. 9 Lover climbs a ladder, phlyakes vase by Assteas, fourth century BC; British Museum*

and codified by Sebastiano Serlio in his familiar illustrations of the Vitruvian stage-descriptions (*Architettura*, 1545) (Fig. 10). His highly influential, though by no means original, scenic contribution is the sophisticated organization of the houses – the front ones constructions, those further back merely foreshortened paintings on the wings and backcloth – into a perspective picture-frame stage. The difficulty in interpreting Serlio's drawings lies in their being a perspective rendering of a perspective stage. They are, in the words of John Orrell, 'a sort of metascene, or perspective of a perspective'.[4] Serlio's visual conception of the stage is that of an architect and a city-planner. It is not surprising therefore to find it so closely related to contemporary architectural designs of piazzas and cityscapes. In fact, not only did the new stage design attempt to copy the innovations in city planning but also vice versa, city planning and even landscape gardening were theatricalized, planned

*Fig. 10 Comic scene; Sebastiano Serlio, Architettura, 1545*

with view lines and perspective vistas in mind, trying to emulate contemporary stage design.[5]

Purporting to illustrate the Vitruvian Codex, Serlio's stage designs in fact strayed far away from the Roman theatre. Innovation in the guise of interpretation is a familiar stratagem of the period, as exemplified in the various treatises expounding Aristotle's *Poetics*. The Renaissance conception of the stage adheres to the Roman convention of continuous outdoor action unquestioningly, despite the fact that the original theatre architecture which necessitated that conception is no longer followed.

This point is perhaps best illustrated by the still extant Teatro Olimpico at Vicenza, begun in 1580 by Andrea Palladio and finished in 1585 by Vincenzo Scamozzi. Although later in date than the Serlian illustrations, the Olimpico can be seen as an interim stage, incorporating the Roman *frons scenae*, which Serlio had chosen to abandon, within a closed Renaissance building. Palladio's theatre was on a much smaller scale than the ruins of the ancient theatres he had studied. The ceiling which covered the *cavea*, or auditorium, was apparently painted to represent a blue sky with some clouds, to create the illusion of, or just refer to, the ancient, open-air theatre. As it now stands, the Olimpico is roofed, but there is disagreement among scholars about whether the auditorium (as distinct from the stage) was originally covered by a permanent awning or by a ceiling painted to represent a *velarium*.[6] Considered to be the first permanent indoor theatre, the Teatro Olimpico was meant in fact to enclose an outdoor theatre indoors.

While the basic architectural conception of the classical theatre was retained and even canonized, it was also imaginatively developed and enriched by Peruzzi, Serlio and others. These Renaissance artists attempted to accommodate their own predilection for perspective representation and verisimilitude within the inherited tradition. Windows were added as indispensable architectural and ornamental features which could also be used as added links between the outdoors and the indoors. Although Assteas had recorded their use in ancient, pre-Roman farce, windows were not called for in Roman comedy, so that their introduction on the Renaissance stage exemplifies the method of preserving a convention by easing its rigidity.

Still, Serlio's proposals for the comic and tragic scenes set strict restraints on the dramatist and actors, the most serious of which is perhaps that the whole action must be contrived to take place out of doors, without offending propriety and verisimilitude. The development of such an action must depend largely on chance meetings, on characters bumping into each other in the piazza when coming from one of the side-streets or walking out of one of the front houses. (These are the only houses from which a character can enter the stage, for only these are both three dimensional and not excessively foreshortened.)

The effect of such drama greatly depends on the dramatist's ability to orchestrate his characters' movements, on his control of who goes where at what time and who meets whom. This concern with the blocking of movement is quite evident in the extant *scenari* of *commedia dell'arte*. The house door often becomes the focal point of the action, at times almost assuming a wilful life of its own. It may open arbitrarily to introduce characters, or remain obstinately shut, thus hiding a character from sight, or it can be locked either from within or from without, to prevent intruders from entering or the inhabitants from exiting.

In the architectural stage designs of Serlio and his followers, windows figure prominently. These added apertures provide the action with a vertical dimension, extending the theatrical space upwards. Whereas the mere usage of street entrances and house doors dictates a movement on the plane, the window creates a truly three-dimensional theatrical space. A character inside can converse with someone standing down below through an open window, thus circumventing the closed door. In the theatre, recourse to the window is typically associated with some difficulty about the normal functions of the door. Although not as dramatically useful as doors, windows were used to advantage on the Renaissance stage, as can be seen in many *scenari* and plays as well as in illustrations.

The window can be extended into an overhanging balcony, to give a full view of the locked-up character. From both window and balcony a letter can be dropped or a rope-ladder let down to get round the locked front-door, adding ingenuity and excitement to the illicit communication or forced entrance, and transforming the action into an adventure.

These blueprints of dramatic situations can thus be seen as structural permutations derived from the basic scenic conceptions of the Renaissance stage. The limitation imposed by confining the action to the street and blocking off the house-interior provides the impetus for the dramatic invention expressed through the characters' own imaginative stratagems.

The relationship between this architectural conception of scenery and the dramatic invention is intimately tied to the traditional association between woman and her house. The social position of women as well as the exigencies of the plot often relegate the heroines to the indoors, in circumstances not unlike house-arrest. The male guardian of the unmarried girl or the elderly husband expecting to be cuckolded try desperately to sever the young woman's ties with the outside world. Trapped in her house, the window or balcony offer her some opportunity for public appearance. Dropping *billets-doux* becomes her means of communication with her lover. If determined enough, she can let down a rope ladder, while her lover may devise some other clever scheme to gain access to the forbidden house, such as the over-worn music-teacher trick (used by Molière in *Le Malade imaginaire*) or the portrait-painter ruse (as in *Le Sicilien ou L'Amour peintre*).

The house itself is so closely identified with the woman that entering the guarded house becomes a theatrical metaphor for sexual conquest, for that which happens in the scenically impenetrable indoors. The invisible indoors is the feminine domain, while the outdoors is male territory. Thus, the closedness of the house is a symbol of its dweller's chastity, while, conversely, her appearance at the window may be taken for an invitation and a provocation.

This visual symbolism is so old that it can be found in the Old Testament, and so suggestive that it sometimes spills over into the dialogue of a play as poetic metaphor. Two notable biblical examples are the vignettes of Sisera's mother and of Jezebel. In her song of thanksgiving, Debora celebrates the downfall of Sisera. Though arguably the first feminist, she turns her feminine thoughts to the mother of her vanquished enemy:

*Fig. 11 The woman in the window, Phoenician ivory plaque, Nimrud, seventh century BC;
British Museum*

The mother of Sisera looked out at a window, and cried through the lattice,
Why is his chariot so long in coming? why tarry the wheels of his chariots?
(Judges 5:28)

Queen Jezebel awaits Jehu the avenger, all made up, at the window: 'and she
painted her face, and tired her head, and looked out at a window' (II Kings 9: 30).
This terse description of the harlot queen finds its parallel in contemporary
Phoenician and Assyrian ivory tablets, discovered, among other places, in Samaria,
the capital of the Kingdom of Israel (Fig. 11). In some of them, archaeologists have
identified the recurring motif of what they have termed 'the woman at the
window', with possible implications of sacred prostitution.[7]

Entering the palace gates, Jehu lifts up his face to the window, not to answer the
queen's desperate appeal, but to ask: 'Who is on my side? who?' In response, two

or three eunuchs look out at him through the window. In the grim sequel, Jehu orders the eunuchs to throw Jezebel down. They comply, in what might be the first recorded instance of defenestration. Both passages reinforce the traditional image of the woman who stays at home, awaiting the battle news. Like Sisera's mother, Jezebel has just lost her son in battle, but her provocative sensuality is apparent in her last-ditch attempt to save her own skin by making the most of her appearance in the window.

The scenic configuration of woman, house and window becomes the basis for an extended poetic metaphor used by Rosalind in *As You Like It*:

> Make the doors upon a woman's wit, and it will out at the casement. Shut that, and 'twill out at the key-hole. Stop that, 'twill fly with the smoke out at the chimney.

$$(4.1.53-6)^8$$

Verbal references to the constrained amatory uses of windows abound in Shakespeare, ranging from the romantic, 'Thou hast by moonlight at her window sung' (*A Midsummer Night's Dream* 1.1.30), to the ribald description of an adulterous affair, 'In at the window, or else o'er the hatch' (*King John* 1.1.171),[9] or the bawdy 'Those milk-paps, that through the window bars bore at men's eyes' (*Timon of Athens* 4.3.116).

The theatricality and dramatic efficacy of window-scenes accounts for their widespread use in *scenari* of *commedia dell'arte* and in Renaissance and later plays. The convention of the Serenade, from Scapino to Figaro, is a natural outgrowth of this scenic feature (Fig. 12). Variations on the guarded woman theme and on the window-scene are found in three of Shakespeare's Italianate plays: *Romeo and Juliet*, set in Verona, and his two Venetian plays, *Othello* and *The Merchant of Venice*. The window-scene in Ben Jonson's *Volpone*, which also takes place in Venice, exhibits a self-consciousness of its *commedia dell'arte* origins. In *L'École des femmes*, Molière has blown-up the window-scene into a complete play, exploiting its inherent comical and critical potential. Even as late as 1772, the by then totally anachronistic window convention is used by Beaumarchais in *Le Barbier de Séville* for its precious artificiality. Like Watteau's paintings of *dell'arte* comedians, this is a sophisticated attitude, devoid of the immediacy and innocence of the original theatrical constraints responsible for the growth of the window-scene. The romantic icon, reverberating with literary echoes, still crops up in Chekhov's naturalistic *Seagull*, in Konstantin's vow: 'I'll stand in the garden all night gazing at your window.' But his romantic idealism is deflated by Nina's warning: 'Our dog doesn't know you yet and he'd bark' (Act 1, p. 238).[10]

The scenic constraints of house fronts and street defined the theatrical space and

# OPERA NVOVA
## NELLAQVALE SI CONTIENE
il Maridazzo della bella Brunettina,
Sorella de Zan Fritada de
Valpelosa.

CON VN SONETTO SOPRA
l'Agio, cosa molto diletteuole, & degna d'esser
letta da ogni spirito gentile.

*Fig. 12 Serenade;* Il Maridazzo della bella Brunettina, *1585, frontispiece*

at the same time expressed symbolically the relative social position of the genders. The different plots of plays sharing these scenic conventions work out the potential situations implicit in the set itself when taken in conjunction with particular given characters. This is in effect the very essence of the *scenari* of *commedia dell'arte*.

As can be learned from the rich visual material depicting *commedia dell'arte* performances, the basic scenery used when there was more than a makeshift booth-stage was along the lines of the Serlian designs. In some of the illustrations one can clearly see characters joining in from a window. Many of these scenes depict lute-playing lovers serenading their mistresses. The serenade is a prime example of a dramatic, theatrical and operatic convention growing from the scenic constraints. It is in fact a stylized courtship conducted in the piazza between street level and window, as in the first scene of Beaumarchais' *Le Barbier de Séville* and in Mozart's *Le Nozze di Figaro* and *Don Giovanni*. An extended serenade, a mini-opera with three shepherds, appears in Molière's *Le Sicilien*. Of great interest is the feather-collage of Scapino serenading Spineta, who looks down at him from her window. This delightful work, executed in 1618 by Dionisio Minaggio, gardener to the governor of Milan, perfectly illustrates the charming romantic quality of the conventional scene, complete with the different musical instruments Scapino can play, all strung from a tree (Fig. 13).[11]

Window-scenes can also be found in *scenari*. In the scenario *The Doubles According to Plautus* from the Corsini collection, 'Zanni from the window complains to Silvio that his wife Flavia will not sleep with him.'[12] Inside, Zanni's wife obviously reigns supreme. In this case, the window is used by the husband, rather than the wife, to convey information about what is happening indoors and cannot be seen. In another scenario, *The Unbelieving Zanni and The Four Alike*,

> *Lavinio* ... says that he has been away in the country and wishes to visit Silvia;
> at this: *Silvia* appears at the window: he salutes her. She reproaches him and
> dismisses him. He is left anxious, not knowing the reason.[13]

Then Zanni tries to intercede on his behalf with the servant Argentina, but she only abuses Zanni and retires back into the house. Here the protagonist's predicament can be easily grasped in scenic terms: not only is he denied entrance into the house, but he cannot even establish some sort of communication or negotiation with the lady either through window or door.

The transferral of the window-scene from the Italian to the English stage provides yet another example of how a theatrical convention outlives the particular theatrical architecture which gave rise to it. Unlike the Serlian stage with its three scenic options of tragedy, comedy and pastoral, the Elizabethan playhouse offered an unchanging, neutral theatre space. In fact, every performance took up the given

Fig. 13 Scapino serenading Spineta, feather-collage; Dionisio Minaggio, 1618

theatre space, directly transforming it through word, gesture and properties into a theatrical space, without the mediation of any scenic design.

The Elizabethan stage lacks the illusory depth of the Italian perspective stage. This was to be introduced into England only later, by Inigo Jones. In general, the 'scientific' perspective in painting did not catch on in England until relatively late, so much so, that Sir John Harington found it expedient to preface his translation of *Orlando Furioso* (1591) with an explanation of how the illustrations should be viewed: 'That which is nearest seemes greatest and the fardest shewes smallest, which is the chiefe art in picture.'[14]

Quite unlike its Italian counterpart, the Elizabethan multiple stage offered an indeterminate space, one in which the meaning or function of the various components was defined anew within each production. The gallery in particular was a flexible area, even being used on occasion for extra audience seating. Although it had no piazza scenery, the Elizabethan playhouse could easily absorb the Italian convention, making it its own, by assigning the function of window or balcony to the gallery.

It is therefore not surprising to find certain characters, conventions and stock scenes of the Italian *commedia dell'arte* being appropriated by the Elizabethan playwrights.[15] This is especially true of plays set in Venice, the hometown of the *commedia improvvisa*. The English dramatists were acquainted with the city either at first hand or through the accounts of travellers. They seem to depict the realistic as well as the theatrical characteristics of Venice, in order to recreate the special foreign flavour of the place.

The attitude of Venetian society to women is prominent in Thomas Coryat's travelogue (*Crudities*, 1611). He explains the toleration of courtesans in Venice as the necessary concomitant of the Venetians' excessive safeguarding of their wives and their own honour. He notes that

> the Gentlemen do even coope up their wives alwaies within the walles of their houses for feare of these inconveniences ... So that you shall very seldome see a Venetian Gentleman's wife but either at the solemnization of a great marriage, or at the Christening of a Jew, or late in the evening rowing in a Gondola ...[16]

This is the kind of cultural framework within which one should understand Brabanzio's shock at his daughter's elopement and Othello's extreme sensitivity to the accusation that his wife is playing him false. The opening scene of *Othello* with the stage-direction: 'Enter Brabanzio in his nightgown at a window above', is a clear example of the manner in which the Italian window-scene is interpreted on the Elizabethan stage.

Juliet's window does not overlook a piazza but an enchanted and danger-fraught

garden, and the action is set not in Venice but in Verona. Stealing into the
Capulets' orchard at night, Romeo is struck by Juliet's appearance aloft,[17] i.e. on
the theatre gallery:

> But soft, what light through yonder window breaks?
> It is the east, and Juliet is the sun.
>
> (2.1.44–5)

Due to the deadly enmity between their two families, the newly-wed couple will
still need to resort to that old stage property, the rope-ladder, traditionally used for
pre-marital meetings, in order to consummate their marriage. Romeo will need the
rope-ladder both for entering Juliet's bedroom and for making a speedy retreat.
The typology of escapes through windows by means of a cord or a make-shift
ladder goes back at least to the story of Rahab the harlot and the two spies sent by
Joshua into Jericho (Joshua 2:15). But here the two window-scenes (2.1 and 3.5)
and the 'ladder of cords' derive directly from the Italian theatrical tradition, as do
also the father's tyranny and Juliet's incarceration within the house.

In *Much Ado About Nothing*, the pivotal window-scene takes place off-stage, in the
interstice between two scenes. Its vividness is assured through the vast range of
references to it both before and after it takes place, i.e. at the planning stage as well
as when the consequences are labouriously drawn out. The absence of this crucial
scene from the stage allows the full treachery of the plot to unfold step by step.

First there is the hatching of the evil plan (2.2). In order to thwart Claudio's
marriage to Hero, Borachio proposes to stage a false window-scene. Claudio will be
led to believe that he is witnessing Hero's unfaithfulness on the very eve of their
wedding. The knot is tied when Claudio determines:

> If I see anything tonight why I should not marry her, tomorrow, in the
> congregation where I should wed, there will I shame her.
>
> (3.2.113–5)

The villainy is discovered by Dogberry's staunch watchmen, who, under the
cover of night, overhear Borachio boasting of his exploit:

> I have tonight wooed Margaret, the lady Hero's gentlewoman, by the name of
> Hero. She leans me out at her mistress' chamber window, bids me a thousand
> times good night – I tell this tale vilely, I should first tell thee how the Prince,
> Claudio and my master, planted and placed and possessed by my master, Don
> John, saw afar off in the orchard this amiable encounter.
>
> (3.3.138–45)

This scene parallels those in which Beatrice and Benedick are each tricked into
concluding that the other has fallen in love with him. Claudio and Don Pedro are

similarly 'framed', made to believe in the reality of what is a faked scene. Shakespeare has given the conventional window-scene a special twist, in letting the deluded men expect and accept its conventionality unquestioningly. If it were not for the bumbling night-watchmen, the courtly gentlemen would never have discovered how they were deluded by the window-scene.

The structurally central position of this night-scene, which takes place in the theatrical space without, scores its importance as the climax of the plot. Within Italianate scenic convention, the window is an opening in the house- front from and through which communication between the theatrical space without and the theatrical space within is made possible. But Shakespeare relies on the audience's familiarity with the conventional scene and pushes the window from its border-line position between the two spaces further back into the theatrical space without, making a purely dramatic use of the theatrical icon.

*The Merchant of Venice* is the most Venetian of Shakespeare's plays. Although the theatrical space is complicated by the shifts to Belmont, the Venetian scenes lend themselves easily to performance in a piazza-like environment, with Shylock's house in the background. This is not to say that anything approximating the Serlian design should be envisaged for the original production. The playwright was simply using material gleaned from the Italian tradition which would be readily actable in the Elizabethan playhouse.

Abstracted from his more familiar qualities, Shylock is a Pantalone figure, jealously guarding his daughter and his money. Before going to supper at Bassanio's house, he issues directives to Jessica. In this particular case, the father trusts his daughter – mistakenly, as it turns out – leaving her the keys and asking her to look after the house in his absence. He warns her:

> Lock up my doors; and when you hear the drum
> And the vile squealing of the wry-necked fife,
> Clamber not up to the casements then,
> Nor thrust your head into the public street
> To gaze on Christian fools with varnished faces,
> But stop my houses ears – I mean my casements.
>
> (2.5.29–34)

But the servant Lancelot offers Jessica conflicting advice:

> Mistress, look out at window for all this.
> There will come a Christian by
> Will be worth a Jewës eye.
>
> (2.5.40–2)

For this scene, Jessica has been called out of doors, and at its termination she retires, ostensibly in obedience to her father's wishes. She is to lock herself up inside and avoid the temptation of even peering out of the window to catch a glimpse of the gentile merry-makers roaming the streets of Venice by night. In the event, Shylock's fears seem justified, although his preventive measures prove futile. In the following scene (2.6), the masquers appear in the piazza, ready to assist in the elopement. Responding to Lorenzo's call, Jessica appears 'above' (line 25, s.d.), in boy's apparel. The functional stage direction 'above' refers to the architectural space of the Elizabethan theatre, rather than to any implied naturalistic setting. But it is clear from the dialogue and the action that the gallery above should be taken to represent a window or a balcony. From there Jessica talks with Lorenzo and throws down a casket full of gold and jewellery before exiting above and entering below, i.e. on the stage which represents the street.

Elopement is the supreme expression of the daughter's rebellion against paternal domination, it is an escape from the house arrest imposed by a tyrannical father. Jessica's act of disobedience is counterpointed in the play by Portia's submission to the wooing match set up by her dead father. Like the masked Jessica, it is only in male attire that Portia will leave her home in Belmont for Venice. The dramatic convention of the heroine dressed up as a man in order actively to pursue her goals is clearly connected with the inside/outside dichotomy of the Renaissance stage.

Using the convention of the woman in the window presupposes a society based on male authoritarianism and a plot which works out ways of getting round the obstacle posed by the locked door. The erotic drive at odds with the coercive, incarcerating power will of necessity often appear to us as hopelessly romantic, artificial or shallow, for what catches the eye of the lover and his fancy is no more than the image of a woman in a window.

In his masterpiece *Volpone*, Ben Jonson created an elaborate window-scene in which his protagonist is allowed to see Celia. She is first brought to Volpone's notice by Mosca, who whips up his master's sexual appetite by describing her in provocative sensual terms. Mosca also weaves into his description an analogy between the woman and gold (1.5.110–14),[18] thus arousing Volpone's lust to the level of his cupidity. The offensive treatment of woman as an object analogous to material wealth expressed in Mosca's temptation, 'Bright as your gold! and lovely as your gold!' is reminiscent of the comic mingling of the two by another famous dramatic Venetian character lamenting, 'My daughter! O, my ducats! O, my daughter!' (*The Merchant of Venice*, 2.8.15).

This attitude is also shared by Celia's husband Corvino, who makes sure that,

> She's kept as warily as is your gold;
> Never does come abroad, never takes air
> But at a window.
> ...

> There is a guard, of ten spies thick, upon her;
> All his whole household: each of which is set
> Upon his fellow, and have all their charge,
> When he goes out, when he comes in, examined.
>
> (lines 118–26)

Rather than dissuade Volpone, this information whets his appetite, and he declares: 'I will go see her, though but at her window' (line 127). Two serious obstacles complicate the situation: the lady's married status, and Volpone's own pretense of lying on his death-bed. In order to overcome these difficulties, Volpone makes his public appearance in 'an obscure nook of the Piazza' (2.2.38), under Celia's window, disguised as Scoto the mountebank.

The mountebank's appearance is conceived of as a show in the *commedia dell'arte* style, complete with scaffold stage, singing and *zanni*.[19] Volpone establishes contact with Celia by calling on potential buyers of his universal medication to 'toss your handkerchiefs' (line 216) and promising 'a little remembrance' (line 218) to the first to throw a handkerchief. The desired response is indicated in the stage direction: 'Celia at the window throws down her handkerchief' (following line 222). His trick having succeeded, Volpone celebrates with a long monologue in praise of the elixir of youth which he is about to present to her as a gift. His patter, which resembles a modern commercial, discloses that this is nothing short of the elixir of vanity, a powder given to Venus by Apollo, 'that kept her perpetually young, cleared her wrinkles, firmed her gums, filled her skin, coloured her hair' (2.2.237–9). This product is designed to appeal to credulity as well as self-love: passed from Venus to Helen it was lost at the sack of Troy, till it was recovered 'in this our age' by a studious antiquary.

The disguised cosmetics pedlar is surprised by the return of Corvino. The enraged husband beats him up for finding 'no house but mine to make your *scene*' (2.3.2). The *dell'arte* aspect is explored further when Corvino gives vent to his rage in a speech that draws the parallels between the characters of the play and the Venetian masks:

> Signior Flaminio, will you down, sir? down!
> What, is my wife your Franciscina, sir?
> No windows on the whole Piazza, here,
> To make your properties, but mine? but mine?
> Heart! ere tomorrow, I shall be new christened,
> And called the *Pantalone di Besogniosi*,
> About the town.
>
> (2.3.3–9)

Later, in the quarrel scene (2.5), Corvino's absurd accusations serve to sharpen the structural elements of the conventional window-scene. For him, an Italian and not a Dutchman, as he puts it, his wife's appearance 'at a public window' is tantamount to 'Death of mine honour' (line 1). The mountebank's 'drug lectures' have drawn her 'itching ears' (line 5), while

> A crew of old, unmarried, noted lechers
> Stood smiling up, like satyrs.

(lines 6–7)

In his eyes, Celia is guilty of having smiled down at the mountebank, a gesture Corvino interprets as a fanning forth of favours and giving 'her hot spectators satisfaction' (line 9). Celia's smile has condemned her and made him a cuckold.

Although his accusations are monstrous in so far as there can be no doubt of Celia's innocence, they are not far off the mark in regard to the mountebank. Celia's untainted innocence is juxtaposed with the ambiguity of the situation in which she finds herself 'framed'. The window-scene in itself is potentially erotic and fraught with sexual innuendoes, so that, despite their patent falsehood, we do recognize the partial validity of Corvino's hyperbolic accusations.

Celia protests against Corvino's reflex interpretation of what he has seen:

> I could not think
> My being at the window should more, now,
> Move your impatience, than at other times.

(lines 35–7)

But Corvino is adamant in seeing it as a 'parley with a known knave, before a multitude' (lines 38–9), and, embroidering on what he has witnessed, composes as it were his own scenario:

> You were an actor, with your handkerchief!
> Which he, most sweetly, kissed in the receipt,
> And might, no doubt, return it, with a letter,
> And point the place, where you might meet: your sister's,
> Your mother's, or your aunt's might serve the turn.

(lines 40–4)

Corvino thus offers a complementary version to Volpone's original scenario. Both set the scene for Celia as the adulterous heroine. Celia, on the other hand, is a mere 'actor', with the handkerchief as a hackneyed stage property, following a prescribed plot-line.

Corvino now resolves to tighten even further his control of Celia, starting with 'I will have this bawdy light dammed up' (line 50). In his mind, the innocuous window has been metamorphosed into a brothel window. Celia is ordered not to overstep a chalked line three yards away from it, which is to be her new confining threshold. Corvino further asserts his domination over her by his decision to hang the lock (line 57), i.e. the chastity belt, on her very person. Locked within her own

65

house and barred from her own window, it is now her body which is to be locked up, making it into the sole property of her husband.[20]

The supreme importance of woman's chastity and her husband's honour is suddenly dissipated for Corvino when his greed is aroused. Succumbing to the temptation of the expected inheritance, he is prepared to prostitute his wife and will gladly serve as her pander. To show herself an obedient wife, Celia must now gratify him by prostituting herself. Indeed, he threatens to proclaim her 'strumpet, through the streets' (3.7.96) for refusing to sleep with Volpone. Rising to a paroxysm of anger, he promises to punish her even further:

> I will buy some slave,
> Whom I will kill, and bind thee to him, alive;
> And at my window, hang you forth.
>
> (3.7.100–2)

The window's meaning has changed in the course of the play from innocence to experience and now to castigation and public humiliation.

Corvino's male-centred code of behaviour for women is exposed as self-contradictory, coercive, immoral and cruel. Jonson shows that Corvino's concern for his wife's chastity does not spring from a religious abhorrence of sin or a moral concern, but from a self-centered, egotistical view of her as his private property, no better than a bought slave, to be disposed of as he sees fit.

Beyond the dialogue, this idea is clearly expressed by the central *Gestus* of this scene (3.7): Corvino forcefully dragging his young wife to Volpone's bed. Thus the situation has been neatly reversed, Celia having been taken out of her house by her husband in order to perform that which she was previously accused of planning.

In Thomas Middleton's *Women Beware Women*,[21] the convention of the woman in the window seems to be stretched almost to a fault. Christopher Ricks comments on the 'striking sequence of visual effects ... by which Bianca repeatedly appears to our view framed or aloft'.[22] Leaving his young wife in the morning to go to work, Leantio lingers in front of his house, finding it hard to detach himself from her. Bianca's appearance 'above' makes him even less inclined to depart:

> See and she be not got on purpose now
> Into the window to look after me.
> I have no power to go now, and I should be hanged.
>
> (1.2.13–15)

In his soliloquy, Leantio is torn between his desire to re-enter his home and while away the day with his wife, and his reason which tells him it is time to go to work. This struggle between house and street, the domain of love-making and that of bread-winning, re-affirms the conventional gender division between the seen and the unseen theatrical spaces.

In this play the house is shared by mother and wife, and it is both who appear 'above' as Leantio desperately tries to overcome his weakness and tear himself away. After he departs, the two women stay in the window to watch the Duke leading a religious procession. As the procession passes below their window, the Duke looks up and catches Bianca's eye. It is this meeting of gazes from which all the mischief in the play ensues.

The window convention is by now so well established that it becomes a dramatic shorthand, enabling the playwright to complicate his plot quickly. Middleton uses it as a dramatic device, embroidering on the theme of the young wife imprisoned in her home, whose only means of communication with the outside world is the window through which she can see and be seen.

Moving the action to the interior of Livia's house, Middleton makes further use of the theatre gallery in the chess-playing scene. Here the gallery is employed so as to present two actions simultaneously. While Livia distracts Leantio's mother with a game of chess below, Bianca is seduced by the Duke above.

From a sweet-tempered, modest young bride, Bianca now changes into a cross and demanding woman, complaining of the inadequacy of the material circumstances of her house. The unsuspecting Leantio returns home congratulating himself on his happy marriage:

> Honest wedlock
> Is like a banqueting-house built in a garden ...
> ... when base lust
> Is but a fair house built by a ditch side.
>
> (3.2.8–13)

But his is no longer a spiritual banqueting-house, as he soon finds out. Bianca's first complaint concerns the house:

> Methinks this house stands nothing to my mind;
> I'd have some pleasant lodging i'th'high street, sir,
> Or if 'twere near the court, sir, that were much better:
> 'Tis a sweet recreation for a gentlewoman
> To stand in a bay-window, and see gallants.
>
> (3.2.46–50)

When Leantio's suspicion awakens, he instinctively knows that 'Not all the locks in Italy can keep you women' (3.2.131–2) and that his womenfolk have ventured out of the house while he was away on his business. Bianca rebels against his overbearing attitude:

> Do you think y'have married me to mew me up
> Not to be seen?
>
> (3.2.137–8)

Still uncomprehending, Leantio proposes to 'lock my life's best treasure up' (line 166) within a sanctuary in the house. It is only when his wife brazenly declares her intention to accept the Duke's invitation that Leantio finally understands the corruption that has taken hold of his wife.

When Bianca is comfortably installed in court, Leantio comes to see her. Contemplating the luxury of her new lodgings he comments dryly:

> I took her out
> Of no such window, I remember, first:
> That was a great deal lower, and less carved.

$$(4.1.43-5)$$

Leantio's recollection evokes an earlier window-scene which antedates the plot: Bianca's elopement through the window of the Cappelli house in Venice. Bianca's career can be seen as a progression from one house to another, from one window to another. Escaping from her father's house, i.e. from patriarchal tyranny, through the window, she arrives at the beginning of the play in Leantio's house. Through the window she tries first to stop her husband from leaving, but shortly after meets the Duke's gaze, an event which turns out to be her means of escape from her home-confinement as a married woman. Seduced by the Duke in Livia's house, she aspires to a window overlooking the court, and then moves to court, where her lawful husband finds her by another, carved window. Her fortunes rise as her morals drop.

Here the icon of the woman in the window serves a number of functions: elopement, farewell, assignation, lewd invitation and luxury. The play thus moves swiftly through the entire gamut of potential meanings of the theatrical icon, from the romantic to the lewd. Middleton uses up the whole range of stock themes that have sprouted around the image of the woman in the window, making them into so many stages in the career of his corrupt heroine. The series of window moments dwindles into a mere theatrical trick. The convention has hardened into a facile *cliché*.

The theatrical icon of the woman in the window evolved from a necessity, a theatrical restriction imposed by the very conception of the Renaissance stage, to a convention employed in the Elizabethan theatre where other options were possible, and where it needed to be interpreted in quite different visual terms. Recognizing this particular dramatic configuration when it appears may help redress our tendency to treat such scenes as naturalistic, reminding us of their essential artificiality and conventionality and forcing us to admire them for what they are, clever artifacts, new twists to old *clichés*. Beyond that, the theatrical icon embedded in a play is not only a manner of giving shape to the theatrical space but also an expression of the basic values of the society depicted, as only too visible in Middleton's play.

*Chapter 6*

# The useless precaution

A considerable number of Molière's plays employ the traditional public-place setting.[1] But the old house-front scenery is no longer treated as a neutral city-scape. During its long history, that scenery became loaded with meaning and ideology, so that it could no longer be used innocently. Molière radicalized the traditional scenery, making it into a symbol of male oppression, an icon of authoritarianism. The classical division of the theatrical space into a male outdoors and a female indoors had attached quite different values to the two, echoing the separate spheres of activity of the two genders: business and the affairs of state for men, family and domestic economy for women. But with Molière, the interior of the house, originally the woman's stronghold, becomes a female prison.

Male control is expressed by the physical oppression of lock and key, female subversion by wit, ingenuity and cunning. In Molière's *Le Sicilien ou L'Amour peintre* (*The Sicilian or Love the Painter*, 1667), the tyrannical Dom Pèdre is taunted by Climène:

> toutes les serrures et les verrous du monde ne retiennent point les personnes.

> all the locks and bolts in the world will not hold a person.

> (scene 18)[2]

One of Molière's radicalizing measures is to take literally the idea of enslavement. Isidore is a Greek slave, freed by Dom Pèdre, who finds her new liberty an even worse enslavement: ' ... vous changez mon esclavage en un autre beaucoup plus rude'. Dom Pèdre guards his ward Isidore jealously, keeping her under constant surveillance, never letting her out of sight. Dom Pèdre prides himself on his possessive love and excessive jealousy:

> jaloux comme un tigre et, si vous voulez, comme un diable. Mon amour vous veut toute à moi ...

> jealous as a tiger and, if you please, as a devil. My love wants you all for myself ...

69

Isidore's position is no less doctrinaire when she attacks the constraint and servitude suffered by women:

> la possession d'un coeur est fort mal assurée, lorsqu'on prétend le retenir par force. Pour moi, je vous l'avoue, si j'étais galant d'une femme qui fût au pouvoir de quelqu'un, je mettrais toute mon étude à rendre ce quelqu'un jaloux.

> the possession of a heart is not at all assured, when one wishes to keep it by force. As for myself, I admit, were I courting a lady who was in the power of someone else, I would use all my ingenuity to make that someone jealous.

(scene 6)

The conflict between guardian and girl takes on the aspect of an ideological debate. Both the dramatic structure of the play and its definition of the theatrical space (in front of Dom Pèdre's house in Messina) are entrenched in the confrontation of male control and female subversion. The traditional façade is used by Molière as an integral and doctrinal element, dictating not only the theme but also the nature of the plot.[3]

Throughout the play, Dom Pèdre is motivated by his jealousy. The words *jaloux, jalousie*, appear in this short play some fourteen times. Still used in French and other languages to signify persian-blinds, *jalousie* meant in the fifteenth century a window-trellis made of wood or iron, such as was used in the Orient, allowing women to see without being seen (Fig. 14). Thus the word itself carries with it associations of barred windows and male possessiveness. Associated with the inhibiting trellis, the word as an abstract noun expresses the oriental attitude to women exemplified by such oppressive measures.[4]

The jealous guardian in *L'École des maris* (*The School for Husbands*, 1661) is described by the young lover as an Argus, 'a watchful dragon' (1.3). This mythical monster had one hundred eyes, only two of which were asleep at any one time.[5] Mascarille in *L'Étourdi* (*The Blunderer*, 1655) uses a similar image 'a dragon, watching over this rare treasure' (1.4). The very language of the plays joins the themes and plots both to support and to enrich Molière's 'feminist' interpretation of the traditional scenery.

The theme of the heroine's involuntary incarceration was developed and problematized in fifteenth-, sixteenth- and seventeenth-century drama. The plays concerned with her predicament fall into two general types, from the point of view of male control: (1) those dealing with the subjection of the girl to her father, i.e. with the pre-marital stage; and (2) those dealing with the tyranny of the husband, i.e. with the marital stage. From the heroine's point of view, her plight is thus systematized into two plot-patterns: (1) the attempt to prevent a forced marriage; and, if this has failed, (2) a scheme to outwit the distasteful partner and escape his distasteful hold. Despite the apparent social, religious and ethical discrepancies

*Fig. 14* Commedia dell'arte: *Woman behind a* jalousie, *oil painting,* c. *1580;*
*Drottningholms teatermuseum, Stockholm*

between the status of the unmarried girl and the married woman, many dramatists
seem to have sympathized with both manifestations, refusing to indict their
heroines for following their own inclinations, even when offending against the
marriage institution.

This attitude is not surprising considering that, in the *dell'arte* tradition, the
husband foisted on the girl is patently unsuitable. Often he is elderly and clearly
impotent. Her unfaithfulness to him is thus part of the package he has bargained
for and which, in his fear of cuckoldry, he anticipates. His impotence assures her
virginity, and, if the marriage has never been consummated, the transgression
committed can be treated lightly, as the very stuff of comedy. Machiavelli's
*Mandragola* (*c.* 1518) established the rationale of this genre: the childless marriage
of Signor Nicia proves his impotence and justifies, at least poetically, his being
tricked by the young libertine Callimaco. Likewise, we experience no moral
indignation at the sight of Molière's boorish George Dandin, in the play suitably
subtitled *Le Mari confondu* (*The Frustrated Husband*), being repeatedly outwitted
by his upper-class wife Angélique and her aristocratic lover Clitandre. Molière's
idiom is more 'polite' than Machiavelli's, erotically less explicit, but here too the
ill-suited match cancels out the fault.

In both plot-models, of the unmarried-girl and the married-woman types, it is only with the help of her adoring and adored lover that the young woman succeeds in freeing herself from the older man's bondage. The freedom for women advocated in such plays is not unreserved: it is not the freedom to be her own mistress but the freedom to choose her own mate, be it lover or husband. Far from supporting a feminist cause, the playwright adheres to a male perspective, but chooses to identify with the desired lover rather than the coercive father or undesired husband. In indicating his preference for a relationship based on mutual love, he is advocating a new, romantic morality. He prefers the woman to have freedom of choice because, as a male, he stands to gain from her assertiveness.[6]

A playwright who is no longer young may find it difficult to sympathize with his *jeune premier*, since his own predicament is clearly reflected in that of the older character. But he may side with the younger man, remembering himself as he once was, at the same time that he realizes his present affinity to the older man, thus achieving an ironic double-focus. In his repeated treatments of the forced marriage theme, Molière wrote for himself the central roles of the older men: Arnolphe, Dom Pèdre, Dandin, and the various Sganarelles.

In *Le Mariage forcé* (*The Forced Marriage*, 1664), a title that codifies the typology, the fifty-two year old Sganarelle wishes to marry the young and beautiful Dorimène, herself in love with Acaste. Dorimène is the typical *ingénue* who complains of her father's severity at home and looks towards marriage as a liberation from his subjugation (scene 2). When she assures her fiancé Sganarelle that she loves games, visits, parties, presents and promenades, i.e. all the entertainments which worry a jealous husband, he begins to doubt the wisdom of getting married at his age. When, moreover, he overhears the brazen explanation she gives her lover, 'This is a man I am not marrying at all for love, and it is only his wealth which makes me accept him', he determines to pull out of the engagement, but discovers that the girl's father and brother will not let him back out. With a clever twist, the forced marriage in this play rebounds onto the male partner.[7]

In *L'École des femmes* (*The School for Wives*, 1662) Molière succeeded in crystallizing the essential structure of the forced marriage theme. Here the almost allegorical battle of youth and age over the possession of the girl empties the arsenals of both, until the inevitable *dénouement*: the victory of youth. Arnolphe's advantage in cunning and experience is balanced off by Horace's libidinous energy. Arnolphe derives his intelligence from Horace's own inadvertent confessions, and is therefore always able to take the necessary precautions and forestall his rival's next move. The war between old and young, 'thoughtless youth and crabbed experience',[8] suffers constant turns of fortune, incessant *contretemps*, which provide the plot with a rhythmical pattern of move and counter-move. One of Molière's early farces is called *L'Étourdi ou Le Contretemps* (*The Blunderer or The Counter-Plots*, 1655), emphasizing his self-conscious use of this dramatic pattern.

By the very nature of his project, it is Horace who takes the initiative, following the beaten track of dramatic tricks aimed at gaining access to the girl and winning her heart and hand. As of old, the *senex* acts the blocking character, but he plays a losing, rearguard game, while the *iuvens*, armed with a figure to make cuckolds ('de taille à faire des cocus' (1.4)), develops his strategy. Poetic justice, i.e. the victory of innocent, mutual love over calculating, repressed desire, appears as a technical victory, due to the fortunate appearance of the fathers of both young people and the discovery of Agnès's true identity.

The special force of the play lies in its unique combination of the two basic plot-types mentioned above. Arnolphe sees himself as both father and husband to Agnès and, in her struggle to escape his tyranny, she takes on the double aspect of daughter and wife. His attitude to her is not, strictly speaking, incestuous, since he is no blood-relation but only an adoptive parent or guardian. But having brought her up since infancy, the progression from father-figure to husband is morally, if not biologically, of that nature. This central ambiguity of their relationship is generally ignored, but once pointed out it must become a focal and disturbing element in our appreciation of the play.

Arnolphe has brought up Agnès since the age of four, taking great care to shape her character and prepare her to be his ideal wife. She was educated in a small convent, according to her guardian's express orders, to be totally innocent and a complete idiot. Arnolphe prides himself on having attained this goal, as proved by her inquiring,

> Avec une innocence à nulle autre pareille,
> Si les enfants qu'on fait se faisaient par l'oreille.

> With an air of innocence equal to no other
> If the children that one makes were made through the ear.[9]

(1.1)

Arnolphe's own stupidity appears not only in his foolhardy attempt to bring up Agnès in ignorance so as to make a perfect wife for himself, but also in his attempt to legislate against eroticism and sexual attraction, i.e. against human nature itself.

Now that Agnès is seventeen and her education, or ignorization, has been concluded to his satisfaction, Arnolphe intends to wed her. By marrying a fool, he hopes to escape being made a fool himself (1.1). The word he uses, *sot*, is a pun that means both 'fool' and 'cuckold', and is especially *à propos* to Arnolphe, the namesake of the legendary saint of cuckolds.[10] Arnolphe regards himself not only as the adoptive father of Agnès but also as her future husband:

Je la regarde en femme, aux termes qu'elle en est;
Elle n'a pu faillir sans me couvrir de honte,
Et tout ce qu'elle a fait enfin est sur mon compte.

I consider her as wife, being what she is,
She cannot go astray without covering me with shame
And all that which she does is finally charged to me.

(2.1)

In his first confrontation with Agnès after Horace's disclosures (2.5), Arnolphe's chief concern is with her chastity. Gaston Hall, in his essay on word-play in Molière, shows how the covert interest of the scene depends on the technique of avoiding words banned in polite society while bringing them to mind. The humour of Agnès's ingenuous 'Le petit chat est mort' ('The little pussy is dead') lies not only in its obvious inadequacy to Arnolphe's anguished inquiry, but also in its slang meaning, as in English.[11] The double-meaning juxtaposes, in a single word, the extremes of naiveté and indecency that create the comic tension of the scene. The comic interrogation is climaxed by Agnès's surprising admission: 'Il m'a pris le ruban' ('He took my ribbon'). While Agnès in her simplicity thinks she will be blamed for letting Horace take away the ribbon given her by Arnolphe, he is trembling with fear for her chastity. These personal and incongruent subtexts, cleverly communicated though never spoken, are the source of fun in this scene.

In *La Critique de l'École des femmes* (*The School for Wives Criticized*), written in 1663 and performed as a sequel to the earlier play, Molière joined battle with its critics. One of the issues taken up by the *Critique* is the hypocrisy and prudery of those who pretend to squirm at the erotic suggestiveness of the earlier play. In this comedy of manners, the fine company assembled in the *salon* discusses, among other things, that celebrated scene of *double entendre*. The playwright uses the opportunity to squeeze even more fun out of its ambivalence. Climène, who launches the attack, claims to be shocked by Agnès's disclosure of that which Horace has taken from her. In the original text, Agnès is very hesitant, misinterpreting Arnolphe's growing irritation and impatience. Climène, in objecting to the lewdness of the scene, deepens the comic effect because, unlike Agnès, she obviously understands Arnolphe's sexual innuendoes but pretends to be shocked by their grossness. She uses circumlocution to refer to what she sees as unacceptable vulgarity: it is the 'the' she finds offensive, the interchange of hesitant and insistent 'the's which precedes the disclosure of the captured ribbon. When social control dictates the use of equivocation and circumspection, ordinary discourse becomes so suggestive that even the most innocent word or act is loaded with implications.

Another of the assembled ladies pretends not even to know what the word 'obscenité' means, although she supports whole-heartedly its use in disparaging the play (scene 3). Molière's satire is directed at the hypocrisy of polite society that sees sex as dirty and campaigns to purify discourse from intercourse.

The theme of affected modesty is expanded and systematized in *Les Femmes savantes* (*The Learned Ladies*, 1672). In their Platonic Academy, the learned ladies plan to regulate language itself and prohibit the use of certain words for which they have developed a dislike. But their star project will be the suppression of dirty syllables that show up even in the most beautiful of words, scandalizing the auditors. Thereby they will purge language from its store of infamous equivocations which offend female modesty (2.2). The purification of discourse is complemented in this play by a rejection of marriage, 'and all that follows', in favour of platonic love, 'That union of hearts in which the bodies have no part' (4.2).

Molière was forty years old when, in February 1662, he married Armande Béjart, who was nineteen or twenty. *L'École des femmes* was produced in December of the same year and the respective ages of the protagonists are forty-two and seventeen. The contemporary scandal surrounding Molière's marriage provides a suitable background for a discussion of the ambivalent relationship portrayed in the play. Angered by his parodic representation in *L'Impromptu de Versailles* (*The Impromptu of Versailles*, 1663), the rival actor Zacharie Montfleury wrote to the King, accusing Molière of having married his own daughter.[12] Although Louis XIV exonerated Molière, the rumour never died out, and the question has never been settled.

Supposedly the younger sister of the actress Madeleine Béjart, Molière's former mistress, Armande appears to have been in fact Madeleine's daughter. If so, the identity of her father becomes crucial: was he Madeleine's first lover, the Comte de Modène, or was he Molière, who took his place, or another, unknown man? Although the truth about Armande's parentage will apparently never be uncovered, the different options provide an interesting typology of possible family relations. Clearly, if Molière was the father, and only in that case, the marriage was incestuous. If either Modène or someone else was the father, there would be no blood relationship and therefore no incest. But, as the daughter of his one-time common-law wife, Molière would still be in the morally precarious position of a man who has married his own step-daughter. Today's newspapers are full of stories of step-fathers sexually molesting their step-daughters, an occurrence usually viewed as hardly less repulsive than incest proper.

The unresolved biographical question is instrumental in fixing our attention on the wider issue of the unacceptable passage from father-figure to sexual partner. At the risk of completely diluting the concept of incest, one could even claim that there exists an incestuous element in any couple between whom there is so big an age gap that it blurs the distinction between paternal affection and sexual attraction. From the strict religious, moral and social taboo on marrying close kin, through the stigma of a sexual liaison with in-law relatives, to the faint impropriety of marrying

75

someone who, by his age, could have been your child, one can see a receding gradation of incestuous relations. The concept of incest is thus widened to mean a double family tie, a sexual liaison with a family member, or as Hamlet puts it 'my uncle-father and aunt-mother'.[13]

Arnolphe is dramatically cast in such an equivocal position, as would-be father and husband. He is totally motivated by the fear of his future wife transgressing against another taboo, i.e. being unfaithful to him. To avoid this calamity he has reared and trained her to be his ideal of untainted womanhood. The complete programming of the girl from infancy is the means of establishing his total possession of her as both daughter and wife, to insure himself against cuckoldry. But this fantastic scheme of male self-gratification, mindless of the girl's own wishes, turns out to be a useless precaution.

Agnès is shaped by her guardian, as by the playwright, into the complete opposite of the depraved woman of misogynistic literature. But Arnolphe is basically a misogynist who attempts to circumvent what he regards as the innate evils of womankind. This is clearly a paradoxical undertaking, since what is innate cannot be changed. Despite all the efforts to subvert it, her nature asserts itself in her candid response to Horace.

Although written as comedy, with the rivals 'pulling fast ones' on each other, the play leaves no doubt about Molière's basic stance: for him, as for Horace, keeping a girl in ignorance should be a punishable crime. Arnolphe's sole redeeming feature is his love for Agnès, the true emotion which makes its appearance only after he has been defeated by Horace.

It seems to have escaped notice that at the end of the play Arnolphe suffers a double loss: not only does he lose Agnès as bride, but he loses her also as daughter, when her natural father, Enrique, appears to reclaim her. Enrique's unexpected appearance is a true *coup de théâtre*: the biological father appears to give his daughter away (the phrase is revealing of the social attitude!) to her young suitor. No wonder Arnolphe is left speechless at his sudden demise.

The dual role of guardian and fiancé is underlined by the double identity of Arnolphe as M. de la Souche, the bourgeois and the would-be aristocrat. Horace sees him as an old friend of his father's, but Arnolphe sees himself as Horace's rival in love. Arnolphe's whole being collapses when his duplicity is revealed.

Molière's tight plotting is especially noticeable when the play is compared to its principal source, Scarron's picaresque *nouvelle* 'La Précaution inutile' ('The Useless Precaution', 1661), itself an imitation of a Spanish story by Maria Zayas y Sotomayor.[14] Scarron's story begins with Don Pedro witnessing his affianced giving birth to a baby girl and abandoning her in a derelict house. He adopts the child, names her Laura and entrusts her to the care of a female relative. Before embarking on his travels, he orders that Laura be educated in a convent, 'and above all, to take particular care that she should know as little as might be of the affairs of the world'.[15] The bulk of the story is then devoted to the sexual misadventures he encounters on his peregrinations. When he finally returns home to Granada, towards the end of the story, he is attracted to the now grown up Laura by her strong resemblance to her mother, with whom he had once been in love, and marries her. He is well pleased with her excessive simplicity, the fruit of her convent education: 'Il la trouva belle comme tous les Anges ensemble, et sotte comme toutes les réligieuses' ('He found her as beautiful as all the angels put together, and as foolish as all the nuns').[16] Like Arnolphe, he furnishes his house with the most foolish servants he can find and sits down in a chair to give moral instruction to his youthful wife while she stands before him. But, in his absence, she falls easy prey to a young gallant, thus proving Don Pedro's educational program to have been a useless precaution, hence the name of the story.

Molière condensed this story, leaving out the hero's amorous career and beginning the play at the point in which Arnolphe's marriage-project is on the point of being successfully concluded. Just as Arnolphe is about to reach his goal, Horace appears on the scene. From this unforeseen event springs the dramatic conflict between the two over the possession of Agnès, which constitutes the plot. Molière picked out from Scarron only the frame-story, expurgated the humourous licentious scenes, discarded the libertine features of the hero, and kept his heroine pure and innocent. But he was clearly attracted by the idea of the useless or ineffectual precaution, the idea of a character being motivated by his fear of cuckoldry to the extent of trying completely to mold and control his future wife from infancy. The character study of Arnolphe stands in the comic tradition of Theophrastus' *Ethical Characters* and Ben Jonson's humours as demonstrating the workings of a single dominant trait or obsession.

Male jealousy and the fear of horns are important Renaissance motifs, part and parcel of the widespread authoritarian and patriarchal attitudes in the period. They are the other face of female coercion, of forced marriage. A necessary connection exists therefore between the two types of comedy defined as *mariage forcé* and *précaution inutile*. But for the male perpetrators of the system, it is woman's innate depraved nature that is responsible for their fear and suffering. The misogynistic fear of cuckoldry which drives the comic Arnolphe is shared, *mutatis mutandis*, by Othello:

> 'Tis destiny unshunnable, like death.
> Even then this forkèd plague is fated to us
> When we do quicken.
>
> (*Othello*, 3.3.279–81)

Shakespeare as well as Molière exposes the inanity of this sweeping metaphysical assumption, but the very use of the cuckoldry-motif evidences its importance in a male-centred society. The inevitability of horns is a central cultural myth which shapes the relations between the genders. The traditional division of the theatrical space into an invisible, marginal, female, theatrical space without, and an outdoor, visible, central, male, theatrical space within would seem to reinforce this myth by suggesting that woman's place is indoors and that she should be kept there forcibly if her inherent licentiousness is to be pre-empted. But Molière uses the dramatic and scenic convention in order to expose and dissipate the myth, thereby making the convention, which had represented that misogynistic doctrine, obsolete. Molière re-uses the old codes to create a new message, to subvert the very convention in which he is writing.

*L'École des femmes* is set in 'une place de ville', a town square. One of the houses overlooking the square represents the house Arnolphe has acquired for Agnès and in which he keeps her guarded as in a prison. The scenic conception seems at first to be a mere repetition of the traditional Renaissance iconography of house and woman, old guardian and young lover, over-hanging balcony, *billet-doux* and ladder. However, this is no re-hash of thread-bare theatrical tricks but an examination of their ideological basis. The articulation of the theatrical space conveys directly the protagonist's obsessional fear of cuckoldry and his basic misogyny.

The artificial world which Arnolphe has created around Agnès is a world he has dreamed into existence, a male wish-fulfilment in which all male anxieties have been laid to rest. He has thought up the most monstrous of schemes, a totalitarian control of female nature, a complete physical, intellectual and moral enslavement. Molière has taken the theme to such an extreme that it must erupt in farce and end in reversal.

Before handing Agnès the Precepts of Marriage, which apparently he himself has written for her, Arnolphe lectures her on woman's place:

> Votre sexe n'est là que pour la dépendance:
> Du côté de la barbe est la toute-puissance.
> Bien qu'on soit deux moitiés de la société,
> Ces deux moitiés pourtant n'ont point d'égalité:
> L'une est moitié suprême, et l'autre subalterne;
> L'une en tout est sousmise à l'autre, qui gouverne.

> Your sex has being only for dependence:
> The beard has on its side the entire power.
> And while we are two halves of one society
> These halves are not, however, on a par:
> The one is the superior, the other the inferior half;
> The one submits in all to the other, which governs.

> (3.2.699–705)

For Arnolphe, the wife must obey her husband just as the soldier should his general, the servant his master, a child its father, or a monk his superior.

In his frontispiece to the first edition of the play (1663), François Chauveau chose to depict a scene that gives visual expression to the main theme: Agnès is shown reading out the Precepts of Marriage to Arnolphe, played by Molière (3.2) (Fig. 15). Whether a parody of the Ten Commandments or a travesty of *Les Précepts de mariage de Saint Grégoire de Nazianze*,[17] the Precepts are the distillation of unabashed male authoritarianism. They are to be accompanied by daily exercises and are introduced by Arnolphe as devotional duties, the failure to observe which entails the frightening prospect of eternally burning in hell. Agnès is required to apply herself to the careful study of these precepts as a novice to her vocation.

In this scene Arnolphe is sitting on a chair which he has ordered the servants to bring out of the house, while Agnès stands in front of him. Molière's *mise-en-scène* thus reinforces his dramatic ideas. Chauveau has succeeded in conveying the central *Gestus* of this scene as well as of the play as a whole. Not only does he show Agnès 'like a novice standing before her superior in a convent',[18] but he actually illustrates the opening lines of the scene in which Arnolphe instructs her to put aside her sewing, lift her head and fix her sight on him while he is talking. A stage direction adds that Arnolphe points his finger at his forehead. In the picture, Arnolphe holds the book of Precepts in his left hand while pointing his right index finger at his forehead. In the context of threatening Agnès with divine vengeance should she fail to be faithful to him, this gesture focuses the spectators' eyes on the redoubtable forehead, making its potential for growing horns almost palpable.

In his interesting research on 'The décor of Molière's stage', based on the original illustrations of the plays, Roger Herzel criticizes Molière's scenic conception of *L'École des femmes* as depicted in Chauveau's engraving:

> The exterior location ceases to be an entirely appropriate environment for the play. Some aspects of the action – the chance encounters, the long-lost fathers – could only occur in the traditional farce setting of the public street; but other moments in the play belong in the privacy of an interior, most notably the scene between Arnolphe and Agnès that Chauveau has chosen to illustrate.[19]

Herzel identifies the play as a transitional work which has over-stretched the scenic outdoor-convention. In his view, this inadequacy or even failure opens the way for the intimate scenes set in the bourgeois *salon* of Molière's mature comedies. Thus considered, the play becomes of pivotal importance in the revolutionary switch from the outdoors to the indoors, from the public place to the intimacy of the private room. In some later plays, e.g. *Le Tartuffe* (1664)[20] or *Le Malade imaginaire* (*The Imaginary Invalid*, 1673), the audience can watch the heroine being forced to marry against her will, within the confines of her own home.

Fig. 15 L'Ecole des femmes: *Agnès reading out the* Precepts of Marriage *to Arnolphe*; *François Chauveau*, 1663

To argue that the reading of the *Précepts de mariage* belongs 'in the privacy of an interior' is to criticize the scene for its lack of verisimilitude and for the manner in which its scenery seems to get in the way of the action, rather than serve it. Molière himself underlines the artificiality and theatricality of the scene by letting Arnolphe order the servants to bring out a chair for him into the fresh air. Analogous stage-business is undertaken earlier, with Arnolphe instructing the servants in 1.2 and again in 2.2 to send Agnès downstairs, i.e. outdoors, to the theatrical space within. This last instance is extended into a wholes sequence when Arnolphe changes his mind and goes in to call her out himself, leaving the comical servants outside to give their version of male control: 'La femme est, en effet, le potage de l'homme' ('Woman is really man's cup o'soup') (2.3). He then comes out alone and in a soliloquy tries to make the scenic convention appear more natural by explaining that he has asked her to come out for a stroll, 'Sous le prétexte d'y faire un tour de promenade' (2.4). When Agnès enters, she is greeted with 'La promenade est belle'. Clearly, this is an attempt to accommodate the embarrassing discrepancy between scene and setting, but Molière is consciously straining the convention to its very limits.

Already in *L'École des maris*, written a year earlier, Molière had found it necessary to provide an explanation for the outdoor negotiations. The scene is a public place in Paris, surrounded by the houses of Sganarelle, Valère, Ariste and the Commissaire. The action evolves conveniently between the neighbouring houses, chiefly those of the guardian and would-be husband Sganarelle and the lover Valère. Imprisoned in her guardian's house, the heroine has no recourse to Valère, so she turns her jailor into her love-messenger. The familiar dramatic situation is thus brought to its logical end, *ad absurdum*. This is a risky game in which she wins Sganarelle's confidence by feigning to resent Valère's advances, and sends him on various duplicitous missions. When Valère asks Sganarelle into his house and is rebuffed by the latter, he orders that a chair be brought out for his unexpected visitor (2.2). This obvious pretext for holding the conversation outdoors is extended into a dramatic sequence that contrasts Sganarelle's boorish behaviour with Valère's natural civility.

In *L'École des femmes* the action calls only for a single functional house, although Chauveau's illustration may represent faithfully the scenery used (Fig. 15). Despite the thematic similarity between *L'École des maris* and *L'École des femmes*, the later play exhibits a much greater mastery of aesthetic form, and its dramatic plotting is much tighter. It is in this play that the scenic convention and the social position of woman implicit in it reach a climax and a dead end. Both the theatrical *topos* and the social thinking that had nourished it have exhausted themselves simultaneously. The traditional street setting has been laid bare: Molière conducted in *L'École des femmes* a thorough investigation into its social and ethical preconceptions. He based his whole plot on the scenic conception of the closed house in which Agnès is kept. All other characters are re-defined in relation to her imprisonment: her guardian becomes her prison-warden, her servants – her watchmen, and her lover – her liberator. Her narrated biography extends the disciplinary system to which she is subjected: brought up as a child in a convent, she is also threatened with confinement to a convent if she refuses to marry Arnolphe (5.4).

The play makes use of all the conventional scenic tricks associated with the heroine's isolation, but it does so in narrative rather than dramatic fashion, and sets each trick so that it rebounds upon itself. When Agnès obeys Arnolphe and throws down from her window a brick on Horace, she attaches to it a love letter which negates her hurtful action. All this is confided by the trusting Horace to Arnolphe (3.4). Horace's attempted nocturnal entrance to Agnès's chamber by climbing up a ladder to her window is foiled by Arnolphe and his servants (5.1). Although these exploits are recounted rather than shown, they evoke mental images of previous theatrical usages. Thus, the actual theatrical cliché is avoided, recounted only to be immediately overthrown.

Molière turned again to the street décor in some of his later plays, notably in *Amphitryon* and *George Dandin* (both written in 1668), and in *Les Fourberies de Scapin* (*The Rogueries of Scapin*, 1671). The outdoor Theban setting of *Amphitryon* was no doubt influenced by that of its Plautine original, and the Neapolitan street scene of *Scapin* by its *commedia dell'arte* antecedents. Although no theatrical source has been traced for *George Dandin*, two stories from Boccacio's *Decameron* serve as its narrative source.[21] The play's subtitle, *Le Mari confondu*, the frustrated husband, points to the new twist introduced into the traditional plot, or the new angle from which the familiar web of relationships is viewed.

The scene is set in front of George Dandin's house, in the country. Driven by social aspiration, this wealthy farmer has married the aristocratic Angélique de Sotenville. On her side, Angélique has been forced to marry far beneath her social rank by the pecuniary situation of her parents. This is the background to a comedy in which the husband tries to forestall his cuckolding by a young and debonair rival. The play clearly belongs to the second type of forced-marriage plots, i.e. those in which the forced marriage has already taken place prior to the opening of the play, so that the heroine's struggle is aimed at deceiving her husband. In its general outline the plot is pedestrian, but it gains in interest thanks to the cunning inventiveness of the heroine, who repeatedly turns the tables on her husband whenever he seems to have scored a point, creating a *contretemps*.

By locking Angélique out of the house after her nocturnal rendez-vous with her lover, Dandin seems to have at last gained the required proof of her inconstancy (3.6). The action now focuses on the locked door and the open window through which the jealous husband thrusts his head to taunt his deceitful wife. Eager to preserve her dignity, especially with her parents, Angélique tries to negotiate a settlement with her husband: she promises to be the most faithful of wives from now on if only he will be generous and allow her back into the house. Despairing at his persistent refusal to pardon her, she takes out a knife and threatens to commit suicide, pointing out that he will no doubt be suspected of having murdered her. Calling her bluff, Dandin remains unperturbed, saying that people do not kill themselves any longer, 'la mode en est passée il y a longtemps'. Now it is again her turn to move. Under cover of night, she plays out her little suicidal charade, this time achieving the desired effect. When he comes out to investigate, the young lady and her servant slink in quietly through the door he has left open, shutting it behind them. The positions are now neatly reversed, with Angélique at the window, mocking her husband, and Dandin locked out.

The play works out the different structural options of within and without presented by the scenery. Initially, Angélique is a young woman, forced into a distasteful marriage, who declares that she has no intention to renounce the world and bury herself alive to please a husband (2.2). She therefore uses every means to escape from her prison and arranges clandestine meetings with her lover, while her husband spies on her, attempting to collect incriminating evidence against her. In the scene analyzed above, she finds herself locked out of the house instead of in it, clamouring to be admitted, and it is her jailor who has barricaded himself indoors. This paradoxical situation is reversed yet again when she cunningly gets him to come out and hurries in to lock him out. This game of in-and-out is further accentuated through the opposite 'innings-and-outings' at the window.

When Dandin's in-laws arrive on scene, they are easily taken in by their daughter's dissembling and the evidence of their own eyes: clearly, as it seems, Dandin has spent the night out and is falsely accusing Angélique. Although the spectators know Dandin to be speaking the truth, they can also see that appearances are against him. From the beginning he is obsessed by the injustice of appearing to be in the wrong: 'J'enrage de bon coeur d'avoir tort, lorsque j'ai raison' (1.6). Moore sees in this a deeper philosophical motif concerning the difference between essence and accident,[22] but the point seems to be that Angélique's *contretemps* depend on the persuasive, though false, interpretations she offers for the situations in which she finds herself caught.

*George Dandin* is no longer a play about the plight of the girl forced into an distasteful marriage but about the consequences of such a marriage to both wife and husband. Angélique's superior manipulative ability compromises the natural sympathy we might feel towards her as a victim of the patriarchal system. In this play, the themes of forced marriage and useless precaution, female grievance and male grudge, seem to even out. It is as though, having exhausted the scenic potential of the woman imprisoned in her house by the guardian turned husband, Molière had now discovered a new series of formal permutations of in-and-out, expressive of different power patterns. In *George Dandin* the heroine is strong and cunning, more than a match for her jealous husband. Although her parents deny her wish to be separated from him (3.7), it is clear that Angélique will never suffer her married state to interfere with her free life-style. But Angélique's liberation from bourgeois morality is aristocratic in nature, and not open to a girl brought up in bourgeois propriety.

Having exhausted the old Serlian and *dell'arte* scenic convention and demolished its ideological basis, Molière progressed into the interior of the bourgeois home, violating its sanctity in order to take a closer look at the intimate conflicts played out there. Notable examples of plays with interior settings are *Le Tartuffe*, *Le Misanthrope* (1666), *Le Bourgeois gentilhomme* (*The Would-be Gentleman*, 1670) and *Le Malade imaginaire*.

The relations of outside and inside become reversed, with the theatrical space within now representing the interior. Inside the house there are male as well as female family members, so that the strict demarcation line between men and women represented by the threshold disappears. Although the woman's problem is no longer the focus of the play, as it was in *L'École des femmes* or *George Dandin*, it is still of significant and even crucial interest in Molière's 'interior' plays. The self-centred male protagonists of these plays try to manipulate their womenfolk callously but are outwitted and exposed by the females of their household.

Seen within the wider family context, the depiction of the woman gains in the refinement and depth of its probing. The surrounding home and family reflect on the woman's social position, education and culture, and her conduct is brought under closer scrutiny, allowing for a more complex characterization. Inside the house, although still subjected to forced marriage, her personality and wishes can be better explored than when she was glimpsed at in front of her house, the icon of her imprisonment.

Mariane in *Le Tartuffe* and Angélique in *Le Malade imaginaire* are both studies of young and helpless innocents being forced into marriages advantageous to their fathers but contrary to their own wishes. Both are in love with suitable young partners, but, in the old *dell'arte* tradition, are being used by their fathers to further the old men's interests. The poor girls are caught up in the dilemma of obeying their fathers or remaining true to their lovers.

*Le Tartuffe* is set in the wealthy bourgeois home of Orgon in Paris. Although we can assume the interior setting to be a reception-room, it is not defined either through dialogue or stage directions. If we look to the illustrations of Chauveau and Jean Lepautre for visual information, we find that the room depicted is unfurnished except for the table covered by an ample tablecloth required for Orgon to hide under (Fig. 16).[23] The absence of furniture is also noticeable in Lepautre's depiction of four of the scenes in a roundel.[24] The later list of scenic requisites compiled by Mahelot calls also for two chairs.[25] The vagueness of the interior space facilitates the easy entrance and exit of the various household members as well as visitors, although not quite as easily as in the chance meetings of the older street setting.

This interior space is largely characterized through the people who inhabit it. The play begins with the peremptory leave-taking of Madame Pernelle who, with the privilege of age, tells each in his turn what she thinks of him, thereby providing us with an initial, though biased, characterization. She finds fault with each and everyone, complaining of their lack of respect and loud voices, but especially of their lack of due reverence for the holy man, Tartuffe. She is also very critical of their hectic social life, thus building an impression of the bustling atmosphere of the house. The sparse guardian-girl-lover relationship associated with the outdoor scenery is replaced in the interior of the house by the fullness of the bourgeois family, including grandmother, father, step-mother, uncle, brother, sister, lover and servant. The returning master of the house, Orgon, is clearly out of step with this easy-going, sociable family, having fallen under the influence of the heinous outsider who has wormed his way into their midst.

The noisy household evoked so vividly in the opening scene of the play serves as a background for Mariane's conflict with her tyrannical father. Although as a character Mariane is of secondary importance, the drama of her forced marriage forms a significant part of the plot. It is played out in the intimacy of the room, with Orgon attempting to keep it 'en secret' (2.1). To Mariane's astonishment, he begins his move by examining first a cupboard to make sure nobody is eavesdropping there. This may be the same cupboard Damis hides in later to spy on Tartuffe's interview with Elmire. The question of privacy is thus problematized rather than assured by moving the action indoors, into the close-knit family atmosphere.

Having made sure that they are alone, Orgon now approaches the subject of Tartuffe, the designated husband. But while he talks, in sneaks the servant Dorine, taking up a position behind him and breaking into the conversation when she can no longer keep quiet. Dorine is the self-appointed champion of the helpless Mariane against her autocratic father. At first she pretends disbelief – it must be a joke; then she changes tack, pointing out the unsuitability of the proposed match for both father and daughter; when this fails to convince, she produces the fidelity argument:

> Sachez que d'une fille on risque la vertu,
> Lorsque dans son hymen son goût est combattu,

## LE TARTVFFE

*Fig. 16* Le Tartuffe; *attributed to François Chauveau, 1669*

Que le dessin d'y vivre en honnête personne
Dépend des qualités du mari qu'on lui donne.

Know that one risks a daughter's virtue
When one marries her against her taste,
And that whether she lives in honesty
Depends on what a husband she is given.

(2.2)

Cuckoldry is thus demystified by the level-headed Dorine: rather than an inherent female evil and the inevitable fate of man, it is simply the natural consequence of forced marriage.

The timid Mariane finds it impossible to oppose her father, 'un père absolu', but she cannot reconcile her filial obedience with her love for Valère. In her misery she turns for help to Dorine, who reproaches her young mistress for failing to insist that she must marry to please herself, not her father (2.3). When Mariane declares heroically that she will kill herself rather than marry Tartuffe, Dorine mockingly congratulates her on finding such a clever way out and then loses her patience, ironically recommending Tartuffe as the best possible choice, until she succeeds in provoking Mariane into a more belligerent mood.

Mariane's opposition to her father in the question of the forced marriage thus assured, attention is now shifted to her relationship with Valère. Piqued by the rumour of Mariane's proposed marriage to Tartuffe, Valère questions her about it and she, in turn, is hurt by his manner. Both are sensitive and easily offended, so that the initial misunderstanding of each other's intentions leads quickly to an impassioned 'lovers' quarrel', in the tradition of the *dépit amoureux*.[26]

What follows is a comedy of misunderstanding and reconciliation, focused on the two side-doors of the room. Miffed, Valère repeatedly pretends to be leaving Mariane for good, but is so keen to hear her calling him back that he imagines she does, and so turns back just before he reaches the door. His wavering between hope and despair is thus graphically rendered in his movement away from the door and towards it. Mariane's hurt pride leads her to follow his example and run for the opposite exit.

It is her insecurity that leads Mariane to treat Valère spitefully, instead of revealing her true emotions towards him. The weakness displayed in the confrontation with her father is counter-balanced by the false pride that prevents her from expressing her love for Valère. Both the impotence in resisting the father and the force of rejecting her lover's pleas for a sign of fidelity spring from Mariane's conception of female propriety, 'la pudeur du sexe' (2.3).

The motif of the lovers' quarrel complicates the woman's problem: it is no longer just the marriage foisted on her by her father, but also her own inability, due to her education, to express her love freely and directly without feeling she has committed a social sin. Like the forced marriage, this too is a recurring literary and dramatic theme. Physical incarceration is thus replaced by misguided moral compulsion, the burden of etiquette in polite society, that dictates propriety rather than sincerity, social pride at the cost of personal happiness.

The notion of *bienséance*, of the correct way of behaving in the *salon*, is closely allied to the new theatrical space of the indoors and the evolving comedy of manners. Inside the *salon*, physical constraint is replaced by social and pseudo-moral inhibitions. The consequent interiorization of social restraints, a more refined form of authoritarian control, is part of the network of pressures exerted in the privacy of the home.

Opening up the interior for inspection, Molière discovered that it was not only the actual lock on the door that kept the woman imprisoned in her house. Even with the passing away of the older conventions, both social and theatrical, she continued to be imprisoned, though in a more subtle manner, by the social code she had accepted as natural law. These internal bonds proved to be even more durable than the externally imposed ones.

Two characters in the play refuse to conform to the binding social decorum: Tartuffe, who knows how to take advantage of the social mores without himself subscribing to them in any way, and Dorine, who as a mere servant has no social pretensions. Molière developed the traditional comic figure of the servant into a character who is exempt from social propriety. Dorine saves the lovers from their own self-righteousness by speaking out for them those words each wants to hear but neither dares speak: she is absolutely devoted to you; he is in love with you and has no other wish but to marry you.

Dorine pronounces these words after having physically dragged each in turn back from the opposing doors they attempted to use for a highly theatrical exit. Running back and forth between the two, she finally succeeds in holding them together, forcing them to join hands and make peace. When they threaten to start all over again with their recriminations, she quenches the new argument by reminding them of the real danger to their happiness – the proposed match with Tartuffe. Promising to engage Elmire and Damis to help the young couple, Dorine now tries to disengage them, propelling each in the direction of the same door they had tried to use earlier. Once again that movement is arrested, then reversed, as the lovers find it difficult to part. The repetition of the pattern of movement, now conveying love and tenderness instead of offense and anger, is a powerful structural scenographic effect which makes full use of the interior setting of room with facing doors.

The denser tissue of relationships developed within the house allows Molière to contrast the *ingénue* with a maturer, married woman. In *Le Tartuffe*, as in *Le Malade imaginaire*, this woman is cast as a step-mother, although the two are diametrically opposed in that the one loves her husband and step-children, while the other is a money-grabbing, self-seeking woman. Together, step-mother and daughter create a double focus on the role of woman. The other two women in *Le Tartuffe* are Madame Pernelle, the bigoted old lady, originally performed by a male actor,[27] and Dorine, whose sexuality is confirmed by Tartuffe finding her *décolté* too provocative to remain uncovered (3.2). Mariane's youthful timidity is naturally contrasted with the self-assured comportment of Elmire, the woman who knows how to use her sexuality without compromising her integrity, in order to get her own way with her husband and with Tartuffe. She goes to great lengths, seducing Tartuffe so as to convince Orgon, who is hiding under the table, that he is seduceable and far from saintly. This famous scene, depicted by Chauveau, Brissart and Jean Lepautre (see above, p. 84), makes full use of the new theatrical space, bringing the action to the brink of intimacy while carefully guaranteeing the heroine against it by keeping her husband hidden under the table. This undignified position of witnessing his own cuckolding serves to punish him for trusting Tartuffe and doubting Elmire. Such a scene is wholly dependent on the indoor setting.

Although the scenic change from outdoors to indoors was not Molière's innovation but a natural development of the theatre of his time, he made it his own by integrating it into his artistic and ideological development. Experimenting with the *dell'arte* forms, he brought them to maturation and eventually made them come apart, then took his drama indoors for a close-up view. Playing around with the simple, constitutive elements, as with a kaleidoscope, he achieved each time new variations and permutations. The migration of the theatre into the interior was an important step towards the individuation of character and especially a more penetrating investigation of women. In his later plays, Molière creates independent women, women who pursue their own financial interests (like Béline in *Le Malade imaginaire*), and women with intellectual aspirations who refuse the traditional role of wife and mother.

## Chapter 7

# Inside the drawing-room

The lengthy stage-directions at the head of Henrik Ibsen's middle-period realistic dramas carefully define their particular theatrical spaces. The original productions of Ibsen's plays aimed at realizing faithfully the theatrical spaces required by the plays. Such were the world première of *A Doll's House* at the Danish Royal Theatre, Copenhagen, in 1879, and the Norwegian première at the Christiania Theatre, a year later (Fig. 17), which tried to translate into visual terms the verbal description of the drawing-room; such was also the conception of Max Reinhardt and Edvard Munch for their 1906 production of *Hedda Gabler* (Fig. 18).

The drawing-rooms called for by *A Doll's House* (1879) and *Hedda Gabler* (1890) are very different from each other, reflecting the difference in social position, upbringing, culture and character of the two heroines. The furnishings are not just a background of naturalistic objects but a living presence that characterizes the protagonists, their taste, income and style, all of which are constitutive elements of the action. Nora's inexpensive but tasteful furniture is as relevant to her play as are the missing slip-covers on Hedda's elegant chairs and sofas. The realistic appearance of the drawing-room functions both as an environment for the action and an expressive means of characterization.[1]

The drawing-room is the fixed theatrical space within of these plays. The reality of this perceived space is bolstered by its extension to the unseen theatrical space without. This merely conceived space is as real as the perceived space. The two unseen empty rooms in the Tesmans' house, potential nursery rooms, are no less real than the drawing-room or the inner room on stage. Characters enter the drawing-room from the other rooms in the apartment, or use the front door to leave the house and go to their own homes or to visit other people, some of whom, like Mademoiselle Diana in *Hedda Gabler*, are not characters in the play.

Characters congregate in the family drawing-room coming from far-off places, thereby complicating the plot that is developing in the perceived space. The spectator knows that a character leaving the room is an actor who has moved off-

*Fig. 17* A Doll's House *at the Christiania Theatre, 1880; Universitetsbiblioteket, Oslo*

stage, but the reality of the theatrical space within is easily carried over to these other, implied satellite spaces. These conceived spaces allow the continuous flow and the great concentration of the action. They in fact guarantee the observance of the three 'classical' unities, strange as this may seem at first sight in a realistic play.[2]

Whether adjacent, as another room or a flat on another floor, or further off, as a different location in Christiania, the reality of these conceived places is extrapolated from that of the visible room. The more vividly perceived it is, the more vividly conceived they are. And the reality of the actor moving between them strengthens the impression of their actual existence. In the Greek theatre, the theatrical spaces without were either designated as interiors behind the *skene* or had geographical reality as actual place-names, but the theatrical space within was more symbolic than representational. In Molière the vagueness of these off-stage places merely complements the rather general nature of the on-stage street or *salon*. But the particularity and individuality of the drawing-room in Ibsen's naturalistic drama, together with its localization in contemporary Christiania, make these unseen places into extensions of the supposedly perfect illusion of everyday reality on stage. Conversely, the merging of these off-stage places with the reality of Christiania and the ability of characters to move off-stage and into town, as it were, strengthens the audience's sense of the reality of the visible theatrical space, of the fictional drawing-room.

*Fig. 18* Hedda Gabler, *Edvard Munch, 1906; Munch-museet, Oslo*

The classical convention of the theatrical space within has by now been completely reversed. Instead of depicting the outside of a house, the perceived space now represents an interior. But the basic spatial relations of the perceived space and the conceived close-and-removed spaces have been preserved, creating an illusion of a continuum of theatrical spaces, only a small section of which is visible.

The formal drawing-room was the only room into which a nineteenth-century guest would be invited, and therefore it is the only part of the house which the audience is allowed to see by theatrical convention. To a degree, the drawing-room shares the public aspect of the outdoor space of earlier plays. Here, and not in the bedroom, husband and wife play out their conflicts in short intervals of privacy. The nature of this room, where much of the family life is conducted, restricts the degree of intimacy between husband and wife and predetermines the nature of the dialogue and of the relationship between them.

If the *oikos* used to be the heroine's fort, now that she has turned middle-class, she shares the same space with her husband, and the space she has to herself has been further curtailed. The formality of the drawing-room pushes the woman's true self further indoors: Hedda to the inner room, to which she moves her few personal belongings and to which she retires to kill herself, and Nora to her bedroom, where she shuts herself up to work. The move indoors, which seemed to promise a closer and less restricted view of the woman's problem by shifting the scene from the threshold and into her own territory turns out to be disappointing. Now the woman becomes confined and hampered by the drawing-room itself, retreating to an inner room of her own.

Both Nora and Hedda have secrets which they keep from their husbands. Nora has forged a note so as to get a loan needed to finance the trip south which saved her husband's life. For eight years she has been paying back the loan, working in the secret of her room and saving household-money in order to meet the monthly payments. She keeps this to herself as also Krogstad's attempt at blackmailing her. Hedda's secrets are all connected with her erotic nature: her pregnancy, her love for Lövborg and her interest in forbidden pleasures. The intimacy of the family home only increases the sense of alienation between the characters who live side-by-side but do not share their innermost thoughts and experiences.

The dramatic and theatrical change from the depiction of the outdoors to the depiction of the indoors, goes along with the shift from women's secluded quarters to family home. The male space of the *agora* has now invaded the home: Helmer's study and Tesman's library are delimited as male sanctuaries. The differentiation between female and male spaces within the family home has left the drawing-room as the meeting place of husband and wife.

The drawing-room is seen as a bourgeois hallmark of success, the concrete proof of happiness and prosperity. The house is no longer an organic part of the family economy, a means to an end, but an end in itself. The parlour is a pretentious, ostentatious show-case of the upwardly mobile who have cast aside the middle-class, Protestant ethos of hard work, modest living and thrift. Helmer still adheres to the old values, reprimanding his wife for being a spendthrift. But Tesman has clearly forgotten his humble origins and strict education, buying an expensive house which sinks him into debt. Thus, the house is not just a scenic fixture but is itself drawn into the action.

The true state of the owners' affairs, a central issue in the plot, throws an ironic light on the realism of the drawing-room setting and of everything which is said or takes places in it. The famous 'photographic similitude'[3] and, the 'allegiance to material reality',[4] are turned through this irony into conventional and false icons concealing instead of revealing the protagonists' position and power. The revelation of the uncertain financial foundation of the house is followed by the disclosure of the unsound foundation of the marriage tie. Thus, the self-congratulatory ostentation of the drawing-room is exposed as doubly deceptive. The concrete representation of reality in the theatre is used by Ibsen ironically to destabilize its own message.

The misleading appearance of the room alerts the spectator to the communication that lies behind the spoken dialogue, not in it. The dialogue, like the setting, is treated ironically, pointed by abundant stage-directions, which need to be translated in acting into voice inflections and expressive gestures. The extreme terseness of the dialogue is such that, in the words of Edmund Gosse, reviewing *Hedda Gabler* on its first performance, even

> The stichomythia of Greek and French tragedians was lengthy in comparison with this unceasing display of hissing conversational fireworks, fragments of sentences without verbs, clauses that come to nothing, adverbial exclamations and cryptic interrogations.[5]

The spectator is forced to attend carefully to the various clues and innuendoes in the dialogue if he is to make out the sub-text, and 'the strain on the audience becomes almost intolerable'.[6]

Viewed today, Ibsen's realistic room, like his naturalistic dialogue, appears as an embodiment of a 'realistic' convention. Far from natural, everything about it is calculated to produce the right effect and interact with the spoken word. Contrivance and artificiality are evident in the counterpointing of characters and their symmetrical biographies and destinies, and in the aesthetic patterning, so far removed from chaotic 'reality'.

Molière's dramatic analysis of patriarchy in *L'École des femmes* as a system in which the male wishes to dominate the female in the double role of father and husband is, surprisingly, echoed in Henrik Ibsen's *A Doll's House*. Towards the end of the play, Helmer comments on the immense satisfaction experienced by a man who has forgiven his wife:

> It's as if that made her doubly his – as if he had brought her into the world afresh! In a sense, she has become both his wife and his child.[7]

He believes he has now strengthened his hold on her, becoming her father as well as her husband. But in fact, despite their eight years of married life and three children, Helmer has been treating Nora all along as a child-bride in need of being pampered, guided and protected. Nora has 'passed out of Papa's hands' and into Helmer's (p. 226).

The governing image of the play is indicated by its title.[8] The Helmers' home, meticulously detailed in the stage directions and realistically portrayed on stage, looks like the real thing, a real home, but its reality is illusory, it is only a doll's house or a stage-set. This warm and pleasant room, embodying the bourgeois values of hard work, parsimony, prosperity and the family, turns out to be a fake when Nora discovers that

> our home has been nothing but a play-room. I've been your doll-wife here, just as at home I was Papa's doll-child. And the children have been my dolls

in their turn. I liked it when you came and played with me, just as they liked it when I came and played with them. That's what our marriage has been, Torvald.

(Act 3, p. 226)

Up to this final moment of truth and self-discovery, Nora has been Helmer's willing play-mate. Their role-playing game has stuck to the stereotypes of responsibility and seriousness for the male, flightiness and coquetry for the female. Helmer's protective attitude towards Nora has been expressed by the diminutive imagery of his endearments: 'little twittering skylark', 'little song-bird', and 'scampering little squirrel', and of his playful reprimands: 'my little featherbrain', 'little scatterbrain' and 'little prodigal'. In Act 1, Nora accepted and even encouraged these epithets, which seemed to flatter her femininity. Far from resenting his superior airs, she seemed to enjoy being pampered and treated as an infant with a sweet tooth.

But this pleasure on one plane of existence was accompanied by the constant effort needed to hide her real self and lead a double life. Helmer's posture of benign, condoning husband trying to wean his child-wife of being a spendthrift suited Nora because it helped her conceal from him what she was really doing with all that money, namely paying back the loan.

The second Nora, the one who took the loan so as to save her husband's life and who has been working at night, doing copying and sewing work in order to repay her debt, is a very private and lonely person. She is a victim of a society in which a married woman of her class was not supposed to work and in which she did not have the financial independence to take a loan in her own name. Nora was forced into committing the forgery by her insupportable position. Therefore, her second, clandestine, and even illegal, self is relegated to her own room, where she locks herself up to do her work. Unlike the pride her husband takes in his job, she must hide what she is doing, inventing excuses to explain why she locks herself in for long hours.

In terms of the theatrical space, the drawing-room is where Nora plays her 'feminine' part and her unseen room is where she can be herself. In order to heal this rift in her personality, Nora must leave the house altogether. When she reaches that conclusion, the traditional spatial definitions, social as well as theatrical, are thrown into disarray. The woman's passage out of the home and into the world leaves the male in the house and severs the woman's ties with her home as her unique space.

The scene which leads up to Nora's dramatic exit is carefully constructed. It begins with Helmer's flinging his study-door open, the condemning letter in his hand, at the same moment that Nora, wrapped up in her shawl, is about to rush out of the house to commit suicide. This scene takes Nora from this lowest point of despair and a sense of having betrayed her family to the high point of self-realization as a woman and a human being with a life of her own. When she does quit her house at the end of the scene, it is in order to start a new life for herself, not to commit self-immolation. This is a scene which unsettles the social framework represented by the stage-set and advocated by Helmer, and to which, up to now, Nora has acquiesced.

Krogstad's incriminating letter, which Helmer holds in his hand, forces the couple to face up to the truth of the situation and of their own natures. Their pseudo-harmonious relationship is shattered by the violence of this experience and by the discovery of the other's true self behind the role-playing. Helmer's earlier playfulness, gentleness and erotic passion make way for cold self-interest and livid anger. He even uses physical force against Nora, preventing her from leaving, first by holding her back, then by locking the front door. As Nora takes in his reaction, she too begins to change. Her initial expression of love for him and eagerness to carry all the blame give way to a new comprehension of who he is and what his feelings towards her really are. While he declaims self-righteously against her depravity, 'I find that you're a liar, a hypocrite – even worse – a criminal' (Act 3, p. 221), she becomes visibly alienated from him.

Their conversation is a verbal *pas de deux*, which moves through a whole spectrum of emotions. The playwright has painstakingly prepared all the materials in order to show the awakening of the female consciousness. Without a word of criticism about Helmer's conduct, the audience is made to see through his moral posturing and take note of his excessive self-centredness: ' ... my happiness... my whole future... I'm in the power of... ' (Act 3, p. 221).

Helmer is mainly concerned with saving appearances: 'the thing must be hushed up at all costs', hinting at his willingness to be blackmailed by Krogstad. They must continue to lead their lives as before, 'but only in the eyes of the world, of course' (p. 221), preserving 'the mere façade' (p. 222). Nora is to remain 'here in my house' (p. 222) but without any contact with him or with the children. Helmer, no less than Nora, realizes that his home has been based on deceit. But unlike Nora he is too pusillanimous and conventional to admit this openly, and prefers instead to carry on and even deepen the illusory nature of their relationship.

When the maid brings in a second letter from Krogstad, addressed to Nora, Helmer appropriates it for himself, then cries out joyously: 'I'm saved! Nora, I'm saved!' Nora's piercing response 'And I?' underlines Helmer's insupportable egotism. To Helmer's great relief, Krogstad has returned the bond. Helmer now tries to be conciliatory: 'I've forgiven you everything. I know now that what you did was all for love of me' (Act 3, p. 223). Once again he extends his guiding male hand: 'I shouldn't be a proper man if your feminine helplessness didn't make you twice as attractive to me', and tries to return to his 'little song-bird' imagery, promising that 'my great wings will protect you' (p. 223). But the quaint little-animal images no longer suit Nora, nor can Helmer's protective attitude hide the widening gulf between their different perceptions of the situation.

Having recovered from his panic, Helmer reverts to his old self, offering protection and refuge, as well as moral guidance ('I'll be both your will and your conscience', p. 224). But Nora has in the meantime taken off the 'fancy-dress' both literally and metaphorically. It is she who insists now on a serious talk. Her home has been a 'play-room' and she herself a 'doll-wife' and she realizes that her upbringing and education have been inadequate. She feels she must cut herself off from her home and family in order to educate herself and grow up. In response to her husband's expression of religious and moral indignation at her neglecting her most sacred duty to her husband and children, she discovers another sacred duty, 'My duty to myself'.

Nora's awakening self-consciousness is the awakening of woman herself. She refuses to accept any longer benign patriarchy. She is shocked into self-awareness by the extreme egotistical response of her husband to Krogstad's disclosure, as compared with her own readiness to sacrifice herself for him. At her moment of need he has failed her completely, thinking only of his own skin.

It is interesting to note the absence of a similar scene of direct confrontation between husband and wife in *Hedda Gabler*. Hedda goes to her death without Tesman ever discovering what was on her mind. Had Nora left to commit suicide just prior to the discussion scene, as she had indeed intended to, there would have been no *anagnorisis*, no mutual recognition and understanding. Technically, Hedda's confrontation with Tesman is prevented by Thea's sitting down to work with Tesman. Unlike Nora, who believes in Helmer's potential for transcendence, Hedda has no illusions about Tesman. Her analogous expectations were pinned to Lövborg, who is now dead. *Hedda Gabler* ends where the final scene of *A Doll's House* begins.

Nora's secret wish that Helmer would shoulder the blame, should her forgery be discovered, has been criticized as hopelessly romantic and childish:

> She blames him now for not thinking of undertaking precisely the kind of
> knightly rescue of a damsel in distress which would assert his male superiority
> all over again.[9]

Such criticism, though rightly interpreting Ibsen's ironic portrayal of Nora's adolescent dream, seems to miss the basic seriousness that lies behind the ironic, realistic façade. Nora's repeated use of '*det vidunderlige*', the wonderful or miraculous,[10] is Ibsen's way of circumventing his own self-imposed realistic restrictions.

The miracle which Nora has been hoping for and dreading at the same time is the miracle of Helmer's taking upon himself the burden of her '*skyld*', both her debt and her guilt.[11] It is a miracle because it cannot happen, and it is totally unrealistic of her to expect this. But it is realistic to portray people entertaining dreams, even if their dreams are unrealistic. Nora's dream has sustained her through all the years of secret struggle to repay the debt, and as such has an objective existence.

Helmer's taking upon himself the blame, the hoped-for miracle which, being a miracle, can never happen, is understood by Nora as the supreme expression of love, in imitation of Christ.[12] These religious associations are emphasized by the prominence of Christmas in the play.[13] Only the generosity of love could have redeemed Nora's fallen world. The reality of everyday existence, like the reality of the *décor*, is thus dependent on a spiritual and metaphysical regulative idea, a point of reference outside itself, a sustaining ideal which imbues human behaviour with ethical meaning.

In this final *agon* between husband and wife, their whole married life is torn apart. 'With each line of dialogue exchanged between Nora and Helmer in the play's final scene, we feel the gulf between them widening more and more, and it creates a gripping effect to witness this bond being unravelled strand by strand', wrote Vilhelm Topsøe the day after the world première at the Royal Theater in Copenhagen.[14] The last marriage tie to come undone, after the couple have taken apart house, children and the reciprocity of convenience and protection, is love. It is Helmer who brings up these different corner-stones of the marriage institution and Nora who dismisses them one by one. The whole super-structure of bourgeois home and family becomes an empty shell, a doll's house abandoned by a girl who has suddenly grown up and has her own ideas of what 'a real marriage', as she calls it, should really be like.

The naturalistic drawing-room setting serves Ibsen as a laboratory for testing the premises of bourgeois ideology, and the direct confrontation between husband and wife, with which the play ends, is an experiment investigating the nature of marriage itself. Only in the intimacy of the house can such a conversation take place, and even in this carefully laid out space, Nora notes that this is the first time that the two of them are sitting down to have a serious talk (Act 3, p. 225). Her comment works on two levels: it points to a change in the relations between the genders as well as in dramatic technique. Nora's revelation is shared by the playwright who has discovered the power of simple naturalistic dialogue between a man and a woman sitting in their drawing-room, to probe into the basis of their relationship. George Bernard Shaw saw in this 'discussion' a technical break-through.[15]

The dialogue is exciting even today, after many of its personal revelations have been trivialized by becoming feminist commonplaces and slogans. Its excitement is due to this feeling of witnessing a genuine process of self-discovery in Nora, and not an 'instant', faddish, feminist conversion. And the excitement is also due to the sense of the progression of the mutual relations from the playfulness of the beginning to the direct and open confrontation of the final scene.

In the traditional street scenes of older forms of drama, the action moved forward as one character tried to overcome or outwit another. The naturalistic space of the drawing-room sets off the interiorization of the action. Its heroine is no longer an *ingénue* struggling to live happily ever after but a married woman who, due to external events, undergoes an internal process of change. In *A Doll's House*, this crisis of consciousness is long in the making and it actually breaks out only in the first-and-final conversation scene, after the agony of Nora's decision to commit suicide. It is then that Helmer's self-centred reaction to the incriminating letter hits her, wonderfully clearing her mind and changing her despair to inner strength and resilience.

Both the applause and the condemnation with which the play was received by Ibsen's contemporaries attest to the sensitivity of its feminist theme. The opposition voiced by Pastor M. J. Faerden saw in the heroine's emancipation from family bonds a serious threat to the marriage institution. For Faerden, woman's place remains 'in the innermost sanctuary of the home' and she herself is still, as in Greece, a priestess of Hestia. He interpreted the emancipation of woman as the freedom to leave her home and family at will, which, from his point of view, is immoral. He envisaged the new woman poised at the door, suitcase in hand, ready to depart.[16] The reversal of outdoors and indoors in the theatre thus reached its logical conclusion with the heroine's voluntary exit from the home which had for so long been represented as her prison.

The Tesmans set up home as soon as they return from their prolonged, five- or six-months-long honeymoon. The house, a distinguished old residence, is mortgaged and the elegant furniture has been paid for with another mortgage, on the aunts' meager pension. All these financial arrangements have been negotiated by the ever-obliging Brack. Heavily in debt, Tesman has been counting on his prospects of receiving an academic appointment and with it a fixed salary. The apparent prosperity reflected by the drawing-room stage-set is thus discovered to be merely illusory, lacking a solid basis. There is a grim irony in the setting itself, in its solid concreteness, in its expression of material values. This irony is also extended to the social and moral values attached to the seeming display of financial well-being.

The entire action of *Hedda Gabler* takes place in the Tesmans' drawing-room and the inner room attached to it. This serves as a social centre where the different characters congregate. In the theatrical space without there are three places important to the action: the aunts' home, Judge Brack's quarters and Mademoiselle

Diana's apartments. Unlike Hedda, who is practically always present and never leaves her house, Tesman moves in and out, visiting his aunts twice, and going to Brack's bachelors' party. Lövborg and Brack both visit Mademoiselle Diana, where Lövborg finally finds his death. Other places which give the illusion of the spatial continuum of Christiania are the temporary lodgings of Lövborg and of Thea. Strands of action lead from these various imagined locales to the perceived space of the Tesmans' drawing-room.

The Tesmans are the only married couple in the play, and they are about to start a family. Theirs is the only established home, a symbol of steadfast propriety, towards which the other, single characters gravitate. Hedda brings to their marriage social status and Tesman brings to it the reputation of a serious academic with a seemingly secure future. Superficially a good match, it is quickly exposed as a *mésalliance*. Tesman is blissfully unaware of this, lacking the necessary sensibility to perceive that something is wrong. He continues to congratulate himself on having caught the beauty who had so many suitors. But she finds it difficult to hide the contempt and revulsion she feels towards him.

In her conversation with Brack in Act 2, Hedda reveals how such an unsuitable match could come about:

> But in this ardour for Lady Falk's villa Jörgen Tesman and I met in mutual understanding, you see! It brought on engagement and marriage and honeymoon and the whole lot.[17]

The image of the expensive and respectable house and of the distinction conferred by such a house on its owners took precedence in their relationship over the lack of a mutual attraction or a genuine interest in each other. The tantalizing mirage of the bourgeois home and the values it stands for thus forms the basis for the plot of the play. Both Hedda and Tesman succumbed to the allure of the conventional image of happiness, success and respectability. The house was the meeting-point for two characters with totally different goals and life-styles.

The inauthenticity of their relationship finds expression in their attitude to their new home. Hedda now reveals that she never really cared about the house but only voiced her wish to live in it on an impulse, because she was trying to help out the conversation with the embarrassed Tesman and 'felt sorry for the poor erudite man' fumbling for words. She finds the atmosphere of the house stifling and feels bored in it.

Tesman, on his side, is appalled when he realizes the financial burden of paying back the mortgages and discovers that 'the appointment to professorship might conceivably be contested by another candidate' (Act 1, p. 200). Tesman loses his composure and becomes visibly upset:

We got married on our expectations, Hedda and I. Went and borrowed vast sums. We're in debt to Auntie Julle, too! Because, good God... the post was as good as promised to me. Eh?

(Act 1, p. 200)

Tesman, the 'square' bourgeois, is caught out of his depth, having for once abandoned caution and embarked on an adventure:

Yes... it can't be denied... it was idiotically romantic to go and get married, and buy a house, just on expectations alone.

(p. 201)

Living beyond one's means is the nightmare of the bourgeois brought up on the ethos of work and parsimony. Tesman has acted against his better judgement and upbringing, pushed by Hedda's caprice. He is a person who has been brought up modestly by two maiden aunts. But the upper-class Hedda married on the expectation of being able to entertain, of having a footman and a saddle-horse. Their dubious financial circumstances thus widen the rift between them.

The house and its furnishings are all geared to appease and satisfy Hedda. She is regarded by both Tesman and his aunt as an extraordinary 'catch', a society beauty and a person who must live in style, who cannot be expected to economize. From her maiden home she has brought over her piano, General Gabler's portrait and his pistols. The piano is removed into the inner room between Acts 1 and 2 in preparation for Hedda's playing wild dance music on it prior to shooting herself with one of the pistols, under the portrait.

Perhaps the most important and interesting scene is that of Hedda's *tête à tête* with Ejlert Lövborg in Act 2. The scene is set meticulously with Tesman and Brack drinking and smoking in the inner room, Hedda sitting on the corner sofa and Lövborg on a chair next to her, his back to the inner room, so that he cannot observe the two men there. It soon becomes clear that the photo album spread in front of Hedda and Lövborg serves as a convenient screen to cover up the true nature of their conversation. Hedda especially is quite adept at switching quickly between public and private voices, pretending to show photographs and chat about rock formations with a family friend, while holding a clandestine and emotional conversation with a former lover. This is part of the social game of propriety that she is attempting to play, necessitated by the contradiction between her sensuality on the one hand and her conventionality on the other.

Hedda's duplicity is well-studied, since she has had previous experience in it. Her conversation with Lövborg turns out to be a re-enactment of the secret lovers' meetings they used to hold at her father's house under the very nose of General Gabler. He used to sit by the window, reading a paper, his back turned, while they

102

sat together in the corner sofa pretending to look at a magazine, 'for want of an album' (Act 2, p. 222). Instead of her father, it is now her husband and the portrait of the General that watch Hedda's game from the inner room.

The meaning of this dramatic moment is conveyed by the spatial relations of inner and outer rooms, the relative positioning of corner sofa, portrait, husband, wife and secret lover, and by the gesture of whispering over an open picture-album. The careful spatial arrangement of the scene takes us beyond Hedda's pretence, evoking the past, explaining its significance and relevance to the dramatic present, and picking up what has remained inconclusive despite the apparent finality of marriage.

The married Hedda, like the unmarried Hedda, is always afraid of what people will say. She readily admits to being a coward, and admires and envies Thea's courage to spurn public opinion. The self-control and composure she exhibits while deceiving Tesman about the nature of her conversation with Lövborg is a measure of the dominance of her strong sense of social propriety over her powerful libido.

Lövborg can enter Hedda's house because no one suspects they have had any kind of affair. Because of his dissolute reputation, Hedda never dared to be publicly associated with him in any way and preferred the stability and safety of a conventional, comfortable marriage with her plodding scholar, eager to provide for her.

The naturalism of the dialogue as well as contemporary social and theatrical decorum preclude the spelling out of what went on between Hedda and Lövborg in the past. But the bits of oblique information that do come up in the broken dialogue challenge us to piece them together. The intimate and illicit conversation contrasts with the formality of the drawing-room and the watchful eyes behind the couple. Thus it is the social convention and the theatrical convention that represents it which compel Hedda, in the dramatic present as in the past, to restrain her eroticism behind her drawing-room manners. Her erotic drive is transmuted into curiosity and voyeurism. She used to force out of Lövborg his confessions not because she wanted to absolve him, as he had assumed, but because she wanted 'to find out about a world that... that she isn't supposed to know anything about' (Act 2, p. 223). This is as far as their conversation now probes. But from the scattered references in the play to Mademoiselle Diana, the red-haired singer to whose party, given for a select group of lady-friends and admirers, Lövborg goes after the bachelors' party is over, one may conclude that he had been confessing his debaucheries with her.

Mademoiselle Diana is Hedda's *alter ego*: her libertine relations with Lövborg afford Hedda a vicarious sexual thrill. Sitting primly in her father's presence, but out of his ear-shot, she thus finds substitute erotic fulfilment without compromising her reputation. Ironically, it is in the very heart of institutionalized conformity, within the respectable parlor, that Mademoiselle Diana is discussed and even envied.

Despite leading diametrically opposed lives, the ever-present Hedda and the unseen (due to social and theatrical decorum) Diana have much in common. This is first indicated when Thea tells Hedda despondently that 'There's a shadow of a woman' who stands between her and Ejlert (Act 1, p. 194), someone from his past who when they parted threatened to shoot him with a pistol. Thea concludes this must be 'that red-haired singer' that carried around a loaded pistol and has now returned to town (p. 195). From Hedda's manner and from what we learn from her conversation with Lövborg in Act 2 about her having threatened him with her pistol on parting, it is clear that at least Hedda believes it is her own shadow that has hampered the evolvement of Thea's affair with Lövborg. But both interpretations of the 'shadow' are possible. This ambiguity between the two women is further emphasized at the end of the play when it is not clear whether Mademoiselle Diana, a fine shot in her own right, has killed Lövborg or he has committed suicide at Hedda's behest.

The scene which duplicates in externals Hedda's past meetings with Lövborg points to her sexual repression. Her condition is exacerbated by her marriage. The interpretation of this enigmatic scene, widely ignored in critical literature, is essential to the understanding of the play as a whole, since Hedda's destruction of Lövborg and subsequently of herself and her unborn child all emanate from the complexity of her feelings towards him. The scene is structured so as to exhibit the relationship between the two in the present, evoke the past history of that relationship and point out the unresolved erotic tension between them.

With Brack she can flirt and talk suavely, with her husband she is contemptuous and ironic, but with Ejlert Lövborg Hedda is passionate. Lövborg recognizes this as their common bond, 'our common lust for life' (Act 2, p. 223). But he too is repressed, going to Mademoiselle Diana for release and retaining a platonic, intellectual relationship with Thea. 'Like two good companions' or 'comrades', is the phrase that denotes the way he regards his relationship first with Hedda and then with Thea. There is an unbridgeable duality in his nature between his spiritual and his carnal desires.

The extreme circumspection with which human sexuality, and especially female sexuality, is treated in the play is itself an index of the repression Ibsen is attempting to convey. Similarly, the realism of the setting expresses directly the repressive social environment of the formal drawing-room.

For release, Judge Brack invites his friends, the married Tesman included, to a 'lively' bachelors' party in his own home, where they will indulge in drink and from which they will proceed in the early hours of the morning to Mademoiselle

Diana's lodgings. Hedda's voyeurism becomes apparent when, seeing the men out and speaking of herself in the third person, as if to distance herself from her daydream, she wishes she could join them unseen:

> Ah, if only that lovely lady could come along as an invisible onlooker... So as to hear a little of your liveliness... unexpurgated.

(Act 2, p. 230)

She resents the sexual freedom enjoyed by the men and the double standard of late nineteenth-century society which allowed men to come and go between respectable society and brothel but confined the well-brought-up woman to domesticity. Lövborg can move between Hedda Gabler and Mademoiselle Diana, but women can only be either the one or the other, either respectable or dissolute.

Whereas Lövborg can find partial relief in his dissolute life-style, which he carries on in the theatrical space without, Hedda remains constantly on view, and her only means of escape is into sexual fantasy and reverie. At the climax of her conversation with Lövborg, she makes an unexpected confession:

> That I didn't dare to shoot you... that wasn't my worst cowardice... that evening.

(Act 2, p. 224)

The spectator may find this rather baffling, but Lövborg 'takes her meaning' and 'whispers passionately':

> Now I think I see what it was that lay behind our comradeship! You and I... ! So it was your lust for life...

(p. 224)

Hedda's response is to shut herself up yet again, warning Lövborg not to assume anything. Presumably, Hedda's greatest failure of courage was that she failed to seize the moment in which Lövborg tried to go beyond their customary conversations. She recoiled from the 'imminent danger that the game would become a reality', refusing to change from a friend and companion to a lover, and threatened to punish him for his sexual overture with her pointed pistol. By denying her strong sexual attraction to Lövborg, she lost the opportunity, condemning herself to a life of boredom and frustration with Tesman. Even her honeymoon with him she found exceedingly boring, wishing that Brack had been with them to entertain her.

Being so repressed, she will have nothing with the fruit of sexual relations. She refuses to admit her condition or to let others refer to it. The rapid progress of time, evidenced by the yellow autumn leaves and Thea's reminder that it is September already, arouses in Hedda the feeling of being trapped. She 'walks about the room, raises her arms and clenches her fists as though in a frenzy' (Act 1, p. 183). A little earlier, Tesman has spoken smugly to his aunt of how Hedda has 'filled out beautifully on the trip' and alluded to the intimacy between them, both of which Hedda peremptorily denied. She reacts similarly to Brack's circumspect suggestion that she is about to face a 'sacred' responsibility, by totally rejecting the possibility: 'Be quiet! You'll never see anything of the sort!' (Act 2, p. 213). The bachelor Brack can obviously see she is pregnant and considers this a potential for female self-fulfilment, a natural 'vocation', as he puts it. But Hedda has already decided at this early stage of the play against having the child.

The only other character who has noticed Hedda's condition is the maiden aunt, who tries to draw Tesman into a conversation about it but is too shy and modest to broach the subject directly. Instead, she asks him about whether he has any special prospects he would like to tell her about. His self-satisfied nature comes through his complacent answer: 'I have the best prospect in the world of becoming professor' (Act 1, p. 176). His lack of sensitivity and intuition becomes apparent when he fails to respond to his aunt's broad hint about the two spare rooms coming to good use in the future. All he can think of is extending his library into those two rooms. The figure of the maiden aunt yearning for a new baby in the family but unable to speak openly about her expectations is central to this inhibited society.

The pregnant Hedda, who stands at the centre of all this attention, denies in word and deed the life-giving aspect of her female body. In discussions of her suicide it is often overlooked that in killing herself she also murders her unborn child, that she in fact kills herself in order to prevent its birth and her own motherhood. The repression imposed on her by society results in her denying a future to that society, either in the form of a child or in the form of a book on the future.

Until Hedda brings herself to reveal her pregnancy to him, an act of desperate self-defence after she has burnt Lövborg's manuscript, Tesman remains unaware of his wife's condition. The honeymoon had been almost six months long and Hedda's pregnancy is not all that obvious yet. It would have been too scandalous for Ibsen to suggest that Lövborg fathered this child on that one occasion in which he took advantage of her. In Hedda's words: '...how could you offer such violence...to your confidential companion!' (Act 2, p. 223). At the same time, Hedda rebuffs Tesman's boast that he has opportunities to see her undressed and complains of the boredom of their honeymoon. At least intellectually, and perhaps also physically, Tesman is portrayed as impotent and contrasted with the virile, libidinous, imaginative and passionate Lövborg. All that can be concluded on the basis of the scant information provided is that Ibsen left us in the dark about the identity of the father.

The theatrical space of *Hedda Gabler* is sterile, unable to accommodate happiness and fulfilment. The protagonist is held back from following her own drives by social convention and psychic repression, forces much more subtle than external patriarchal control. George Lukács points to this dialectic: 'Modern life liberates man from many old constraints ... But in turn, man comes to be enclasped by an entire chain of abstract bondages, which are yet more complicated.'[18] While external pressure on the Renaissance heroine could be defeated with the aid of an astute lover by elopement or some clever trick, the self-imposed restraint in Ibsen's drama is more difficult to overcome and often destructive. Its origins lie in ancient patriarchalism – hence the emphasis on the fathers of both Nora and Hedda, different as they are – but it is modern in its apparent freedom from external constraint and its internalization of the values and mores of polite society.

Ibsen's analysis of the modern woman's repression as internal rather than external is expressed directly by the meticulously prescribed bourgeois drawing-room. The physical restraint of previous generations, expressed by the theatrical convention of the house front and locked door, have given way to a much freer and more egalitarian life-style in the shared living-room. Enjoying this greater freedom, Ibsen's heroines discover the more subtle fetters, moral and cultural, that inhibit them and force them to act inauthentically. The social propriety that finds its outward form in the formality and elegance of the *salon* is discovered to exert a deadly influence on woman's ability to find self-fulfilment. The room is the gilded shell of an impossible social decorum, a pretence and an imposture that attempt to cover up the vacuity of the underlying moral justification.

## Chapter 8

# Preferring insecurity

The Ibsenite drawing-room forms a static theatrical space in which significant, yet minimal, modulation is achieved through re-arranging the furniture or altering the lighting. The apparent solidity and respectability of this room, supposedly expressive of the well-being of its inhabitants, is gradually undermined by the action of the plays and exposed as a false icon. For Chekhov, on the other hand, what the house represents is authentic enough, but the house itself becomes subject to the passage of time, part of the general process of change that affects its dwellers.

Chekhov is the playwright of change, recording the momentous social and cultural transformations of his period,[1] analyzing them in relation to technological and economic developments, evaluating their impact on the individual, and searching for a suitable artistic vehicle to express them. Chekhov's outlook is Heraclitean in its basic perception of reality as in constant flux. In the words of Marc Slonim, 'What he sought to achieve was the illusion of the actual flow of life, of the texture of existence'.[2]

It is sometimes claimed that nothing much happens in Chekhov's plays. But a synoptic view of each play reveals the extent of the momentous changes that take place between opening and ending, often bordering on the melodramatic, as in unrequited love leading to suicide. And yet these events seem to develop in imperceptible steps, without ruffling the smooth surface of continuity. The effect is of a superficial calm hiding the strong undercurrent of change, and it is achieved through the depiction of a passive response to events, a clinging to the present moment.

The family members who return periodically to their estates in both *The Seagull* (1896) and *The Cherry Orchard* (1904) have changed their attitude to their country home, but it is also the estates themselves that have changed, becoming unprofitable, a financial as well as an emotional burden, rather than an asset. The plays record the crumbling of the aristocratic estates, the dispersion of the families, the lure of the big cities, the rise of individualism, the intimations of the coming revolution.

Chekhov's characters represent a multiplicity of points of view, from the radical to the reactionary, but he himself adopts a Shakespearean stance of 'negative capability', depicting equally the pain and the hope, the nostalgia and the expectation with which the different characters regard the prospect of change. The winners in Chekhov's universe are those who are adaptable to change. The losers are those whose personality and education prevent them from suiting themselves to the changing circumstances. Instead of looking forward, they cling to memories and to objects suffused with memories.

Chekhov evokes the past as a static background to the events of the plays. The instability and insecurity which he dramatizes are sharply contrasted with the fixity and certainty that has characterized life on the estates for generations. Firs, the eighty-seven-year-old valet in *The Cherry Orchard*, refers to the day of his emancipation as 'the calamity'[3]. On that day, the norms and values of his customary world were shattered, and everything took on an impermanent and questionable aspect.

The static drawing-room setting of Ibsen's realistic plays cannot accommodate the dynamics of change which is Chekhov's particular dramatic idiom. Chekhov therefore manipulates the theatrical space, modifying the setting from one act to the next, shifting the spectator's perspective from one point of view to another, making the very form of his art imitate the flow of life rather than impose on it its own fixedness.

When, in Act Four of *The Seagull*, Nina enters from the garden through the French windows, she looks round the room and notes: 'This used to be the drawing-room' (p. 278),[4] directing our attention not only to the incoherent appearance of the room but also to the distance Chekhov has travelled from Ibsen's formal drawing-room setting. Earlier in the act, Dorn commented on the drawing-room having been turned into Konstantin Treplev's study (p. 270), thus forcing the audience to take note of what the reader already knows from the stage directions, which indicate that alongside the drawing-room furniture there is also a desk, a bookcase and books on window-ledges and chairs.

This already transformed room keeps changing its function in front of our eyes. First, Treplev and Polina come in carrying bed-linen, pillows and blankets to make up a bed for the ailing Sorin in Konstantin's study. Then, a whole group of characters gathers there around Sorin's bath-chair. The sense of invading Kostya's privacy (Dorn: 'We're stopping Konstantin working') is strengthened when the folding card-table is opened by Arkadina for a game of lotto.

Kostya himself declines to play and goes out, returning a little later and going directly to his desk. While the whole company trails off to supper, he stays behind to deliver a long, unnaturalistic soliloquy in which he agonizes over his own artistic incompetence in comparison to Trigorin's facile technique. His isolation from his family and his creative despair are vividly conveyed through his remaining alone at the desk with his manuscripts, the manuscripts that he will tear to shreds after

Nina's brief visit. At first arousing his hopes, this visit ends in his realization of the finality of their parting. As the others gather again in his study after supper, Kostya commits suicide in the theatrical space without.

Each of the four acts defines a different theatrical space, a different part of the estate and the house. This multiplicity of settings and perspectives is an aspect of Chekhov's modernity.[5] The play moves from two outdoor to two different indoor settings. The action unfolds in a large park with a lovely view (Act 1), in a croquet lawn and a large terrace (Act 2), in a dining-room crammed with the bags and suitcases of those who are about to leave (Act 3) and in the drawing-room turned study (Act 4). The four different theatrical spaces of the four acts are spaces *manqués*. The first three acts avoid the central drawing-room. Instead, the action moves through a dispersed space bearing the nostalgic memories of happier days. Then there was singing on the lake every night (Act 1, p. 243), an accord between man and nature, and a sense of personal and social harmony. When, finally, in Act 4, the action does reach the drawing-room, this is no longer the traditional symbol of the family's permanence and well-being and has itself become an icon of change.

Taken together, the four settings portray a country house which has lost its centre. This lack of a centre is closely linked to the fact that nobody wants to remain in this house, although everyone recognizes its unique beauty and regards it as a source of creative inspiration. It is this ambiguous attitude coupled with the general tension between individual fulfilment and familial bonds that brings about the dissolution of the home, both as a material and as a spiritual entity.

If the play is read from the point of view of the female characters, the theatrical spaces in which the action unfolds become meaningful. In the The *Seagull*, the woman is not at the centre of the action, as in the two Ibsen plays discussed in the previous chapter and in Chekhov's own *Cherry Orchard*. Nevertheless, the articulation of its theatrical space is still determined by female motivation. The fate of the female characters is directly relevant to the protagonist's predicament, to the dissolution of his home and to his inability to achieve personal and artistic success. The falling apart of Konstantin's home is caused by the refusal of the two women in his life, his mother and his beloved, to accept their traditional roles as women and home-makers. The disintegration of the household is primarily due to Arkadina's refusal to stay in her country-home and her lack of interest in her son. The space in which Konstantin moves is blighted by his mother's basic rejection of it, and of him, as part of woman's traditional onus. This experience of abandonment is compounded by Nina's rejection, her preferring a transient affair with Trigorin to Kostya's whole-hearted and idealistic devotion. Chekhov follows the fortunes of his emancipated heroines beyond the slammed door. Both women turn their backs on the security offered by their homes, preferring to remain unattached.

The uneasy settings of the different acts reflect the absence of a woman in the house.

Chekhov characterizes the four female characters of *The Seagull* in relation to the struggle for female equality. They belong to two groups: Polina and Masha, the disaffected mother and daughter, who do not find the way to cut off their links with house and family; and mother and spiritual daughter, Arkadina and Nina, the actresses who have wilfully severed themselves from domesticity. The play deals with the price of this emancipation.

The unhappy marriages of Polina and Masha throw into relief the independent life-style of Arkadina and Nina. The two actresses are progressive in their espousal of free-love and repudiation of institutional security offered by matrimony. Chekhov faithfully records the shift in the attitude of women towards marriage: the security it reputedly affords the woman is no longer sought after. His two emancipated women are totally engrossed in their own career-and-love lives and show no inclination to be tied down by home or marriage. In many ways, their attitude anticipates the Me generation.

Nina, the star of Konstantin's play and his beloved, arrives just in time for the performance after virtually escaping from her home on the other side of the lake. She arrives nervous and flustered because she must be home before her father and step-mother return and find she has spent the evening with Treplev's family, whom they regard as 'wildly bohemian'. They are apparently afraid of that family's bad influence on Nina, i.e. that she too will want to become an actress. Therefore they keep her 'pretty well a prisoner' in her own home (Act 1, pp. 235, 237). Patriarchal tyranny and woman's emancipation still brush shoulders in this twentieth-century drama.

As it turns out, the parents have judged rightly the influence on the impressionable Nina, who is only eighteen or nineteen years old. As soon as she joins the company after the failed performance, Arkadina compliments her on her looks and her performance, the compliment of a famous actress to an aspiring one, and encourages her not to bury herself in the country: 'Your duty is to go on stage' (Act 1, p. 243).

Nina's youth is what Trigorin, who has never been young, as he regretfully admits, is attracted to. For him, she represents the younger generation in her idealism and innocent trust, but also in her naive artistic ambition. On her side, Nina tells Trigorin that she envies him and would like to be in his shoes and lead a meaningful life (Act 2, p. 254). She is not just awed and fascinated by the celebrated writer but actually compares herself to him, assessing her own distance from attaining his artistic renown. Her admiration for him is mingled with envy, indicating that she sees herself as potentially his equal, beyond gender differences.

She too wants to make a name for herself in the world, and this ambition is so strong that it pushes aside all other concerns and considerations:

> If I was lucky enough to be a writer or actress, I wouldn't mind my family and friends disliking me, or being poor and disappointed. I'd live in a garret on black bread, I'd suffer, being dissatisfied with myself and knowing how imperfect I was. But I should insist on being a real celebrity, with all the tumult and the shouting that go with it.
>
> (Act 2, p. 257)

Nina is also prepared to take risks in her love-life, taking the lead and virtually offering herself to Trigorin through the reference to a line from his novel engraved on the medallion she gives him: 'If you should ever need my life, then come and take it' (Act 3, p. 264). Then she takes the big leap and decides to leave home, go on stage and start a new life in Moscow (Act 3, p. 267). In that city she has an affair with Trigorin and gives birth to a child who dies in infancy, after which Trigorin leaves her and goes back to Arkadina – this rather melodramatic action takes place between Acts 3 and 4, i.e. in the narrative background of the play.

As Kostya sees it, 'Nina's private life has been a disaster' and her stage career 'even worse'. She has been playing leading roles, but in the provinces, and 'her acting was crude and inept, with lots of ranting and hamming', although she did have some superb moments. He has followed her career closely, dogging her at hotels, desperate to meet her. But she has only communicated with him in letters which she signed as 'Seagull', from which he sensed that 'her mind was slightly unhinged' as a result of her extreme unhappiness (Act 4, p. 272).

Coming back for a short visit, Nina is forced to put up at an inn, since she is banned from her father's home. Her life is now the life of an actress staying at hotels. When Treplev brings her into his study in the last act, she comments on how warm and cosy the room is and quotes from the Epilogue of Turgenev's novel *Rudin*:

> Lucky the man with a roof over his head and somewhere to be warm on a night like this... And may the Lord help all homeless wanderers.
>
> (Act 4, p. 278)

Still, she rejects Kostya's plea for love. She has long since chosen her course and will not go back, now she is an actress. She recounts how Trigorin had discouraged her and how she had suffered from jealousy while living with him, becoming petty and narrow-minded. Only after the baby had died and the affair was over did she really become an actress and find herself. Now she knows that what counts in life is stamina and that acting is her vocation, and she is no longer afraid of life (Act 4, p. 280). In her professional self-confidence she has left Konstantin behind. It is his realization of his own inadequacy, of his own unfulfilled potential and of the finality of Nina's rejection of him that leads him to suicide.

Treplev's mother, Arkadina, is also in many ways a liberated woman. The mature actress, with the expected ego of a *prima dona*, is living with the famous Trigorin who is her junior by a number of years (she is apparently forty-three, while he is 'nowhere near forty yet', Act 1, pp. 236, 237). She is so absorbed with her own artistic life, 'serving humanity in the sacred cause of art', and with her affair with Trigorin that she has little time and interest for her twenty-five-year-old son, not even to the extent of helping him financially. Kostya records his anguish:

> I can't help being a bit selfish, as anyone should in my position, and I'm sorry to have a famous actress for my mother – feel I'd be better off if she was just an ordinary woman.
>
> (Act 1, p. 236)

Because of the nature of their profession, actresses were always in the vanguard of women's emancipation. Chekhov shows the ambiguity of the actress' social position: on the one hand, there is the romantic image of the actress consecrating her life to the theatre and, on the other, the conservative repudiation of the loose morals of the actress who lives in sin. These views are represented in the play by Shamreyev and by Nina's father, respectively. Arkadina's reputation as an actress allows her to be in the forefront of women's liberation without any self-conscious effort. However, Nina's struggle to become another Arkadina is almost a martyrdom, a long journey achieved at great personal cost.

Masha and her mother Polina are portrayed as more conventional women. Polina's life-long obsession with Dorn comes to nothing and she continues to suffer from her husband Shamreyev. Masha repeats the pattern, marrying Medvedenko in-between acts, in a desperate effort to drown her love for Kostya in domesticity. But her whole nature revolts against this self-imposed oppression. She treats her husband as a nuisance, refusing his entreaties to go home with him and even his repeated appeals to her maternal instinct. Masha repudiates this emotional blackmail: 'Now it's all baby, baby, baby, home, home, home. That's all you ever say' (Act 4, p. 268). Her irate emphasis on cutting herself loose from home and baby directs our attention to the actresses' revolt against these two traditional female duties. Her chafing at her bonds leads to nothing more than frustration, and her independent spirit asserts itself only in her habits of taking snuff (Act 1, p. 247) and drinking. She scorns Trigorin's suggestion that she drinks too much: 'Women drink a lot more than you think. A few do it openly like me, but most keep quiet about it. Oh yes they do. And it's always vodka or brandy' (Act 3, p. 258).

The refusal of both Arkadina and Nina to take upon themselves the traditional roles of mother and home-maker is in effect an attempt to put an end to the association between woman and house. It also means that the theatre can no longer take the domestic theatrical space for granted. This explains perhaps Treplev's sense of the inadequacy of the naturalistic three-wall setting (Act 1, p. 236). He senses that naturalism has degenerated into yet another convention and attempts to replace it with a new, symbolist technique. Guided by his artistic intuition, Konstantin sees the discrepancy between the falling apart of the institutions of family and home and the impression of security conveyed by the cosy room-setting. Treplev's search for new forms in art is a search for an appropriate vehicle for expressing this loss of a secure centre. It is the two women in his life who thus determine not only the quality of his life but also the nature of his art.

The whole point about Konstantin's playlet is that it tries to avoid the challenge of everyday strife by escaping into metaphysical reverie: in the absence of material change there can be neither pain nor passion but only pure spirit, a crystallization and conglomeration of all memories. Kostya has written this play for a single actress, Nina, and also for a single member of the audience: his mother. In the conversation with his uncle just before the performance, Kostya claims that his mother is jealous and angry because Nina and not she will be acting (Act 1, p. 235).

Arkadina's awareness of herself as unique addressee may already be indicated by her quotation from Gertrude: 'O Hamlet, speak no more: / Thou turn'st mine eyes into my very soul' (Act 1, p. 240). From the start, she is an antagonistic spectator, perceiving the play to be directed personally to her and at her, and disrupting the performance with her scathing comments. She intervenes both in self-defence and in retaliation, dismissing its subject-matter as boring ('We're fast asleep anyway', p. 240), its dramatic form as iconoclastic ('This is something terribly modern', p. 241), and its theatricality as childish ('Oh, a stage effect', p. 241). Treplev's imploring interjections say it all in just one word: 'Mother!'

The performance of the play within the play constitutes the most effective showdown between Treplev and Arkadina, conducted under the cover of a family entertainment, with all the normal strain of such an affair. The simmering conflict flares up when Arkadina provokes her son by cracking a joke at the expense of his play, and he brings down the curtain, cutting short the performance. Arkadina, for one, realizes that Kostya's aim was 'to show us how to write and act. I've really had about enough of this! These constant outbursts and digs against me' (Act 1, p. 242). She is evidently piqued by the performance, denouncing it as 'experimental rubbish' and him as 'a selfish, spoilt little boy' (p. 242). It is only a little later that her maternal conscience begins to torment her: 'I'm beginning to feel rather guilty. Why did I hurt my poor boy's feelings? I'm worried' (Act 1, p. 243).

The analogies of this scene with the performance of the play within the play in *Hamlet* are too many to be pursued in this context. Here, they will serve to underline the parallel configuration of characters in the two plays. Like Hamlet, who is surrounded by his mother Gertrude, her second husband Claudius and his sweetheart Ophelia, Treplev is surrounded by his mother Arkadina, her lover Trigorin, and Nina, with whom he is in love. Hamlet's emotional difficulties with his mother's hasty marriage and Ophelia's lack of commitment are reflected in Treplev's ambiguous feelings towards his mother and in his despair over Nina's falling in love with Trigorin. As Hamlet before him, Treplev feels rebuffed by both mother and sweetheart. The mother's lover is in both cases an object of jealousy and hate, thus rounding off the counter-pointing of the main characters in the two plays.[6]

Arkadina is a mature woman with an artistic career of her own and an ongoing affair with a famous writer. For her, these are more important than her son and what is left of her old home. Although she is still attached to these, she has clearly broken away from traditional life on the estate and is in fact trying to distance herself from it even more. In the course of the play, Nina follows her example, with tragic consequences.

But it is not only the women who try to break away from the country house. Even Sorin expresses his dislike of it, but 'now I'm retired I've nowhere else to go' (Act 1, p. 234). He recalls with nostalgia his life in the city with its cabs and telephones, the instruments of anonymity and solitude, as well as industry. Sorin tries to arouse Arkadina's compassion for Kostya who is 'buried in the country' and needs money in order to leave and perhaps go abroad (Act 3, p. 260). Another variation on the theme of the temptation of anonymity appears in Dr Dorn's memories from Genoa, where,

> leaving your hotel in the evening, you find the whole street jammed with people, and you drift round in the crowd ... you share its life, enter into its spirit and begin to think there really could be such a thing as a World Spirit.
>
> (Act 4, p. 272)

However, all three men, Sorin, Treplev and Dr Dorn remain in the country, and it is only the two actresses who find the strength to leave behind the security of home. Arkadina is always ready to depart, at the slightest provocation. She finds 'the charming country' exceedingly dull and boring, with people lolling around, doing nothing. All in all, 'I'd much rather sit in my hotel room learning a part' (Act 2, p. 251). There it is, the preference for the transitory, unattached life in hotels, and the 'railway carriages, stations, refreshment-rooms, mutton-chops and talk' (Act 3, p. 266), which this new woman prefers to living by her own hearth.

The close association between woman and her house and its implications for the family group and for society at large form both the framework and the inner core of *The Cherry Orchard*. In this play, the action not only takes place within the theatrical space of the family estate but is also concerned with the very fate of this estate. The country house from which all the characters of *The Seagull* struggled to free themselves is now itself the focus of the drama.

Chekhov made the whole action revolve around the fate of the estate and at the same time created an image of it on stage, fashioning his theatrical space as the estate, the house with its orchard. He thus achieved the unique effect of foregrounding the background. In the *Cherry Orchard*, theatrical space itself becomes the subject-matter, at the eye of the storm, at the heart of the plot. It is both subject and object, both the issue and the spectacle.

Lyubov Andreyevna Ranevsky is the centre around which the house will stand or fall. At the beginning of the play she arrives by carriage from the railway station after a long train journey. She has been brought back in order to try and save the family home from being sold to cover debts. As has often been pointed out, Lyubov will not betray her aristocratic values by accepting Lopakhin's sensible plan.[7] But her refusal to bow to economic pressures jeopardizes her family's welfare, as do her insistence on her independence as a woman and her determination to pursue her own happiness.

Mme Ranevsky's attachment to her home has been attenuated prior to the opening of the play by a whole series of reported events: the death of her husband, her love affair, the drowning of her son, her voyage abroad, the purchase of the villa in Menton and her move to Paris. Bringing her back is a last ditch, half-hearted attempt to save the house.

Unlike the villa in Menton, the estate cannot be viewed simply as a financial commodity which can be sold to cover debts without much fuss. It is a home in the deepest sense, full of memories, emotional attachments, family ties, culture. Without it, Ranevskaya's family will disintegrate, each member going his own way. The sale of the villa in Menton is easily overlooked as a gratuitous narrative detail, but it is in fact a crucial piece of information, highlighting Lyubov's inability to act equally rationally when it comes to the cherry orchard.

In this play, the idea of home is broadened to include not only the four walls, conventionally represented on stage as three, but also the cherry orchard adjacent to the house. For some of the characters even that is a reductive, limited view, for 'All Russia is our orchard'[8].

The breaking up of the family and the insolvency of the property and accumulation of debts have been going on for some time, since Lyubov's departure for France. But the imminent sale of the estate, which is on the dramatic agenda, calls for the characters to face up to the finality of this process and recognize that unless they adopt stringent measures there will not be a home to return to. If they wish to prevent the sale of the estate, the demolition of the house and the cutting down of the trees, they must act swiftly and decisively.

In his letter of 5 February 1903 to Stanislavsky, Chekhov insists that

> in Act One cherry trees can be seen in bloom through the windows, the whole orchard a mass of white. And ladies in white dresses.[9]

If, however, we turn to the opening stage directions, we see that although 'the cherry trees are in bloom', 'the windows of the room are shut'. The reader is thus provided in advance with information which will become available to the theatre audience only when Yepikhodov announces that 'the cherry trees are in full bloom'. The orchard becomes visible when the action calls for the windows to be opened. Rather than begin with a view of the trees, Chekhov heightens the effect by throwing the windows open half-way through the act and making the audience join his protagonists in gasping at the sheer beauty of the white blossoms. This effect had already been used by Chekhov in *The Seagull*, where only after the curtain is raised on Kostya's stage does the lake become visible. There too the opening stage directions already inform the reader about what the spectator will see only later.

Varya is the first to open a window and stand transfixed by the enchanting view:

> The sun's up now and it's not cold. Look, Mother, what marvellous trees! And the air is glorious. The starlings are singing.
>
> (Act 1, p. 157)

Gayev opens another window and, addressing his words to his sister, comments on the orchard 'being white all over' and gleaming on moonlit nights. Only now does Ranevskaya look out at the orchard, but it is her impassioned speech that conveys the full impact of the sight of the flowering trees.

Despite its central role, the orchard is relegated to the theatrical space without, i.e. the theatrical space which must be imagined to extend beyond ᵗʰe visible stage. The stage itself, the theatrical space within, is defined by th  ˉening stage directions as 'a room which is still known as "the nursery"'. This description seems to provide excessive and even irrelevant information. This information will become available to the spectator only later, when Anya pointedly asks her mother whether she remembers the room, to which Mme Ranevsky replies, and these are, importantly, her first words in the play, 'The nursery' (p. 147).

This recognition sparks off an emotional response in Ranevskaya, which explains the peculiar choice of the former nursery as the setting for this act. Carried away by tender recollections of her childhood, spent in this very room, she feels again like a little girl. Even the book-case and table, which were hers as a girl, elicit from Lyubov terms of endearment and kisses.

Nursery and orchard, indoors and outdoors, the theatrical space within and theatrical space without, are integrated into a comprehensive view in Lyubov Andreyevna's speech:

> Oh, my childhood, my innocent childhood! This is the nursery where I slept and I used to look out at the orchard from here. When I woke up every morning happiness awoke with me, and the orchard was just the same in those days. Nothing's changed. [Laughs happily.] White! All white! Oh, my orchard! After the damp, dismal autumn and the cold winter here you are, young again and full of happiness. The angels in heaven have not forsaken you. If I could only shake off the heavy burden that weighs me down, if only I could forget my past.
>
> (Act 1, p. 157)

The constituent elements of the theatrical space become meaningful through their intimate relationship with Lyubov. The nursery evokes memories of her childhood while the cherry trees carry a promise of renewal, every spring they are 'young again and full of happiness'. The cyclical nature of their bloom stands in contrast to her own inability to shake off her past.

The whiteness of the cherry trees suggests the innocence of childhood and arouses a longing for that innocence. Transported in her imagination to her childhood, Lyubov has a vision of her mother. The sequence of generations is delicately pointed when Gayev exclaims that Anya looks so much like her mother and 'you were just like her at that age, Lyubov'. The family's ability to rejuvenate itself through reproduction, through a continuous line of young women, is analogous to the annual blooming of the orchard.

The orchard is a pregnant symbol of regeneration, as well as of innocence, purity and beauty. It is essentially a romantic symbol of the redemptive power of nature, contrasting the finite existence of the individual with nature's continual cycle of death and rebirth. But, as it is a romantic symbol, it is out of date and must be axed at the end of the play.

Even at this early stage, the moment of nostalgia is punctured by the dishevelled appearance of Trofimov, who in his very person embodies the coming revolution and is also associated in Ranevskaya's mind with the tragic drowning of her son. His very appearance provides an oblique comment on what has been said, for, unlike the orchard which periodically grows beautiful, Trofimov has grown old and ugly (p. 158).

The stage directions for Act Two introduce the spectator to a scene very different from that of the nursery with its windows looking out on the cherry orchard. The earlier enclosed room is replaced by open country. Chekhov instructed

Nemirovich-Danchenko: 'In Act Two you must give me some proper green fields and a road and a sense of distance unusual on the stage'.[10] House and orchard have been shifted into the background, while the foreground is made up of a number of old and slightly curious relics: an abandoned old chapel, a well, some old tombstones and an old bench.

A clue as to how one should approach these scenic elements can be found in Leonid Andreyev's view that Chekhov was a panpsychologist, for whom 'things are *not* things, but the scattered thoughts and sensations of a single soul'.[11] Although the metaphysical claims implied in the notion of the 'single soul' are too demanding, Andreyev is on to something very important when he claims that Chekhov's 'landscape is no less psychological than his people'. This has practical, theatrical consequences, for Chekhov's plays must be performed not only by people but also 'by tumblers and chairs and crickets and military greatcoats and wedding rings'.[12] Looked at differently, Chekhov's settings and props are not occasional or arbitrary any more than his seemingly casual dialogues, and all require to be interpreted, related and integrated.

One must try therefore to relate the various scenic elements of Act Two to each other. The old chapel, tombstones and bench endow the scene with a special kind of timelessness encountered in places that bear the marks of past generations. These are human marks so old that they have become almost elements of the landscape, parts of nature itself. The decay into which these human monuments have fallen has become part and parcel of the natural process of decomposition. The appearance of the hungry and drunken passer-by, the very image of homelessness, and the threatening sound that 'seems to come from the sky and is the sound of a breaking string' (p. 171) add to the uneasy atmosphere created by purely theatrical means.

The stage directions recede from one plane to another, as in a landscape painting, thus increasing the depth of the picture, and a road is provided to help negotiate between the different planes. The furthest distance is formed by the dim outlines of a big town. As the estate is connected to the foreground by a country road, so the far-off town is connected to it by a row of telegraph poles.

The telegraph poles are perhaps the most puzzling element of this picture. There is no further mention of them in the play, and they seem at first sight superfluous. The chapel, well and tombstones are also decorative rather than functional, but they are used to set the elegiac tone of the second act, and especially of its overture. But what are the telegraph poles doing here?

Clearly, the row of telegraph poles provides a sharp contrast with the ageless stones in the foreground. Past and present are made to clash in the landscape itself. The poles provide for this provincial backwater communication with the big town and beyond. The messages they convey find their voice in the play in the endless string of telegrams which Lyubov keeps receiving from Paris, from her rejected lover, and which finally make her return to him. The telegraph poles connect the estate with a more bustling and vigorous modern world and bring modern technology and progress to its very doorstep.

The intrusion of modern means of communication is represented not just by the avalanche of telegrams but also by the preponderance of the railway system. The play is framed by the arrival and departure of the protagonists by rail, and trains figure prominently in their conversation. Lopakhin opens the play with the announcement that: 'The train's arrived, thank God', after which he tries to establish how late it was. The railway timetable is a central concern, controlling the lives of people, as are the watches whipped out at various times. These contrast with the natural time scheme of the day and the seasons: for post-romantic man, time is no longer regulated by nature but has become artificial and discretionary.

Cables and train-rides, like today's faxes, electronic mail and jet-flights, have revolutionized man's conception of space and time. Stefan Zweig was alert to the changes effected by the new means of commuting at the beginning of the century:

> The mountains, the lakes, the ocean were no longer as far away as formerly;
> the bicycle, the automobile, the electric trains had shortened distances and
> had given the world a new spaciousness.[13]

This new spaciousness pulls the characters of *The Cherry Orchard* away from their provincial home. Kharkov, Moscow, Paris, are all now within their easy reach.

The telegraph poles stand in an interesting relation to the cherry trees. Whereas the trees are organic, living, growing, the poles are man-made, felled wood. They introduce an element of modernity that balances the old chapel and ancient tombstones in the foreground. Thus, the receding spatial planes indicated in the setting of this act are re-enforced by their temporal overtones of past, present and future.

At one time, the orchard was economically viable. The trees were productive, and the cherries were dried, preserved and bottled, and used for the making of jam. The dried cherries used to be sent to Moscow and Kharkov and 'fetched a lot of money' (Act I, p. 154). But now the orchard, although still beautiful, has become unproductive. The practically minded Lopakhin can see no economic reason for its continued existence and has worked out a plan to solve the family's financial problems, making the most of the rise in the value of the property due to the laying of new rail-tracks. His level-headed, unsentimental approach is that of the developer, eager for new economic opportunities, taking advantage of technological advances.

However, the speech on the merits of progress is characteristically – and ironically – given to the down and out student Trofimov. He strikes a heroic posture, declaiming 'Mankind marches on, going from strength to strength', and berating the Russian *intelligentsia* for not working. But it is Lopakhin who turns the tables on him through his own unpretentious words: 'I'm always up by five o'clock ... I work from morning till night, and then – well, I'm always handling money ... ' (Act 2, p. 170).

The move out of the house and into the open air has provided a panoramic view of the estate. From this wider perspective, and led on by Petya's ideological fervour, Anya finds her attitude to the orchard changed:

> Why is it I'm not so fond of the cherry orchard as I used to be? I loved it so dearly. I used to think there was no better place on earth than our orchard.
>
> (Act 2, p. 173)

For Trofimov, the cherry orchard with its aesthetic, social and emotional values has become dated, an immoral relic, dependent on human exploitation; but from now on, 'All Russia is our orchard'.

The idealistic coming together of the revolutionary student and the youthful heiress of the estate has definite romantic overtones which are encouraged by the rising moon and the playing guitar. But this perfect setting for romance, the moment of the shared dream of happiness, is exploded by Varya's annoying chaperoning, thus bringing the second act to its abrupt ending.

In the third act we are back inside the house, although in another part of it: the drawing-room, through which the ball-room may be seen. Throughout this act a ball is going on, with a display of the 'ladies in white dresses' of Chekhov's letter to Stanislavsky quoted earlier. The ball is the swan-song of the old way of life on the estate.

The dance scene, an old and almost hackneyed favourite,[14] is here endowed with ironic touches which give it its special bite. The conventionality of the genteel dance is undermined primarily by the choice of guests, which include the post-office clerk and the station-master. Even the maid Dunyasha is asked to dance because of the scarcity of young ladies. To a sensitive symbolist like Andrei Bely, the dancers appeared like 'masks of horror'.[15] The ball, a symbol of the aristocratic living of the past generation, has dwindled into this mockery, still conducted ceremoniously in French but with the customary champagne replaced by soda-water.

But the most cruel touch is the timing of the dance: it takes place while the estate is being sold. The auction, the central event of the play, which determines the fate of everyone in the household, takes place in a distant theatrical space without, while the protagonists try as it were to dance it off. The characters' behaviour in the theatrical space within is counterpointed by the unrelenting advance of the action in the theatrical space without.

Maurice Valency has commented on the singular relationship between plot and character in Chekhov:

> Chekhov's characters do not serve the plot at all. At best, they accommodate themselves to it like unwilling passengers on a train which is taking them where they have no desire to go.[16]

Valency is interested in the freedom from the exigencies of the plot enjoyed by the characters. This freedom permeates the whole fabric of the play, permitting the separation of the seemingly static situation from the powerful current of momentous events that runs in the background. Nowhere is it more visible than in the disjunction and juxtaposition of ball and auction. While, without, the house is being auctioned off, we are shown, within, the members of the household still striving to keep the show going on.

The fate of the orchard is sealed with Lopakhin's answer to Mme Ranevsky's question as to who bought the orchard: 'I did'. He is reeling with brandy and with the tremendous feeling of triumph that he, who ran round barefoot in winter, now owns 'the most beautiful place in the world' (p. 186). However, this realization does not prevent him from boasting that, now that he will 'get his axe into that cherry orchard, watch the trees come crashing down'. At this point, Ranevskaya sinks into her chair, weeping bitterly. Now, at last, she has fully realized the irrevocable change in her life, the loss of her family home. Muzhik that he is, Lopakhin is moved by her sorrow, yet cannot help gloating over the reversal in their relative fortunes: 'Here comes the new squire, the owner of the cherry orchard!' (p. 187).

The act is not allowed to end with Lyubov's weeping. A note of optimism, the result of seeing things from a different angle, is struck once again by the entrance of the young idealists, Anya and Trofimov. Anya rushes to her mother to comfort her with the promise of the future, 'we shall plant a new orchard' (p. 187).

Chekhov has managed to end the first three acts with the upbeat mood of his two young protagonists. But his last act will end on a dark note, with the death speech of the old and ailing Firs, forgotten and locked in the house with which he identifies himself.

The fourth act returns to the theatrical space of the first act, thus creating a circular structure. Once again we are in the room which used to be a nursery. That there will never be another baby in this nursery, scheduled, together with the rest of the house, for demolition, is underscored by Charlotta's ventriloquist act of a crying baby while she rocks a bundle as if it were an infant (p. 193). The unfulfilled yearning for a baby thus expressed by Charlotta points to the highly uncertain future that awaits Anya and Varya now they too have become homeless. The importance of the character of Charlotta, which Chekhov regarded as 'the best part' in his play,[17] lies in her embodiment of the homeless, uprooted person. This motif is further underlined by the haunting appearance of the drunken vagabond in Act Two.

The play opened with the arrival from the station, and now everyone is on their way out again. But the appearance of the room has changed. The walls are bare of pictures, the windows denuded of their curtains, and the furniture has been gathered into a corner 'as if for sale'. The circularity is marred by the realization that this departure at the end of summer is not seasonal but final, that there will be no future homecoming. Ranevskaya's leave-taking registers the breaking away from the natural cycle:

> Good-bye, house. Good-bye, dear old place. Winter will pass, spring will come again and then you won't be here any more, you'll be pulled down.
>
> (Act 4, p. 192)

As the trees will not bloom again, so there will be no more family reunions. Cutting down the orchard and knocking down the house mean disrupting the cyclical nature of time with its yearly potential for revival and redemption. From now on time will be linear, vectorial, technological, progressive.

The various members of the household are about to disperse, Lopakhin going to Kharkov, Trofimov to Moscow, Lyubov to Paris, and so on. Once again the rail network lying in the theatrical space without becomes instrumental in establishing world-wide links which replace the provincial insularity of the estate.

The dispersion of the family is viewed by the forward-looking Anya as 'the start of a new life' (p. 192), and she seems unaware that 'life has ended in this house', as Lopakhin realizes (p. 195). Trofimov regards what has happened as a positive development, a sign that 'Mankind is marching towards a higher truth, towards the greatest possible happiness on earth' (p. 190). Like all naive, optimistic, ideological assumptions, this too is highly suspect, highly questionable, despite the obvious sincerity of the speaker.

It is interesting to compare Trofimov's idealism with that of Vershinin in *Three Sisters*: 'In two or three hundred years life on this earth will be beautiful beyond our dreams'.[18] These sayings parallel Chekhov's own remarks to Alexander Kuprin on the latter's visit to Yalta,

> 'Do you know,' he suddenly added *with an earnest face and in tones of deep faith*. 'Do you know that, within three or four hundred years the whole earth will be transformed into a blossoming garden? And life will then be remarkably easy and convenient.'

Ronald Hingley, who quotes the conversation, treats Chekhov's words with the ironic disbelief they deserve.[19]

In their last tearful farewell to the house, Lyubov and her brother return to the themes of the beginning, invoking once again their youth and their dead parents, taking in the full meaning of the moment. Ranevskaya's reverie about her own mother is interrupted by Anya's call 'Mother!', again tying together the three generations, but also pointing to the rupture in the continuity of the family. The sounds of the breaking string and the axe striking down a tree are the sounds of the death throes of the estate.

The various characters will go their different ways, pursuing their vocations, dispersing along the railway lines. But the cherry orchard will cease to exist and with it the whole ecological equilibrium around it, the eco-system of a civilization, the culture and values which went with a particular socio-economic set-up. The dynamic principle of periodic regeneration in nature has been abandoned, making way for an ideal of vectorial progress. The cherry trees have been supplanted by telegraph poles.

Woman's refusal to accept her traditional role as home-maker is the obstruction that brings the customary flow of life to a grinding halt in both plays discussed. To want to carry on with the old life style, attractive and civilized as it may be, is seen as a reactionary and provincial attitude; to look forward to change, any change, is seen as progressive and open-minded and a mark of belonging to the *intelligentsia*, or to the international set. Those who travel, who have cut themselves off from their country-home are active, successful, fulfilled. Those who stay behind are the failures who have preferred the comfort of home, who have not dared to take risks, to trust their own talents, to face hardships. The theatrical space of the home has become a dated convention, out of pace with social, political and economic changes.

Woman's new egotism, which Pastor Faerden had dreaded,[20] is now firmly established. The mature and widowed heroines Arkadina and Ranevskaya are both intent on furthering their own goals, whether in love or in career, and for this they are prepared to neglect their children, not to sacrifice themselves. The young actress Nina is even more extreme than the elder women, completely flaunting social decorum, convenience or security, in her search for self-fulfilment and in the strength she gains through utter loneliness and total self-reliance. More than anything else, it is woman's emancipation that has overthrown the traditional scenic conception, because it has severed her emotional bonds with her house.

## Chapter 9

# Constructed rooms

*The Room* is the name of Harold Pinter's dramatic *début*. This deceptively simple title underlines Pinter's central interest in the play. Originally meaning 'space', the word 'room' denotes that part of space confined by walls created for dwelling or protection. The title also conveys the sense of the shrinking home, the wear and tear it has suffered over the ages, the flimsiness of the security it can still afford. The minimalism of Pinter's art is thus already apparent in the sparseness of the home reduced to its basic, atavistic functions.

In his early plays, Pinter sees the room as a basic unit of space, within which skeletal situations can be developed. In the programme notes to the Royal Court Theatre performance of *The Room* (1957), Pinter outlines the various possible permutations of the interaction between a man, a room and a visitor:

> Given a man in a room and he will sooner or later receive a visitor. A visitor entering the room will enter with intent ... The man may leave with the visitor or he may leave alone. The visitor may leave alone or stay in the room alone when the man is gone. Or they may both stay together in the room, etc.[1]

The traditional supremacy of the dramatic component of theatre, i.e. the causal chain of events, is neglected here in favour of a structural analysis of the theatrical scene that takes as its starting point the relationship between a man and his spatial environment. The same spatial analysis supplies the building blocks not only for *The Room* but also for other early plays, such as *The Birthday Party* (1958), *The Dumb Waiter* (1960) and *The Caretaker* (1960).

Pinter's artistic approach to the articulation of the theatrical space is minimalistic and conceptual. Like a painter who reduces a holy icon to a set of geometrical shapes, he discards the dramatic conventions of characterization, plot, and cultural and historical setting in order to expose the dispassionate outline, the basic structure of the theatrical event. Pinter toys with different combinations of the abstracted theatrical elements, much as Kandinsky plays with the confrontations between straight and curved lines or between different colours.

Cleared from 'dramatic' elements, the connotations that adhere to the theatrical structure itself become more pronounced. In an interview with Kenneth Tynan, Pinter attributed a highly emotive value to the within and the without, seeing his characters as

> scared of what is outside the room. We are all in this, all in a room, and outside is the world ... which is most inexplicable and frightening, curious and alarming.[2]

The fear Pinter is speaking of does not grow from any specific predicament, but is inherent in the very nature of our perception of space and the articulation of space in the theatre.

The central theatrical division between the within and the without is formulated by Pinter as an existential experience, demonstrating that this is not merely a topological distinction. The without, described in terms reminiscent of Eliade's 'chaotic space, peopled with demons and phantoms'[3], represents an unknown menace, threatening to intrude upon the relative and fragile security of the within. Between the two separates – or connects, as the case may be – the door. As Pinter puts it: 'The world is full of surprises. A door can open at any moment and someone will come in.'[4]

Clearly, Pinter wishes to tap this hidden source of theatrical energy he has discovered in the articulation of the theatrical space: the room, the world outside, the connecting door. At least at the beginning of his career as a playwright, Pinter felt that within his seemingly constricting theatrical formula there was scope for almost endless permutations. His early plays are therefore attempts at offering different syntheses of his spatial analysis of the theatrical event.

Tricked up to look like a naturalistic play, *The Room* is designed to thwart all our expectations for motivation, perspicuity, meaningful action. At first glance another kitchen-sink drama, it evinces no social interest and uses naturalistic detail for texture rather than for message. The play is so close to Pinter's formula of 'given a man in a room', that it is not clear whether it adheres to the formula or whether the formula was created on its basis.

The title points to the spatial dimension and away from the unfolding of events. A door opens onto the landing and a window looks out to the street, allowing Rose to glimpse and report on the theatrical space without. Outdoors it is freezing cold and getting dark, and the roads are treacherous, while indoors there is a gas-fire and the homely pleasures of bacon and eggs and 'nice weak tea' (p. 103). The naturalistic details reinforce and fill out the basic opposition of outdoors and indoors, the theatrical space without and the theatrical space within.

The outdoors menaces the safety and comfort of the bed-sitter in which Rose has barricaded herself, securing a small habitable and hospitable haven within the large boarding house. She regards it as 'a very nice room', warm and cosy, and speculates about who has taken up the tenancy of the damp basement.[5] In this room she lives with her husband Bert Hudd, her junior by ten years, whom she mothers and pampers incessantly. The house itself is engulfed in darkness and uncertainty. Underneath is the basement, in which a blind black man is lurking, waiting for his chance to enter the room. His enigmatic figure threatens to destroy the temporary refuge Rose has succeeded in building for herself.

In the course of the play, Bert goes out to drive his van and comes back home, and the other characters intrude upon Rose's privacy, but she herself never leaves the room. She attempts to exit once, with the bin, but is prevented by the unexpected visitors, Mr and Mrs Sands, whom she discovers standing just outside her door. The room takes on a double nature as a place of refuge, in which Rose chooses to hide from the world, and a prison which she is stopped from leaving.

Rose seems perfectly content with her humble surroundings, constantly praising the room as a warm shelter from the cold. It is a home which provides the basic needs: warmth, light, food, a roof and, most importantly, protection from the undefined threat of the world outside. Rose keeps insisting on all these blessings, as if to reassure herself as well as the silent Bert. Not only is she happy here, but also 'nobody bothers us' (p. 103).

But she is soon to be bothered, in succession, by the elderly landlord, the young couple in search of a room, and the blind black tenant who lives in the basement. These intrusions are threatening because they are perceived by Rose as attempts to expropriate her room. Mr Kidd recalls unexpectedly that this room used to be his own bedroom (p. 107), and although he affirms that all his rooms are occupied (pp. 109, 118), the Sands learn from the man in the basement that room number seven is to let. Number seven is Rose's own room.

When Riley, the black man, enters, he delivers a puzzling message to Rose: 'Your father wants you to come home' (p. 124). The word 'home' is then repeated, questioned and asserted, making Rose capitulate and revert to some older layer in her biography. The transience of the hired dwelling is contrasted with the home to which she is being recalled, and the father-figure evoked asks Rose to leave her absent husband. Returning, Bert re-asserts his dominance over Rose first through verbal aggression, referring to his van as to a subservient woman, 'I caned her along' (p. 126), then by the use of brute force against the black man. Rose's painstaking attempt to construct a provisional asylum from the world fails as her past catches up with her.

The hyper-realistic style of the play, concocted of the minutiae of behavioural patterns, is shaken by occasional intrusions of improbabilities, as when the landlord is unable to answer the simple question, 'How many floors you got in this house?' He says he used to count them in the old days, but can no longer keep track of them

(p. 108). The dialogue suggests half-heartedly that Mr Kidd's bizarre answers are due to age and deafness, but also that they should not be taken at face value, on a merely naturalistic level. Equally unsettling is the fact that Rose does not seem to know which room in the house is occupied by the landlord himself.

Dwindled and shrunk into a rented bed-sitter, the home is still associated in this play with the woman who tends the fire, keeps the house warm and does the cooking. And the male who braves the frosty night running an errand with his van still cuts a heroic figure, manifesting courage, technical know-how and brute force.

*The Room* might seem at first sight like yet another variation on Ibsen's drawing-room, leading off to other spaces both inside and outside the house. But Pinter's house has been stripped bare of all appurtenances before being re-decorated with naturalistic detail. This stripping has transformed the house from an imitation house, similar to 'real' houses, into a basic structure which organizes space in a particular manner, attaching relative meanings to the different spatial units. Although it is re-decorated to look like a real room, the room no longer represents an ordinary room. Its meaning depends on its position within the other spaces defined, but not depicted, in the play.

As has frequently been pointed out, the 'two men in a room' formula is not followed in *The Homecoming*.[6] But the starting point of the play is still structural and spatial, dealing with the ironical questions of who comes home and what kind of home it is he or she comes back to. In the course of the play, Teddy's attempted re-integration into his childhood home fails. The apparently straightforward title of the play turns into a double ambiguity: in a typically Pinterian trick of displacement, it is his wife Ruth who 'comes home', while Teddy picks up his suitcase and leaves once again for the alternative home he has built for himself in the New World.

The very minimal plot-line of *The Homecoming* (1965) assumes a mock classical appearance: like Agamemnon before him, Teddy returns home after a prolonged absence (six years). The victorious hero has dared and sailed far away, made a name for himself, proved himself, and is now asking to be re-admitted home. The spatial configuration supports this classification, juxtaposing the old home depicted on stage with an image of life in the New World.

Teddy's 'victories' have been won on the American college campus, the respectable, but anemic, conceived theatrical space, which is contrasted with the closer and more sordid texture of life in the London house, in the perceived theatrical space. Teddy celebrates his successful academic career and family life in America by touring the old world with his wife. Their stay in Venice is singled out presumably as an indication of how far Teddy has travelled in the world, both literally and metaphorically.

However, Teddy's triumphal homecoming is spoiled by the late hour of his arrival, after the various members of the household have already retired, and by his use of the old entrance key to let himself in. Instead of making a triumphal entry, Teddy sneaks in and receives a resentful welcome when his presence is discovered in the morning.

The fixed setting of the play is the living-room of an old house in North London. This traditional room has been enlarged by the removal of the back wall, so that the hall with its entrance door and the staircase leading to the bedrooms are visible. According to John Bury, the designer of the original 1965 Royal Shakespeare Company production, the knocked-down wall is meant to provide a pretext for the visibility of the hall and staircase, because Pinter hates composite sets. Rolf Fjelde sees in the setting a meaningful design: 'A traditional, confined environment has been transformed, somewhat violently, into an "open living area", suggesting the old claustrophobic pattern of life partially broken out of, first here and then more extensively in America.' But there is no sense of renewal in either the house or the family, no feeling of a breakthrough or significant change in life-style. The renovation has obviously not created an open living area since the kitchen has remained closed off. John Bury's functional interpretation seems more relevant to the action and appropriate to the stage directions than Fjelde's realistic reading.[7]

Except for the rather unsettling fact of the missing back wall, there is nothing remarkable about the room and its furniture. But the traditional living-room encapsulates the breaking of all familial norms of behaviour. This sense of the ordinary, casual and conventional surroundings is a studied effect intended to increase our surprise at some of the things said or implied. A wide gulf is created between the shocking revelations and the staid appearances.

The entire movement of the play leads towards the filling of the gap left in the home by the demise of Jessie, the wife and mother. The all-male household is comprised of two generations, two brothers in each. Max, who is seventy, informs us that since his wife Jessie died there has been no woman in the house. None of the other males in the house has married or had children. Jessie's figure, both revered and maligned, is conjured up again and again in the play in ambivalent terms. As it transpires, the romanticized and vilified wife and mother was also employed by the family as a prostitute who was driven around by her brother-in-law Sam in his cab. Esslin notes this essential ambivalence of the female as 'the oscillation of the image of woman between that of mother/madonna/housewife and that of the whore/maenad', and sees it as 'one of the dominant themes of Pinter's writing'.[8]

The vacuum left in the house after Jessie's death draws in a substitute figure, Teddy's visiting wife. Ruth is instantly recognized by both Max and his middle son Lenny as a 'tart' and is therefore offered Jessie's vacant position in the household.

Ruth is invited to stay with 'the family'[9] as Teddy prepares to leave, and it is he who delivers the invitation, insisting 'I don't mind. We can manage very easily at home … until you come back' (p. 75).[10] Liberated from her domestic duties in her American home, Ruth is free to accept the offer. The two homes, the overseas college-professor's home in the conceived theatrical space without, and the violent and libidinous North London establishment in the perceived space, are constantly contrasted, as are, by extension, the new and old countries.

A third residence is fancifully constructed in the theatrical space without: the town-flat in which Ruth is to spend a couple of hours every night. In the circumspect manner employed by the characters when discussing the *demi-monde*, it is made clear that this flat is to remain distinct from Ruth's home, 'in the bosom of the family' (p. 76). Ruth demands that the flat have three rooms and a bathroom (p. 77). Although Lenny tries to cut on his costs by maintaining that two bedrooms should be quite enough, Ruth makes him bow to her demands, demonstrating her superior power. The flat is to have all conveniences and Ruth is promised a personal maid, an ample wardrobe and, in effect, anything she might require.

The flat is in fact a mock-home dedicated to Ruth's 'professional' needs, while the traditional family home has become an empty shell, a parody of itself. The three houses offered to Ruth provide alternative aspects of womanhood. But she is not called on to make an ethical choice between different modes of living. As there is no longer an essential link between the woman and her house, the different homes merely represent different poses which Ruth can assume or abandon at will, they are manipulative rungs on the ladder of her career as woman.

On concluding their deal with Ruth, Max and Lenny remind her that apart from her 'employment' she will have the whole daytime free, so that she can 'do a bit of cooking', 'make the beds' and 'scrub the place out a bit' (p. 78). As it turns out, Ruth is still expected to pursue the traditional female tasks, except that she has considerably strengthened her position through her avoidance of any emotional response or attachment and her readiness to join battle with the men who try to use her. What is striking in her manner is the assertiveness and aggressiveness with which she pursues her deals.

In the *Lysistrata*, the problem of raising the class consciousness of the women was caused by their difficulty in tearing themselves from their households and family duties. In the test case of Cinesias and Myrrhine, Cinesias tried to get his wife to come back home by appealing to her motherly instincts.[11] Ruth is fortified against any similar emotional blackmail. Teddy reminds her of their boys back home who will at this hour be swimming in the pool (p. 54) – but to no avail. She is a liberated woman in the sense that she feels no necessary bond with her husband, children and home.

The business negotiations and hard bargaining which lead to Ruth's contract with her husband's family are handled in the matter-of-fact manner of a purely financial matter. The effect of the whole sequence is disturbing because Ruth agrees to forgo her status as college-professor's wife and work as an upper-class prostitute without a qualm. She is completely self-possessed and detached, showing no emotional or moral misgivings. Her shocking immoral conduct is displayed in a totally amoral manner. She abandons husband and children with far less regret than most of us would leave an old job or part from a passing acquaintance.[12]

Ruth's conduct is carefully tailored both to exasperate and to amuse us by frustrating our conventional expectations based on everyday experience and mediated by our ethical upbringing. Similarly, our reactions to the peculiar home depicted in the play are dependent on tapping our ordinary associations and then deliberately thwarting them. The various household members come home to eat the dinner prepared for them by Max, their mother-surrogate, thus keeping up one of the oldest of family rituals. Max both enjoys and resents his maternal functions: 'Go and find yourself a mother', he bawls out at Sam and Joey, then puts on the disgruntled-housewife act, 'You expect me to sit here waiting to rush into the kitchen the moment you step in the door?' (p. 16). The idea of home as a haven and the ideal of harmonious family life are parodied and dissolved by being juxtaposed with the cruelty and hatred between the family members.

The savagery of their relations may seem at some stage to be due to the absence of a female figure in the house. But the choice of Ruth and the definition of her tasks provides an ironic perspective on the position of woman in the household. The customary relations between genders and generations and the intersection between these two sets, particularized within the family as husband, father, son, brother, wife, mother, daughter-in-law are grotesquely distorted. Ruth's acceptance by the family, their readiness to have her fill Jessie's place, is basically incestuous: 'you're kin. You're kith. You belong here' (p. 75). Similarly, when Max taunts Sam about not having married, he offers the latter's non-existent bride hospitality: 'You can bring her to live here, she can keep us all happy. We'd take it in turns to give her a walk round the park' (p. 15), thus suggesting that she be shared among them.

Father and sons compete over the favours of the woman who has suddenly been brought into their midst, who has come home, thus acting out their Oedipal fantasies. In this context of male rivalry old age is a serious handicap. Expressions of fatherly or brotherly love are cynically exploited by the characters as conventional routines behind which and through which they spar for strategic superiority.

As in many realistic plays, the family home serves as a battleground and the family members are the warring parties. But despite the realistic trappings, the source of conflict is disturbingly missing. The participants are not battling over social or economic positions or in order to gain freedom or recognition. Ruth is not a woman struggling to liberate herself from patriarchal male oppression or dreaming of romantic love or self-fulfilment. Her piecemeal biography, the social context in which she finds herself and the particular dramatic moment (i.e. her arrival in the middle of the night with Teddy, on the way from Venice back to America), are the hallmarks of realism according to Hippolyte Taine's theory.[13] But in this play they do not add up to a perspicuous character portrait. They seem rather to have an arbitrary and contrived air and to be thrown in as a smoke-screen behind which the reader or spectator struggles pointlessly to discover an explanation or a motivation for Ruth's astounding behaviour, both in aggression and complicity.[14]

The dramatic conflict is here a battle for dominance pure and simple, without a closed and coherent causality. Raised on Realism, we try in vain to piece together apparent clues. Pinter toys with this rational need of ours, letting us follow false scents, then making us realize we have been tricked as the characters change tack, refashioning their positions. As pointed out by Bert O. States, the characters who are constantly inventing their world are in possession of superior knowledge, 'the very reverse of the familiar "dramatic" irony in which *we* know but they don't'.[15]

Pinter is no crusader-playwright campaigning for reform, he is not out to chastize society, he does not start from any set of values towards which he wishes to direct his spectators. In other words, his own outlook is amoral; he refuses to offer his audience a convenient morality. He precludes ethical judgement or even sympathy with or condemnation of his characters.

The issue of ethics is approached by Max in his long disquisition on the late Jessie, who taught the boys 'all the morality they know', 'every single bit of the moral code they live by' (p. 46). The moral code they live by turns out to be that of pimps, so that Max's conventional eulogy of his dead wife is exposed as a vacuous phrase, inherited from a different cultural and social sphere.

The complete dissociation of human sexuality from morality finds its boldest expression in Lenny's questioning of his father about the circumstances of his own conception. Transgressing one of the deepest cultural taboos, he inquires about the sexual intercourse which led to his begetting; ' ... that night with Mum, what was it like?' (p. 36). The traditional absolutism of one's parents is abolished by this question, and replaced by an egalitarian attitude that sees them as equally appetitive creatures.

Emancipated from the coercive morality of previous ages, the characters are left with their own sexuality both as an end in itself and as a tool to achieve power and control. In a world in which morality has become obsolete, selling one's body for photography or for sexual intercourse is no different from making a living by one's other gifts.

But the nihilism within the theatrical space is calculated to shock an audience that does not share its values. Pinter's cool handling of the sexual wranglings among his characters is meant to create an explosive effect. When Ruth threatens Lenny, 'If you take the glass ... I'll take you' (p. 34), the whole thrust of her directness is in the listener's registering that although the same verb is repeated, taking Lenny sexually is quite different from seizing a glass of water.

In the taut linguistic universe constructed by Pinter, the recurrence of 'take' in Lenny's attempt at drawing his college-professor brother into a philosophical discussion cannot pass unnoticed: 'Well, for instance, take a table. Philosophically speaking. What is it?' His friends, with whom he drinks at the Ritz Bar, say: 'Take a table, take it'. To which he responds: 'All right, I say, *take* it, *take* a table, but once you've taken it, what you going to do with it? Once you've taken it, what you going to do with it?' (p. 52). His attempt at philosophizing glides from the suppositional, technical use of the word in regard to the idea of a table, to its everyday meanings of occupying and then holding, lifting and removing a concrete table.

Groping around the contours of the word does not get Lenny very far, but it focuses the listeners' attention beyond the referential function of the words ('table' refers to something which can be sold, according to Max, or chopped up for firewood, according to Joey) to the communication that lies behind them, which circumvents the apparent meaning and is conveyed through the combined effect of innuendo, gesture and context. Ruth seizes the opportunity of the conversation about tables to exhibit herself as supreme master in the art of such suggestive communication. Infinitely provocative, she directs her listeners' attention first to her leg and then upwards along her body:

> Look at me. I ... move my leg. That's all it is. But I wear ... underwear ... which moves with me ... it ... captures your attention. Perhaps you misinterpret. The action is simple. It's a leg ... moving. My lips move. Why don't you restrict ... your observations to that? Perhaps the fact that they move is more significant ... than the words which come through them. You must bear that ... possibility ... in mind.

(pp. 52–3)

It is the movement of the lips, like the movement of the leg, that is more significant than the actual verbal information, according to Ruth. The audience is mesmerized into total concentration on the beautiful body of the former nude-model and on her provocative movements.

In poetic drama such as Shakespeare's, the characters express themselves through complex lyrical poetry far beyond their own poetic capacities. The beauty or seductiveness of a heroine is expressed through her accomplished figural speech and flowing verse lines. In naturalistic drama, the prose must sound natural and credible and a character's speech is restricted to his own fictional personality and upbringing. For Guido Almansi and Simon Henderson, 'nothing is duller per se than a piece of Pinterian conversation' and the only interest of the recorded-like text 'lies in the mental speculation it provokes'.[16] However, the conversation appears to be dull only if read with no regard for its immediate dramatic and theatrical contexts. Beyond its surface naturalness, the Pinterian dialogue is rich with movement, humour, violence, provocation, but it does not reveal psychology or biography. Its interest lies not in what can be pinned down in words but in the words' suggestiveness.

In Pinter's plays, the room becomes the hub of life – not only for woman but also for man. His male characters retreat into its embryonic safety, seeking the proximity and warmth of a maternal figure. Instead of the hero's struggle to gain maturity, to prove his prowess, these men prefer to revert to a fetal position, to regress back into the womb. Thus, the home is still used as a metaphor for the womb, but the ambiguity of male penetration/regression into the house is extended and ironized.

The men who choose the indoors impinge on the female's domain and stronghold, usurping her space as well as her functions. The male family members of *The Homecoming* have taken up the domestic duties of cooking, washing-up and cleaning. They can certainly manage the practical aspects of house-keeping without a woman (although Lenny complains about Max's lousy cooking, Ruth praises the lovely meal he has cooked). But they yearn for a female presence as such – not in her function as home-maker. The quality of femaleness they seek takes on a different aspect for each of them, as conveyed visually by the positions they take up in relation to Ruth in the final tableau or family portrait: Joey is kneeling at her feet, his head in her lap, while Lenny stands by watching them, Sam lies still, and Max, on all fours, lifts his face towards her, begging for a kiss.

Teddy is different from the rest of the family because he has severed himself from home – and he repeats this action in the course of the play. He has left home twice. The theatrical space without, the new country, America, thus becomes an important option for the man able to cut his umbilical cord and go his own way, change his inherited way of life, become socially and professionally mobile. It is Ruth who is drawn back to a home of the kind she seems to know, rejecting the new life they have found abroad.

The embryonic aspect of this home is emphasized by Max's recollections of his own childhood, in the same house. He sees himself as both father and mother: he boasts that he himself has given birth to the three boys and suffered the birth pangs. This male self-sufficiency tightens the bonds between the family members in spite of their mutual hatred.

The division between the spaces of man and woman, the outdoors and the indoors, have been obliterated and man is no longer the heroic commander sailing on epic missions and returning home victorious, nor is he the bread-winner and provider. Ruth exhibits her superior business acumen in negotiating her terms of employment with the family. Conversely, being a pimp, Lenny makes money from the 'work' of Ruth and her likes, and in fact Ruth is expected to earn her own upkeep. Thus, home becomes a parody of home, with the disintegration of the male/female stereotypes. What remains is memories, snatches of what life was once like or supposed to have been like, nostalgic recollections of harmonious family life, interspersed with memories of conflict and hatred.

The playwright, on his part, refrains from systematizing or regularizing these 'memories' into a coherent, logical sequence in the naturalistic manner. Some critics attempt to do it in his place, offering 'realistic' interpretations. Sometimes they do so despite their better judgement that no such interpretation is called for by the text, that it purposely provides irreducible factual contradictions, thus wilfully preventing us from forming a causal, linear interpretation. After setting out to analyze *The Homecoming* as a play that shocks 'not only by the casual and matter-of-fact way in which sex and prostitution are discussed in it, but also, and even more, by the apparently inexplicable motivations of its main characters', Martin Esslin seems to reverse his position, announcing his conviction that the play 'can also stand up to the most meticulous examination as a piece of realistic theatre',[17] and proceeding to discuss the play as a perfectly realistic and perspicuous text. Rolf Fjelde, Ibsen's translator and interpreter, discerns an affinity with Ibsen in the way Pinter shows the past working itself out in the present lives of the characters.[18] Following Barry Supple's lead, Baker and Tabachnick piece together a 'Jewish' play about the perils of intermarriage, even suggesting a biographical parallel between the playwright and his characters![19] Like other attempts to systematize the play into a coherent structure, the hunting after Jewish clues is basically ridiculous, resulting in a distorted and restrictive 'ethnic' reading.

Pinter can be pigeon-holed no more than his characters. He uses familiar elements of speech to create an impression of naturalistic characterization in the same way that he constructs his theatrical spaces from everyday pieces of furniture. What Pinter's characters say is often self-contradictory and self-cancelling, so that it can have no reference in reality. The world of his characters is wholly contained in their words. We understand the words because they resemble the things we say everyday, just as the room in which they move resembles a familiar room. But instead of an imitation of an action, what we get is a disjointed imitation of words imitating words, and objects – objects. The realism of detail produces a hyper-realistic effect without fusing together into a meaningful structure. Although the superficial impression created is of theatrical realism, the disparate elements do not coalesce into a meaningful mimetic structure.

Pinter chooses to represent the raw texture, without attempting to regularize it into a rational, causal system. George Wellwarth sees this as a refusal to provide the audience with the illusory, comforting assurance offered by realistic drama that human behaviour is explicable. Pinter's gaze is directed instead to 'outside the theatre', where 'human beings are incomplete, mysterious even to themselves, and anything but logical'.[20]

The inconsequentiality of many of the statements made by Pinter's characters and their contradictoriness have led Almansi and Henderson to suggest that

> The particular endgame that Pinter seems to have alighted on is a sort of round game known popularly as 'consequences', a parlor game ... in which each player writes down a part of the story, hands over the paper, and passes it on to another player who continues the story. After several stages, the resulting (nonsensical) stories are read out.[21]

A more comprehensive and self-conscious game is played by the husband and wife in *The Lover* (1963). In addition to their sober and respectable married life, they engage in a fully developed fantasy game, in which they are having an extra-marital affair with each other. In the course of the play the husband seems to get tired of the game and attempts to bring it to an end. It is at this point that Sarah accuses him of trying to play a game.[22]

When, in his persona as husband, Richard decides to stop the visits of his wife's 'lover' in his house, he suggests alternative sites for her future *rendez-vous*:

> Take him out into the fields. Find a ditch. Or a slag heap. Find a rubbish dump. Mmmm? What about that? Buy a canoe and find a stagnant pond. Anything. Anywhere. But not my living-room.
>
> (p. 191)

But the illicit romance flourishes in the much more comfortable setting of the upper middle-class, suburban living-room. The house is located in the vicinity of Windsor and Richard has to travel every day into the city, through the traffic jams, to get to his office. Sarah is left alone in the village for the whole long day. They have been married for ten years and apparently the children are away at boarding school. This life-style seems to suit them, for both agree that 'It's wonderful to live out here, so far away from the main road, so secluded' (p. 173).

Instead of leading a double life with another partner, the couple are leading a double life with each other and in the same spatial setting. The living-room setting is here extended beyond that of *The Homecoming*. The stage directions call for a split-level scenery: a short flight of steps leads to the bedroom and balcony on the left, and on the right is the living-room with a small hall and front door up centre, and the kitchen off right. The use of the bedroom is restricted to the married couple, wearing pyjamas and nightdress, performing the conventional rituals of bathroom and dressing-table, getting into bed with books, and switching off bedside lamps. On awakening, they perform the appropriate morning rites. The bedroom is thus characterized as an environment that stifles romance and eroticism. The 'illicit' love games take place in the living-room, which leaves more options for invention and improvisation. This distinction between the two rooms is not clear-cut, since the married couple also share sophisticated drinks in the living-room.

The entrance hall functions as a transitional space. In the cupboard that stands in the hall are stored the game-props: the bongo drum, the high-heeled shoes and the briefcase. Also in the hall is the hook on which Richard hangs his bowler hat and the mirror in which Sarah checks whether she is dressed for the right part.

In the opening scene the couple display their broad-mindedness and openness with each other's affairs. Sarah finds out that Richard frequents a whore and expresses her distaste and surprise. With hindsight one must remark that this is how Richard chooses to describe his afternoon visits to his wife in his persona as Max. At this early stage in the play, he explains to Sarah why he seeks a prostitute:

> Why? I wasn't looking for your double, was I? I wasn't looking for a woman
> I could respect, as you, whom I could admire and love, as I do you. Was I?
> All I wanted was... how shall I put it... someone who could express and
> engender lust with all lust's cunning. Nothing more.
>
> (p. 169)

In their extra-marital relations, the couple display a sensual abandon and adventurousness that are at odds with their decorous, 'square' behaviour as husband and wife. They dress differently (she: high heels, and very tight, low-cut dress; he: suede jacket, no tie), they play out erotic scenes from books and films (attempted rape, the park-keeper, crawling under the table), and above all they enjoy their own duplicity and the danger of being found out by the neighbours – and yet they play it safe.

The lonely wife blossoms into a voluptuous seductress when her husband returns home in the guise of an ardent lover. The pretence allows both to release their inhibited selves and act out their repressed desires. Their assumed characters complement their everyday, couth appearances.

The game the couple plays reflects the game the playwright plays with his audience. In the beginning he misleads us into believing that the play is about a classical triangle. The only reason for introducing the milkman scene seems to be in order to justify the appearance of John on the list of characters along with Richard and Sarah. John's entrance arouses the audience's expectation that he is the lover, especially since the scene has been carefully set for the lover's arrival. The bathos of his entrance creates a humourous surprise that prepares the audience for the shock of recognizing that the lover Max is Richard.

There is a rift in Sarah's life between her sexuality and her other female attributes that bind her to the house. On his part, Richard takes

> Great pride, to walk with you as my wife on my arm. To see you smile, laugh, walk, talk, bend, be still. To hear your command of contemporary phraseology, your delicate use of the very latest idiomatic expression, so subtly employed. Yes. To feel the envy of others, their attempts to gain favour with you, by fair means or foul, your austere grace confounding them. And to know you are my wife. It's a source of a profound satisfaction to me.
>
> (p. 187)

As Max, he finds her too bony, and yearns for 'voluminous great uddered feminine bullocks' (p. 184). Sexuality, especially female sexuality, is thus extricated from, rather than integrated into, the complete personality. In *The Homecoming* Ruth decides to abandon her husband, children and home in America, and her image of respectability, for the free expression of her sexuality as prostitute. Sarah too cannot integrate these different aspects of her character, and she can keep them all intact only through leading a double life with her husband. This is why she fights back when he tries to terminate the game and merge his two personae into one.

The unifying element behind the double life of the characters is the house. Rather than abandon his 'two people in a room' formula, Pinter has invented a new variation, in which the room itself joins the people as one of the variables. As the male character exits and enters, he not only alters the relationship between the male and female protagonists but also the relationship between them and the house. Although visibly unchanged, the house alternates between being a staid, conventional dwelling, and a love nest. The unity of the theatrical space is preserved at the cost of a rift in the woman's personality as well as in her husband's attitude towards her. But the integrity of the house, like the integrity of the woman living in it has been split into two separate functions.

The fixed *décor* of *The Lover* serves alternatively as the solid home of an established, married couple and an adventurous meeting place for the same two people involved in a passionate love affair. In *Old Times* (1971) the theatrical space of the two acts of the play remains essentially unchanged (the same furniture 'but in reversed positions', p. 47),[23] although its meaning changes from sitting-room to bedroom, with all the consequent alterations. The door which led to the bedroom in the first act, now leads from bedroom to bathroom, the front door now leads off to the sitting-room, and the sofas are transformed into divans. The sofas doubling as divans also look back to the beds in the rented London room that Anna and Kate shared in the past and which Deeley visited.

Thus, with a single setting, Pinter creates three different rooms, two of them seen consecutively on stage, the third referred to as a past and off-stage room. The spareness of the modern furniture, insisted on in the opening stage directions, emphasizes the structural sameness of the three rooms, all furnished with two beds and an armchair. The versatility of this parsimonious setting is underlined by Deeley:

> We sleep here. These are beds. The great thing about these beds is that they are susceptible to any amount of permutation. They can be separated as they are now. Or placed at right angles, or one can bisect the other, or you can sleep feet to feet, or head to head, or side by side. It's the castors that make all this possible.
>
> (p. 48)

The possible permutations in the relative arrangement of the furniture are matched by their combinations with the characters. Observed from the point of view of the theatrical space, the action appears to be a game of musical beds-and-chair. Odd Man Out, as the film they all saw in the past is called, is he who occupies the chair. The spatial distribution of the three characters within the room is the source of the dramatic conflict. Seemingly settled in the past with Kate's marriage to Deeley, the conflict over who will share the bedroom, or, in cruder terms, the conflict between hetero- and homo-eroticism, is re-opened with Anna's visit.

Kate's casual and ambiguous statement, 'We were living together' (p. 15), elicits a slightly belated and obviously perturbed response from Deeley, 'You lived together?' He repeats this question and ponders over the answers he receives, claiming ignorance of the fact, although 'I knew you had shared with someone at one time' (p. 17).

There is here a *double-entendre* between the innocent and the sexual senses of 'living together'. The sharing of the underwear and the complementary roles of the two women, one self-centred, the other protective and supportive, can be interpreted both as 'straight', girlish behaviour and as an expression of sexual attraction. The play seems to be saturated with this ambiguity.

When Anna joins the other two, she sits down on one of the sofas, while Kate is curled on the other and Deeley is slumped in the armchair. Then Kate gets up to serve coffee, returning to her sofa with her own cup, while Deeley gets up to offer brandy and remains standing. Anna recollects a similar scene, when she returned home one night and found a man sobbing, his face covered by his hand, 'sitting in the arm-chair, all crumpled in the armchair and Katey sitting on the bed with a mug of coffee' (p. 32). She goes on to recount how she got into bed, how the man eventually came over to her but she refused him, how he left and how she woke up in the middle of the night to find him lying across Kate's lap. Gradually, Anna re-asserts herself, awakening the old bond that tied Kate to her. She coaxes her, gives her advice on what to wear, offers her little services, such as reading to her or running her bath.

One of the ways in which the struggle between Deeley and Anna over Kate is conducted is through what Tetsuo Kishi has described as a 'lyrical' boxing match, i.e. a sort of party game that is at the same time a *quid pro quo* of lines from songs popular in the 'fifties, which they distort to score their points.[24] There are two singing matches in the play, one in each act (pp. 27–9, 57–8).

In Act Two, Deeley fights back to regain Kate. While Kate is having her bath, he compares notes with Anna on the details of her baths. Thus both acknowledge each other's interest in her. Delicate shades of love between women are sketched in when Anna describes how she used to borrow Kate's underwear and then tell her, in the dark, about her sexual experiences. Deeley comments wryly: 'Sounds a perfect marriage' (p. 66). Then he voices his distaste of the conversation, attempting to assert himself as husband. Kate, who has been quiet for most of the time, comes out on Anna's side when she suddenly hurls at Deeley: 'If you don't like it go' (p. 67). Trying to save appearances, Anna declares that she has come 'not to disrupt but to celebrate' (p. 68).

It is the reticent and seemingly passive Kate who finally settles the power struggle over her by pronouncing her own version of the past. In a fantasy-sequence she envisions Anna lying dead in bed, her face covered with streams of dirt. With complete equanimity she proceeds to take her bath and then to sit naked by the dead body. After ridding herself symbolically of Anna, and indicating that Deeley had inherited her bed, Kate goes on to annihilate also her husband. She recounts how she smeared him with dirt, thus humiliating his sexual desire for her. Shamed in this manner, Deeley starts to sob, and then gradually the earlier scene described by Anna is acted out, leading up to the final, brightly lit tableau, with Deeley in the armchair, Anna lying on a divan and Kate sitting on the other divan.

The conflict between Deeley and Anna over Kate is conducted in a symmetrical manner, devoid of sentimentality or morality. Gender differences no longer follow the old guidelines as one of the women competes with a man over another woman and her femaleness is expressed not through her sexual preferences but through the delicacy of her understanding of the other woman. Pinter prefers to keep the lesbian theme under cover because he is interested in adumbrating the ambiguous nature of human sexuality. Hovering between male and female attraction, woman's association with her home becomes irrelevant. The traditional spatial dichotomy of indoors and outdoors, female and male spaces, is after all a cultural manifestation of heterosexuality.

The shift from the sitting-room to the bedroom and the insistence on the intimate details of Kate's bath, taking place out of sight, in the theatrical space without, indicate that the movement from the representation of the outdoors in front of the *skene* to the indoors is still in progress. The penetration of the privacy of the house has progressed from the formal interiors of Molière's later comedies, to Ibsen's naturalistic living-rooms and the modern stage bedrooms, as in *Old Times*, stopping short on the threshold of the bathroom. This development reflects the modern trend of opening the whole house, not just the drawing-room, to visitors. Zooming in onto the private spatial interior of the home goes along with probing sexual intimacy on the one hand and the inner self on the other. This is practically as far as the theatrical space can go in its voyage into the interior without abandoning its mimetic dimension.

If the bedroom and bathroom point towards woman's erotic dimension, the kitchen represents her domesticity. Woman's role in the kitchen stretches all the way back to the tending of the hearth or Hestia's fire in the Greek *oikos*.[25] In each of Pinter's plays discussed above, some reference is made to the preparation of meals. *The Room* is equipped with a gas-stove on which Rose cooks Bert's meal. Her much diminished cooking space is in keeping with the general shrinkage of the home into a room. In *The Homecoming* the kitchen is out of sight but a heavy stress is laid on Max's appropriation of woman's function as cook. The hungry husband of *The Lover* is dismayed to find time and again that his wife has failed to prepare a hot dinner, commenting that he himself can hardly be expected to prepare dinner after a long day of 'high finance in the city' (p. 188). The left-over ham and salad which she offers him is a clear sign of her stalling at her traditional duties. In *Old Times* Deeley talks about the casserole Kate has prepared for dinner and worries about Anna's husband, alone in his Sicilian villa, 'living hand to mouth on a few hardboiled eggs' (p. 67).

In *Betrayal* (1978), a play devoted to an extra-marital love affair, the erotic impulse becomes ironically intertwined with domesticity. The flat that Emma and Jerry rent to serve as their meeting place quickly evolves into a duplicate home. Emma decorates this love nest, bringing a fancy tablecloth from Venice, and gladly spends time cooking lunch for Jerry, thus willingly coupling her daring role as lover with the traditional function of homemaker.

In *The Birthday Party*, breakfast is constantly served in Meg's 'listed' Bed & Breakfast from the off-stage kitchen. Meg's motherliness is expressed in terms of her nourishing function, both shopping and cooking, which is also bolstered obliquely by Goldberg's dubious 'Jewish' recollections of his mother and wife preparing for him gefilte fish and rollmops. By contrast, in *The Caretaker*, a wholly male play, the gas stove in the room is significantly unconnected and out of order, so that the characters have to eat outside, at the 'caff', or share the cheese sandwiches brought in by Mick.

The setting of *Landscape* (1968) is the kitchen of a country house. There is no cooking or warmth in this kitchen which only serves as a non-functional backdrop. The *dramatis personae*, if we can call them that in the absence of any dramatic action, are the staff who run the house. The play can be seen as a variation on Strindberg's *Miss Julie*, but instead of the man-servant having an affair with the young mistress, it is the woman-servant who has had an affair with the master. Strindberg's highly dramatic naturalism is replaced by a total lack of action, emphasized by the characters sitting throughout and talking, without appearing to hear each other, as indicated in the opening stage directions. The 'dialogue' consists of two interwoven internal monologues. These separate reminiscences do not interact dramatically, but contain narrative threads which sometimes run parallel and occasionally intersect.

Sitting in the same kitchen, each of the two speakers recalls an outdoor experience, tied up with a particular landscape, in which the other had no part. Beth's landscape is the fresh sea shore and hot dunes with her dozing lover and the staring women. Duff's landscape is the pond in the park during a downfall of rain and the tree under which he found shelter with his dog. His lonely walk in the park turns out to be a repetition of a shared walk after disclosing that he had been unfaithful to her on his trip North, with their master, Mr Sykes. Beth has obviously been more reticent, not sharing with Duff the secret of her love affair with Mr Sykes. Duff would like to draw Beth out of the house, to make her join his walks, but she excludes him from her cherished memory, in which she appears to herself as beautiful and an object of gentle adoration, an image which appeals to her and satisfies her in a way her present existence cannot.

This reading of the play seems to be contradicted by Pinter's own interpretation, in a letter to Hans Schweikart, the director of the first German production of *Landscape* and *Silence*. There Pinter states categorically that 'the man on the beach is Duff' and that 'I do not believe that Mr Sykes and Beth were ever lovers. I formed these conclusions after I had written the plays and after learning about them through rehearsals.'[26] Whether Pinter was responding ingenuously or disingenuously to an impossible query, he claims to have formed this opinion *after* completing the play and in the process of rehearsals, not to have intended the play to mean that. In fact, Pinter has always insisted on possessing incomplete biographical data about his characters and disclaimed any privileged access to the meaning of their talk.[27]

The visible theatrical space of the naturalistic country-house kitchen represents the dull and unsatisfying 'reality' from which the protagonists escape into their private landscapes, i.e. totally conceptual theatrical spaces. Dropping any pretence of communication between his characters, Pinter opts here for letting them voice their thoughts. The process of thought goes round in circles, picking up fragmented memories, coming back to particular details, elements of landscape or conversation, picturing it all as in a film.

It is up to the listener to piece together Beth's recollections of walking towards the beach, then back to the dunes, naked underneath her beachrobe, lying down beside her lover and asking whether he would like a baby. The dialogical structure pushes the spectator to try and co-ordinate Beth's experience with Duff's memories, and the information thus gleaned must somehow be related to the perceived theatrical space. A surprisingly clear story emerges of a romantic triangle, the missing side of which is the absent master, Mr Sykes, who hired the couple to look after his country house. The story itself, like the story behind *Betrayal*, is hardly worth mentioning, but it is the manner of its unfolding which is a true work of art.

In the absence of any action, the naturalistic setting of *Landscape* is almost redundant, beyond providing a socio-economic framework. Paradoxically, its presence serves to accentuate the superiority of conceived over perceived space in this play. The man and woman sitting side by side in the kitchen, each absorbed in his own thoughts, stretch the two-men-in-a-room formula to its breaking point.

Pinter's investigation of the space of the room is reminiscent of the obsession of such artists as Kurt Schwitters (1887–1948) and El Lissitzky (1890–1941) with the construction of rooms. During his life-time, Schwitters constructed three different rooms which he called 'MERZbau'. The first MERZbau was 'a three-dimensional assemblage to which new elements were "merzed on" for sixteen consecutive years until, eventually, it grew upwards through two storeys and downwards into a cellar in Schwitters' house in the Waldhausenstrasse in Hanover'.[28] Lissitzky's 'Proun Rooms' are regarded as forerunners of present-day environmental art. The Proun Room is 'a cubic space of habitable size designed as a visual unity (incorporating floor and ceiling as well as the walls as display-space)... All available surfaces were integrated into a single "environment".'[29]

Schwitters and Lissitzky were constructivists eager to free their art from mimetic subordination. Pinter too may be regarded as a constructivist building synthetic rooms. However, his construction materials are recognizable everyday objects, ostensibly serving in their ordinary functions, so that the overall superficial impression is that of a mimetic space. The deceptively naturalistic look of Pinter's 'rooms' has led some critics to claim that Pinter's theatrical space is conservative.[30] But in fact Pinter's special analysis of the theatrical space has enabled him to create synthetic rooms that express his basic view of man as a verbal construct, lacking a coherent, definable character.

Pinter went a step further in *Silence* (1969), attempting to do away completely with mimetic space, simply indicating three acting areas with a chair for each of the speakers. In this latter play, the disappearance of the theatrical space goes along with the complete interiorization of the action. In this play, co-ordinating the three separate recollections seems a more difficult task for the spectator, perhaps due to the absence of the even minimally binding theatrical space. In *Landscape* the kitchen setting provides a tangible link with everyday reality. In *Silence* the lack of a comparable link is somewhat compensated for by the snatches of conversation that take place when one of the characters moves towards another.

The play is further complicated by the discrepancy between the ostensible ages of the characters as prefixed to the play and as they perceive themselves: while Ellen is described as 'a girl in her twenties', she speaks about her youth and about being old (p. 36). At one point she reflects on her age: 'I seem to be old. Am I old now? No-one will tell me.' Similarly, Bates who is 'a man in his middle thirties' speaks about someone having called him Grandad, adding 'Were I young ... ' (p. 35). It seems that Pinter is simply reversing the convention of providing information about the present age of the characters (as he himself does, for example, in *Landscape*), giving instead their ages at the time of the recollected events, as they remember themselves.

The play seems to suffer from the absence of a firm point of reference either in time or in space. Without such an anchor in reality, the fleeting reminiscences seem so private that they fail to interest and intrigue us. After this experiment with a totally abstract setting, Pinter reverted to recognizable theatrical spaces such as a hospital ward (*A Kind of Alaska*, 1982), taxi station (*Victoria Station*, 1982) or prison (*Mountain Language*, 1988).

Pinter's one attempt at getting away from a mimetic theatrical space seems to be influenced by Samuel Beckett's experimentation. Ellen, Rumsey and Bates are reminiscent of M, W1 and W2, the man and the two women stuck in urns who are the speakers of *Play*. But, whereas Beckett is a metaphysical writer, dealing directly with the universal problems of existence, Pinter's mode is strongly attached to the surfaces of everyday speech and behaviour. It is from this ordinary, daily experience that the fear of the unknown and the horror of non-being arise, and this is the source of the menace tapped by Pinter in his plays. The universality of his theatre is derived from its particularity, its attention to minute local details. Beckett's idiom is philosophical and symbolic, while Pinter's hyper-realism is universal only by implication. Therefore Beckett's natural idiom is abstract, but Pinter's is concrete.

## Chapter 10

# Abstract spaces

The theatrical space of Beckett's plays is very different from Pinter's rooms. It is an abstract space, unlocalized and indeterminate, and totally uniform. The essential difference between abstract space and the articulated living spaces created by man is characterized by Martin Heidegger. In his view, man relates to space through building himself dwellings, through clearing for himself enclosed spaces. Man's building activity creates locations and it is only through locations that man relates to space:

> The spaces through which we go daily are provided for by locations; their nature is grounded in things of the type of buildings. If we pay heed to these relations between locations and spaces, between spaces and space, we get a clue to help us in thinking of the relation of man and space.[1]

Beckett's space has no geography or topography, no within and without. Lacking co-ordinates in the theatrical space, all movement must be related to the stage, to the theatre space: characters enter from 'upstage right', not from next door or the street. This pure space, which has only extension but no location, is quite different from the theatrical spaces I have been discussing so far. These are delimited, hence cut up, forming segments that are related to each other by direction and distance. The most basic of these limited, finite spaces, through which one relates to all other spaces, is the home or the room in which man, or rather woman, lives. The segmented view of space, of spaces on a human scale and the idea of space as dwelling create the basis for the privileged link of woman with space. But the uniformity of space excludes the possibility of spatial gender distinctions.

In *Waiting for Godot* (1955) the whole point of the play is the lack of any specificity or certainty regarding either time or place. The indeterminacy of the country road-with-tree setting is thematic, the subject of Gogo and Didi's speculation about whether they are at all waiting in the appointed place, by the right tree.[2] The other characters who arrive on scene, Pozzo and Lucky and the boy, come from the wings which are not assigned any particular significance. When Vladimir 'hastens towards the wings' saying 'I'll be back', Estragon comically directs him to 'The end of the corridor, on the left' (p. 35), obviously referring to the location of the rest rooms in the theatre building.

John Fuegi deduces that 'The road and the tree are probably somewhere in France because we know that Vladimir and Estragon have missed their chance to jump off the Eiffel Tower together'. But the Eiffel Tower is not used in the play for geographic orientation any more than the biblical references to the Dead Sea and the Holy Land (p. 12). While Fuegi places the action in France he also recognizes that the characters inhabit a 'nonspecific space'. This inconsistency possibly stems from his attempt to draw parallels between Pinter and Beckett in their use of time-space co-ordinates instead of recognizing their totally divergent approaches to the question of space.[3]

*Endgame* (1957) is a play that still bears the external trappings of the conventional *décor*, a room with windows and doors. But these windows do not look out upon an ordinary view. Through them may be seen, with the aid of a telescope, the sea and the ocean, a 'corpsed', gray, leaden world in which nothing is stirring.[4] This apocalyptic landscape wrenches from the room any sense of a protected, homely environment. When Clov pushes Hamm in his wheelchair around the room they are going 'Right round the world' (p. 25), thus reinforcing the wholly abstract, non-mimetic nature of the setting as well as the action.

Beckett is interested in the existential condition of man, not in his particular history. Stuck in a growing mound of earth, the protagonist of *Happy Days* (1961) has no convenient room to protect her. In the absence of any localizing element, she is characterized solely in terms of her cultural rag-bag of reminiscences. With her coquetry and loquacity, Winnie is recognizably 'feminine', in the old-fashioned stereotype. But the mound into which she is gradually disappearing is rather a universal symbol for the human condition than a metaphor for woman's place.

Shari Benstock is undoubtedly right in her general observation that 'The cultural system can continue to function only when woman keeps to her place'. But, although Winnie's fixity is contrasted with Willie's minimal mobility, the guiding metaphor of the play is the gradual burial, in which there can be no gender distinctions. In Beckett, immobility is not a distinguishing trait of women: both Nell and Nagg in *Endgame* are stuck in ashbins, and all three characters of *Play* (1963) are confined to urns. To say that Winnie 'must be anchored because it is her very fixity that allows the smooth running of the system' is to express a feminist truism with little relevance to the text.[5]

The speaking mouth in *Not I* is not only completely stationary but also wholly unfigured. Although Beckett blocks off any image of the speaker, restricting our view to the mouth, the speaker is recognizably female: a female voice (in the theatre this is immediately registered) speaking about a woman, in the third person, in a disjointed, stream-of-consciousness manner, so that the listener gets the impression that she must be speaking of herself. This impression is strengthened by *what* is being said: 'a voice she did not recognize ... at first ... so long since it had sounded ... then finally had to admit ... could be none other ... than her own ... ' This supposition turns into certitude in Beckett's reference, in his final note, to Mouth's repeated recovery 'from vehement refusal to relinquish third person', in the refrain-like sequence: ' ... what? ... who? ... no! ... she! ... ' Thus the use of the third person constitutes an attempted denial of self, a transparent escape into 'not I'.[6]

Mouth speaks of herself as about sixty or seventy years old. Like the old Nell and the fifty-year-old Winnie, Mouth too is of a post-mating and post-fertility age, with her eye fixed on the end of life. Post-menopausal woman is an ideal choice for Beckett since her role in the cycle of procreation, and therefore also her struggle with patriarchalism, are clearly over. Peter Gidal speaks of 'a de-sexing, an un-sexing' of the speaker in *Not I*.[7] However, some feminist readings attribute sexual significance to 'the tongue in the mouth ... all those contortions'. Thus for Ann Wilson, the lips 'are not only the lips of a mouth but suggest the labia of a vagina ... an emblem of the erotics of language.'[8] This rather fanciful reading seems to miss the speaker's concerns, her advanced age and her disembodied psyche, 'whole body like gone'.

The complete darkness of the stage stipulated by Beckett for the performance of *Not I* destroys any perception of space: this is a radical experiment in abolishing the theatrical space. Under these circumstances, all that remains of the 'character' is the voice and words issuing from her mouth, and the audience is denied any visual image of either the person or her environment. Even within this rigorous minimalism, much more restrictive even than Winnie's confinement, Mouth's way of thinking and speaking is culturally determined and gendered. It is not merely the use of the third rather than the first person that reveals her sex, but her attitudes to love, aging, nature, sin – in other words, to herself. And yet, her summary of life, the anguish she expresses, is of universal validity. So, although human experience and the human voice are either male or female, the existential *Angst*, the confrontation with death, is shared.

Because he deals with the ultimate questions, on a philosophical level, Beckett has no use for the problem of woman and hence for the conventions of the theatrical space. The absence of a mimetic theatrical space, either indoors or outdoors, is a clear indication that Beckett is not interested in the traditional conflicts of private and public, male and female. From his point of view, the theatrical space that expresses woman's place becomes unnecessary, perhaps even a distraction and a hindrance for the metaphysical issues at stake. Beckett has in effect cancelled Aeschylus' original intuition of the *skene* as representing a significant division of space. The distant and the close by, the indoors and the outdoors, the upstairs and the downstairs are meaningless in the Beckettian wasteland.

Distancing himself from the mimetic theatrical space, Samuel Beckett has created totally abstract and symbolic theatrical spaces and even experimented with the total abolition of space. Peter Handke has gone further, launching a direct, concerted attack on Western theatre in general, and on the idea of the theatrical space in particular. Unlike Beckett, who uses the theatre as a vehicle or medium of expression, Handke is interested in the vehicle itself. Handke's art is totally self-reflexive, engrossed in its own ontological and epistemological foundations.

In the introductory note to his two *Sprechstücke* (or 'speak-ins', in Michael Roloff's translation), Handke states that these plays 'are autonomous prologues to the old plays'. Whereas the old plays attempted to give a picture of the world, his pieces 'point to the world ... by way of words'. His is an ascetic, self-denying approach to theatre, which eschews not only image-making, story, and action, but also a separate theatrical space.[9]

*Offending the Audience* (1966) sets out to offend the audience by thwarting all its expectations. In this tongue-in-cheek 'play' Handke destroys the ontological foundations of mimetic theatre. After such destruction, it is not clear what new direction the theatre can now take. Handke himself affirms that his piece primarily negates (p. 14), i.e. that it demolishes conventional theatre without offering an alternative beyond its own ironic form. When he is through, it is as though a hurricane had swept through the theatre and its history, leaving only debris in its wake.

The theatrical space serves as one of Handke's prime targets. The four speakers of the piece, undifferentiated even in terms of gender, insist that there can be no 'line of demarcation' or 'magic circle' that distinguishes everyday space from theatrical space. The whole thrust of their words is anti-mimetic and anti-naturalistic: 'This room does not make believe it is a room. The side that is open to you is not the fourth wall of a house' (p. 13). In his highly sarcastic mode Handke 'proves' that his play strictly observes the three unities, as it refers only to the here and now of the theatre, and concludes that, 'Therefore this piece is classical' (p. 20).

*Self-Accusation* (1966) marks the crisis of an art that has become so self-reflective, self-critical, that it is completely solipsistic, enclosed within its own verbal fabrications, unable to relate to a world outside. The foundations of knowledge have been subjected to such thorough-going criticism that we have been left with nothing but skepticism. The divided monologue of this play (a male and a female speaker) deals with our spiritual biography, with our futile attempts to express ourselves verbally and directly or indirectly, through violating written or unwritten codes of behaviour. The writing, acting or watching of this piece, i.e. the three modes of relating to it mentioned in the final sentence of the play, constitute such subversive, anti-social conduct, a rebellion against the tyranny of convention, a desperate attempt at self-expression.

The two speak-ins end in impasse: following the dismantling of the theatre in *Offending the Audience*, *Self-Accusation* is a totally reflexive play that deals with the expression of self, not with the relation of self to world. As such, it has no need of a theatrical space. Thus the creative crisis brought about by the radical critique of the theatrical event in the first of these plays is delayed but not resolved by the second.

Only in *Kaspar* (1967) does Handke begin to reconstruct the theatre, as the protagonist painstakingly builds a world with words and 'creates his own (three) walls for himself' (p. 83). Although Kaspar's room contains recognizable objects, it does not 'imitate' another room. Like the words of his one, inscrutable sentence, 'Ich möcht ein solcher werden wie einmal ein andrer gewesen ist'[10] ('I want to be a person like somebody else was once'), the pieces of furniture too are initially handled by Kaspar as unfamiliar *objets trouvés*.

As the play progresses, he learns to relate words to objects and combines a growing mastery of words with an increasing mastery of the world. He delights in his discovery of the power of rationality to impose order on reality. It is the processes of mastering language and organizing one's world that are being theatricalized, and the room is used conceptually, not naturalistically, as signifying the order imposed on the world through the use of language, not as representing a particular dwelling. In Kaspar's effort to master speech we see our own desperate attempts to achieve control of reality through the use of words, our frustration with the unbridgeable gap between objects and words, our awareness of the ineffectuality of word-manipulation, self-expression, ultimately – of art.

The play is a kind of abstract spiritual biography, devoid of any individualizing experience. This is expressed theatrically through the use of the mask of astonishment in the first part and the mask of contentment in the second, as well as the multiplication of Kaspar look-alikes or clones. The playwright carefully avoids creating a 'character' or involving it in any life-like event or recognizable situation. The well-known source, Kaspar Hauser's unique and enigmatic private history, was chosen presumably because it presents the paradoxical biography of a biography-less person. Hauser was assassinated as mysteriously as he had appeared from nowhere only a few years earlier.[11] But even these few intervening years of life are not dramatized. The historical figure is abstracted and universalized, becoming a Kasper or Kasperle, a traditional German clown or Viennese puppet.[12] This comic figure is then used as a pattern or paradigm of man's struggle to make sense of the world into which he has been thrust.

Handke's debt to Wittgenstein's *Tractatus Logico-Philosophicus* has been widely recognized and this has helped elucidate his rigorous approach to the limitations imposed on human thinking and self-expression by the narrowness of language itself. Though leading to a better understanding of Handke's critique of language, the fixation on this highly visible aspect of the play has been detrimental to its wider interpretation. As indicated already above, the problem of language is intimately linked in the play with the question of reality, the co-ordination of word with object, of 'table' with table. In their technical manner, the invisible 'prompters' (Roloff's translation for *Einsager*) who address Kaspar from all sides work out the different possible combinations: 'Words and things ... Words without things ... Things without words ... Neither words nor things' (p. 77). The whole theatrical get-up of the piece, its carefully orchestrated movements, voices and sounds, setting, costumes and props, all these constitute Kaspar's 'world', though not in the conventional, environmental sense.

One of the few critics who see the play in its theatrical totality is Christopher Innes, who reads it as an 'interior, psychological drama', in which the table, chairs and wardrobe are the furniture of Kaspar's mind and the prompters represent 'the stream of sense data'.[13] But psychological is an unfortunate description for a play that does not presume to demonstrate the workings of the mind, nor can the sentences with which the prompters feed Kaspar be regarded as sense data.

The play begins with Kaspar being 'born' into the room, through the partition between the curtains, onto the stage. He gropes around to make some sense, mishandling the furniture and missing his balance. Gradually he learns to use words effectively, form sentences, speak about the objects that surround him and handle them and differentiate between his own power of speech and the world. Before he mastered language, he 'could not distinguish / among anything', 'could keep nothing apart' (p. 123), and 'all the unknown objects' were obstacles in his way (p. 124). It was the pain of falling that 'helped me drive / a wedge / between me / and the objects'. Thus the consciousness of pain brought about the differentiation between self and world. It was then that 'I learned to fill / all empty spaces with words', to tremble no longer before empty rooms, to keep everything under control (pp. 124–5). In other words, the ability to discriminate with words gave him the power to control the world around him.

But his proud achievement is also vested with irony: for what does it mean 'to fill all empty spaces with words'? Now that he has succeeded in distinguishing between himself and the objects that surround him, the room (in both senses of chamber and space) seems empty and this experience is perceived as frightening or threatening. His manner of containing this threat is by 'filling' or covering-up the vacuity with words: platitudes, common-places, inanities, maxims – in the manner of the 'truths' he was earlier fed by the prompters. Now his stream of words seems to draw him away from the world with which he used to be at one before acquiring the discriminatory power of speech.

The dramatic development of the play stretches from the birth of consciousness to its chaotic dissolution. Learning to speak and to manipulate the objects around him, Kaspar gains control by imposing order on all sides: 'Ever since I can speak I can put everything in order' (p. 78). His room 'gradually begins to look inhabitable' (p. 83), reflecting the accepted wisdom voiced by the prompters: 'Good order is the foundation of all things' (p. 83) and 'Disorder outrages all decent-thinking men' (p. 84). Before the gap widens, before the world slips away from him, Kaspar temporarily achieves poise and equilibrium, a sense of a rational control of experience. At the end of the play, the repeated phrase 'goats and monkeys', Othello's words as he falls into an epileptic fit, marks the disintegration of Kaspar's world.

The texture of the play is very rich and dense, so that any reading of it can only hope to highlight some of its salient features. In the above reading I have tried to emphasize Handke's unconventional use of what may at first seem a conventional room-setting. Without character or plot, the play has no need of a realistic theatrical space. It deals directly with the central epistemological and ontological problems of how consciousness develops and what it can hope to know about a world which, being material, is essentially different and unknowable. Kaspar's room is a theatricalization of a totally solipsistic world, of a consciousness that develops in response to certain stimuli, the origin of which is unknown, and may be internal. Hence the strange term *Einsager*, 'a made-up word meaning "in-sayers" but having something of the force of "indoctrinators" or "persuaders"'.[14] The *Einsager* or prompters serve as a disembodied channel of indoctrination about the world without any indication as to their nature or meaning. To the end, Kaspar remains enclosed in his own consciousness. The proliferation of identical Kaspars which people his world is an attempt to accommodate other human beings within the confines of solipsistic epistemology. Reaching out to the objects, trying to manipulate and control them, Kaspar strives to break out of his world of words. However, this attempt fails when the objects seem to recede from the self, opening up a frightening, unbridgeable, existential void.

Kaspar's 'room' is not a room in the ordinary sense: it does not represent an environment or a dwelling. By not representing a real room in which a particular character lives, the play has broken with the long tradition linking theatrical spaces with homes and women. It is a departure in a totally new direction, an experiment in abstract and conceptual theatre. Interested in its own structure and validity rather than in the problems of men and women, the theatrical space of this theatre is dehumanized. As such it delimits or lies beyond the limits of the female space which held for so long the centre of Western theatre.

The progressive movement of the theatrical space into the ever more intimate interior coupled with the gradual loosening of woman's bonds with that interior have brought about first the fruition and then the decomposition of one of the shaping ideas of Western theatrical space. With the abstraction of the theatrical space, Blake's intuition of the femaleness of space, quoted in the motto to this book, has been dissipated. In fact, the whole concept of the theatrical space has become problematic and in need of rethinking. Woman's special links with space, based on her privileged position in the home, have come to an end. Space is no longer a woman.

# The child's space

With the dissolution of woman's unique bond with space, this book has run its course. But perhaps a coda is needed for a book that has tried consistently to see the development of Western theatre and drama in terms of the spatial representation of the woman's home, a coda that will discuss the revival of that theme in contemporary plays by women. After the theoretical dismantling and dramatic abstraction of the theatrical space, after the dissociation of indoors and outdoors from traditional gender associations, it is the new feminist playwrights who go back to the recognizable, mimetic spaces, to what for them is still the unresolved question of the home. They offer new solutions, suggest new locations, and often change the focus of the home from the woman to the child, the child who still needs the security of the home even if its mother no longer does.

The needs of the child have never been absent from the treatment of the theatrical space of woman, but they remained largely peripheral, as, e.g., the appeal to Myrrhine's motherly instincts in *Lysistrata*, or the question of the two extra rooms in *Hedda Gabler*. A deeper probing into the problem of the children in the context of the breaking-up home was introduced by Ibsen in *A Doll's House*. There the father took charge, declaring Nora to be morally unfit to raise them. Although he relented, Nora still left her home, in spite of Torvald's plea to stay for the sake of the children. The child's space has become an issue in contemporary feminist drama because of the growing interest in the questions of human fertility and parental responsibility, which go together with woman's liberation. The following examples of recent feminist plays will briefly illustrate this development.

Maureen Duffy's *Rites* (1969) is set in a ladies' lavatory, the last wholly female space in our culture. Only there can the women share their thoughts and misgivings about men and develop their class consciousness. The whole action revolves around the notion of the sacrosanct female space which no man should dare enter. In an afterword, Duffy herself compares her play with *The Bacchae*: '*The Bacchae* is Pentheus' story; *Rites* is Agave's.'[1] The women are very jealous of their own space, as seen already in the resentment encountered at the entrance of the 'lifesize toddler boy doll': 'Isn't he a little old to be still coming down here?' (p. 20). The women undress the doll in a 'ritually slow' manner to look at its 'lifesize' penis and compare their attitudes to it (pp. 20–1). Later, having worked themselves up with singing and dancing to an almost orgiastic frenzy, they hurl themselves on their 'victim', the figure they take to be a male who has hidden himself in the loo, an intruder, a peeping Tom. Only after the ritual murder has been committed and the frenzy has subsided do the women, a random collection of all ages and walks of life, come back to their senses and realize that they have actually killed a woman. Duffy has succeeded in locating a last female reservation and making the question of guarding its perimeters against male trespassers into the very subject-matter of her play.

An altogether different female space is created in Pam Gems' play *Dusa, Fish, Stas and Vi*. The opening stage directions specify that the space is not naturalistic, but indicate various pieces of furniture. The emphasis on the room being not naturalistic is probably aimed at directing the attention to the doctrinal aspects of the conversation and away from the specificity of the milieu and the personal nature of the problems. The room belongs to the wealthy, left-wing activist Fish, who shares her apartment with the other three women for ideological reasons. The room serves as a kind of forum in which the four very different women recount their problems to each other, receiving support and comfort. Fish's house is in effect an asylum for unhappy, homeless women. The artificiality of this household is stressed by the manner in which the four life-stories continue running their separate courses, without any dramatic interaction developing between them.

The feminist awareness which gave rise to the play is summarized by Gems:

> It seemed to me when I was writing the play that for all the rhetoric, and the equal opportunities, and the Sex Discrimination Acts, that society had not moved one step towards accommodating the other fifty per cent of us and our needs ... to be told, as women, that we were to be allowed to 'join', as fully fledged citizens was one thing. [But how were we] supposed to do it, and breed and rear our young?[2]

Dusa is defined by the author as 'the breeding bitch'. She is a young mother and her story-line in the play is the kidnapping of her children by her estranged husband. She describes the predicament of motherhood as that of becoming a hostage for life to your children (p. 64). Fish, the fiery revolutionary, expresses her cravings for a baby and questions Dusa about what it is like having babies. To which Dusa retorts that she would have liked to have one every year (p. 52).

The question of the children is taken up perhaps most persuasively in Caryl Churchill's *Top Girls* (1982). The central character, Marlene, is a career woman and an unwed mother who lets her married but childless sister Joyce raise her daughter. Although this has been kept a secret, Angie has guessed who her real

mother is. The closing scene of the play is a show-down between the two sisters, full
of mutual resentment, bitterness and regret, as each realizes what she has lost by
choosing their contrary ways of life. In order to pursue her professional life,
Marlene has left her hometown, family, friends, and given up her own child. Joyce,
who has remained faithful to her people, alone caring for their aging parents, and
has generously offered to rear her sister's child, finds herself trapped in her house.
Abandoned by her husband she is forced to work as a cleaning-woman, and her
relationship with her adopted niece is less than satisfying. Joyce is perhaps most
aggravated by Angie's natural attraction to the glamorous Marlene, the auntie who
leads an exciting life in London, travels to America and brings expensive presents.

This rather parochial and doctrinally structured plot gains in depth by appearing
within the wider context of mythical female history presented in the opening scene.
Top Girls, the name of the women's employment agency which Marlene manages,
refers also to the leading women who assemble in the restaurant to take part in
celebrating Marlene's promotion to managing director. These are the nineteenth-
century traveller Isabella Bird, Lady Nijo, the thirteenth-century concubine of the
Japanese Emperor, Dull Gret, a figure of folklore and the subject of a Brueghel
painting, the ninth-century Pope Joan, and Patient Griselda, of Chaucerian fame.
These five heroines of women's history, part historic figures, part legendary, belong
to different times and places, but share the woman's burden. They tell each other
their stories of love and its consequences, the children wrested from them, which
they were not allowed to keep and bring up. Even for the intellectual Joan, who had
dressed up as a man to pursue her theological studies, and had risen in the ranks of
the Church until she became Pope, the turning point of her life was the moment of
giving birth. Her intellectual achievements, her power, her position, all ended in
ignominy when she gave birth in the middle of a religious procession and was
stoned to death as the Antichrist.[3]

The legendary Patient Griselda, the perfect example of female fidelity and
obedience, coming out of the pages of Chaucer and Boccacio, is a self-effacing anti-
heroine, an emblem of humility. Like other women celebrated in medieval lists and
legends of good women, her virtue appeals to the male, not the female, mind. From
a feminist point of view, the exemplum of this tale ought to be the autocratic
husband who took away Griselda's children, pretending to put them to death, in
order to test her love for him for some sixteen years.

It is only later in the play that we discover that Marlene shares with these ancient
figures the predicament of having been forced to give away her child. She was
driven to find her child a home so as to be able to compete with men in the job
market. The historic perspective provided by the illustrious guests at the restaurant
party thus sheds a gloomy light on the prospects of the contemporary, 'liberated'
woman.

The play sets up different theatrical spaces. It swings sharply between the theatrical spaces of the employment agency which caters for women and the backyard and kitchen of the humble dwelling in which Joyce lives with Angie. This back and forth movement visually demonstrates the two equally unsatisfactory options open to women, the new professional space or the traditional space. While the first is undoubtedly the more attractive, the second is shown as indispensable for the well-being of the child.

Marlene expresses her liberation in choosing to celebrate her promotion by inviting her women 'friends' to a restaurant, the additional theatrical space of the play. In terms of gender divisions, this is 'male' space, an alternative to home and kitchen. Here she assumes the male assertive posture of ordering drinks and hurrying the waitress. The feminist aspect of this scene is underlined by the nature of the occasion and the topic of conversation. Instead of the separation imposed on the women by being each enclosed in her private home, they enjoy the new freedom of meeting in a public place without having to bother about food and drink. They too can buy services instead of rendering them. The female gathering takes place outside the female space of the home, away from the different males that have played such important parts in their lives. Only in such a space can the women meet and compare notes and develop a class consciousness. Paradoxically, within this liberating space and atmosphere Marlene's party-guests share with each other their painful stories about child-bearing.

Charlotte Keatley's *My Mother Said I Never Should* (1987) shares with *Top Girls* the concern of providing a home for the child. The wider historical perspective there is replaced here by the more limited diachronic perspective of four generations of women in one family, who are also seen synchronically as girls playing together. Already their childhood games revolve round the consciousness of the potential fertility of their bodies. The oldest of the four is sceptical about the use of preservatives: 'I'm talking about the *desire*... for little arms reaching up and clinging round your neck... Mother Nature is very hard to fight' (p. 12). As in *Top Girls*, the nineteen-year-old Jackie has a baby-girl out of wedlock, which she decides to let her mother raise, so that she can pursue her studies.[4] A family secret which surfaces late in the play is that the oldest of the women, the great-grandmother born in 1900, was herself illegitimate and grew up in a one-parent family (pp. 21, 24). Thus family history repeats itself, and the progress of women is seen to be illusory. The play moves between the different houses of the adult women, as each of the older three generations – daughter, grand-daughter and great-grand-daughter – offers in turn a home to Rosie. She finally finds peace in the retirement home of her great-grandmother.

In all the plays by women surveyed above there are only female characters. Men are referred to, but not allowed into the visible theatrical space. The problems of motherhood, especially of mothers and daughters, and of liberation from motherhood, are thrashed out again and again between the characters, without any male participation. In other plays by women, notably in Churchill's own *Traps*, *Cloud Nine* and *Fen*, ways of sharing the burden with male characters are sought out, but basically the view is one of stasis and despair, of a sexual revolution and a liberation from the patriarchal system and from the confinement of the home that have ended with the woman having to take alone full responsibility for her children.

The focus on the child highlights the crucial change in the link between woman and home that has taken place in society and in the theatre. As woman has gradually lost her privileged position in the home, she has also freed herself from its confining space, learning to make a living for herself outside. Hence the dwindling interest in the house and the room. But the question of the home has been reintroduced with a vengeance by women playwrights concerned with the well-being of children. If women no longer need the shelter and security offered by the home and the family, children still do. Home thus becomes re-defined as the child's space.

# Notes

### 1 Woman's theatrical space

1 Cf., e.g., Elie Konigson, *L'Espace théâtral médiéval* (Paris, Centre National de la Recherche Scientifique, 1975).

2 For the distinction between theatre space and theatrical space and for the analogy with the sacred space, see my papers 'Theatre space, theatrical space, and the theatrical space without', in James Redmond, ed., *Themes in Drama* 9: *The Theatrical Space* (Cambridge University Press, 1987), pp. 11–26; and 'The undiscover'd country: Theatrical space without in *Hamlet*', *Lieu et temps* (Montpellier, Société Française Shakespeare, 1989), pp. 95–107.

3 Michel de Ghelderode, *La Mort du Docteur Faust*, in *Théâtre* V (Paris, Gallimard, 1957), pp. 207–85, Third Episode. English translation by George Hauger, in Michel de Ghelderode, *Seven Plays*, 2 vols. (New York, Hill and Wang, 1964), vol. 2, pp. 95–150.

4 The term *exangelos* appears to have been first used by Aeschylus. Cf. H. G. Liddel, R. Scott and H. S. Jones, *Greek-English Lexicon*, 9th ed. (Oxford University Press, 1940), *s.v.*

5 I follow Chaim Perelman's distinction, in a note on Salvador Dali, between *espace perçu* and *espace conçu*. Cf. his comment on M. Dufrenne, 'L'Espace dans l'art', in *L'Espace/Space*, Institut International de Philosophie, Entretien de Berne 1976 (Bern, 1978), p. 242.

6 Cf. Michael Issacharoff, *Le Spectacle du discours* (Paris, Librairie José Corti, 1985), p. 69.

7 Cf. ibid., p. 69.

8 Cf. ibid., p. 72.

9 Simone de Beauvoir, *The Second Sex*, tr. H. M. Parshley (New York, Alfred A. Knopf, 1953), p. 450.

10 Virginia Woolf, *A Room of One's Own* (London, Hogarth Press, 1949), p. 131.

11 Cf. Émile Benveniste, *Le Vocabulaire des institutions indo-européennes*: 1. *Économie, parenté, société* (Paris, Les Éditions de Minuit, 1969), p. 296.

12 Cf. ibid., pp. 293, 305, 307.

13 Benveniste, ibid., pp. 289, 313; Mircea Eliade, *Patterns in Comparative Religion* (London, Sheed & Ward, 1958), p. 371; de Beauvoir, *Second Sex*, p. 450.

14 Cf. Jean E. Howard, 'Crossdressing, the theatre, and gender struggle in modern England', *Shakespeare Quarterly* 39 (1988), p. 424, citing Edmund Tilney, *A Briefe and*

*Pleasant Discourse of Duties in Mariage, called the Flower of Friendship* (London, 1587), E2ᵛ-E3. See also Peter Stallybrass, 'Patriarchal territories: The body enclosed', in M. W. Ferguson, M. Quilligan and N. Vickers, eds., *Rewriting the Renaissance* (Chicago University Press, 1986), pp. 123–42.

## 2 *Indoors and outdoors*

1 In my discussion of the *skene*, I treat it as a neutral architectural façade, and refrain from assuming that it was painted to represent particular scenes. On the controversy over Aristotle's reference to *skenographia* (*Poetics* 1449a18), see, for example, A. W. Pickard-Cambridge, *The Theatre of Dionysus in Athens* (Oxford, Clarendon Press, 1946), pp. 124, 170–2; W. Beare, *The Roman Stage*, 3rd ed. (London, Methuen, 1964), Appendix F, p. 276; Erika Simon, *The Ancient Theatre*, tr. C. E. Vafopoulou-Richardson (London, Methuen, 1982), pp. 22–7; Ruth Padel, 'Making space speak', *Nothing to do with Dionysus?*, eds. John J. Winkler and Froma I. Zeitlin (Princeton University Press, 1990), pp. 336–65.
2 Roy. C. Flickinger, *The Greek Theater and its Drama* (University of Chicago Press, 1918; rep. 1973), p. 226; see also pp. 65–6, 228.
3 Oliver Taplin, *The Stagecraft of Aeschylus* (Oxford University Press, 1977), p. 455. The arguments about the origins of the *skene* are summarized in his Appendix C. Although Taplin has relegated his important discussion of the *skene* to an appendix, the force of its conclusions is felt throughout his interpretation of the trilogy.
4 Oliver Taplin, *Greek Tragedy in Action* (London, Methuen, 1978), p. 184, n. 2.
5 Ibid., p. 35.
6 Michel Foucault, *The Use of Pleasure* (vol. 2 of *The History of Sexuality*), tr. Robert Hurley (Harmondsworth, Penguin, 1985), p. 152.
7 Ibid., p. 155.
8 Ibid., p. 157.
9 Cf. Stephen Kern, *The Culture of Time and Space: 1880–1918* (Cambridge, MA, Harvard University Press, 1983), pp. 186–7.
10 Victor Turner, *Process, Performance and Pilgrimage* (New Delhi, Concept Publishing Company, 1979), p. 17.
11 Cf. Jean-Pierre Vernant, *Myth and Thought Among the Greeks* (London, Routledge & Kegan Paul, 1983), p. 128.
12 Ibid., p. 128.
13 Ibid., p. 132
14 W. B. Stanford, *Greek Tragedy and the Emotions* (London, Routledge & Kegan Paul, 1983), p. 153.
15 *Aeschylus*, tr. H. W. Smyth, 2 vols. (London, Heinemann, 'Loeb Classical Library', 1971), vol. 2.
16 Stanford, *Greek Tragedy*, p. 149.
17 For a discussion of the dramatic moment, see my '"Now to die": Zum dramatischen, lyrischen und theatralischen Augenblick in Shakespeares *Othello*', in C. W. Thomsen and H. Holländer, eds., *Augenblick und Zeitpunkt* (Darmstadt, Wissenschaftliche Buchgesellschaft, 1984), pp. 234–50.

18 Pollux iv. 128, quoted by Peter Arnott, *Greek Scenic Conventions in the Fifth Century* BC (Oxford, Clarendon Press, 1962), p. 79.

19 Ibid., p. 79.

20 Cf. A. J. N. W. Prag, *The Oresteia: Iconographic and Narrative Tradition* (Warminster, Wilts., Aris and Phillips, 1985). Cf. also Anneliese Kossatz-Diessmann, *Dramen des Aischylos auf westgriechischen Vasen* (Mainz am Rhein, Phillip von Zabern, 1978), pp. 89–118.

21 H. Lloyd-Jones, Introduction to Aeschylus, *Oresteia*, ed. H. Lloyd-Jones (London, Duckworth, 1970), thinks the *Oresteia* was produced in 458 BC, two years before its author's death (p. iv), and that the calyx-krater was painted about the same time (p. 91, n. on l. 1382). But Prag, *The Oresteia*, dates the calyx-krater 470–465 BC; cf. his plate 3.

22 For a discussion of the net, cf. Lloyd-Jones, ed., *Oresteia*, p. 91, n. on l. 1382.

23 But in a shield band from Olympia, *c.* 575–550 BC, it is Clytemnestra who stabs Agamemnon. See E. Kunze, *Archaische Schieldbänder* (Berlin, Walter de Gruyter, 1950), plate 18.IVd; Prag, *The Oresteia*, plate 2a.

24 S. C. Humphreys, *The Family, Women and Death* (London, Routledge & Kegan Paul, 1983), p. 73.

25 Algernon Charles Swinburne, 'Under the Microscope', in John Jump, ed., *Tennyson: The Critical Heritage* (London, Routledge & Kegan Paul, 1967), p. 318.

26 Stanford, *Greek Tragedy*, p. 128.

27 Ibid., p. 129.

28 Ibid., p. 130.

29 Pierre Vidal-Naquet, 'Hunting and sacrifice in Aeschylus' *Oresteia*', in Jean-Pierre Vernant and Pierre Vidal-Naquet, *Tragedy and Myth in Ancient Greece*, tr. Janet Lloyd (Sussex, Harvester Press, 1981), p. 151.

30 Cf. Lloyd-Jones, Introduction, p. ix.

31 *The Odyssey of Homer*, tr. Richard Lattimore (New York, Harper & Row, 1967).

32 Cf. H. C. Baldry, *The Greek Tragic Theatre* (London, Chatto & Windus, 1971), pp. 51–3.

33 See above, p. 4.

34 For the influence of the Aeschylean Clytemnestra on Euripides see T. B. L. Webster, *The Tragedies of Euripides* (London, Methuen, 1967), pp. 13, 56.

35 Tr. Rex Warner, in *Euripides I*, with introduction by Richmond Lattimore (University of Chicago Press, 1955).

### 3 Reversing gender roles

1 Cf. B. B. Rogers, Introduction to *Lysistrata, Aristophanes*, 3 vols. (Cambridge, MA, Harvard University Press, 'Loeb Classical Library', 1924, 1963), vol. 2, p. 2.

2 The allusions range from the oblique and implied to the explicit: the Women's chorus enumerates the different rites of passage associated with Athena through which they progressed into womanhood (lines 640–8), referring to service rendered at the Erechtheion and to the Panathenaic procession leading to the Parthenon; the Men's chorus sings of the women daring to seize 'the Holy Image' (line 262), i.e. the image of Athena Polias, and of 'Victory, immortal Queen' (line 317); and Lysistrata reveals the

source of a feigned pregnancy as the hidden 'sacred helmet' (line 751), i.e. 'the great bronze helmet of Athene Promachos' (cf. Rogers' notes, pp. 66, 27, 32, 76).

3 Cf. Thucydides 2.15; Nicole Loraux, *Les Enfants d'Athéna: Idées athéniennes sur la citoyenneté et la division des sexes* (Paris, François Maspero, 1981), p. 27.

4 On the intrusion of women into the public domain in Greek drama, see Michael Shaw, 'The female intruder: Women in fifth-century drama', *Classical Quarterly* 70 (1975), pp. 255–66; *contra* Helene Foley, 'The "female intruder" reconsidered: Women in Aristophanes' *Lysistrata* and *Ecclesiazousae*', *Classical Quarterly* 77 (1982), pp. 1–21.

5 Unless otherwise indicated, all quotes are from Rogers' translation.

6 Cf. Dietrich von Bothmer, *Amazons in Greek Art* (Oxford, Clarendon Press, 1957), p. 147; and William Blake Tyrrell, *Amazons: Study in Mythmaking* (Baltimore, Johns Hopkins University Press, 1984), p. 11.

7 Tyrrell, *Amazons*, p. 10, claims that the Amazonomachy in the Theseum was probably done by Polygnotus rather than by Micon, but fails to provide any substantiating reference.

8 Cf. Froma Zeitlin, 'The dynamics of misogyny: Myth and mythmaking in the Oresteia', *Arethusa* 11: *Women in the Ancient World* ((Buffalo, NY, Arethusa, 1978), p. 151.

9 Cf. Tyrrell, *Amazons*, pp. 19–20.

10 Cf. Leo Strauss, *Socrates and Aristophanes* (University of Chicago Press, 1966), pp. 204, 211; Jeffrey Henderson, Introduction to *Aristophanes: Lysistrata* (Oxford, Clarendon Press, 1987), p. xxxv; Nicole Loraux, pp. 157–96, esp. pp. 166 (n. 31), 168, 177.

11 Lampito was a Spartan queen (cf. *Kleine Pauly*, 5 vols., (Munich, Deutscher Taschenbuch Verlag, 1979), vol. 3, *s.v.*) or one of the queens of the Amazons (cf. J. Lemprière, *A Classical Dictionary* (London, George Routledge and Sons, 1898), *s.v.* Lampeto); the tomb of the Amazon Myrrhine is mentioned in *Iliad* 2.814.

12 Froma Zeitlin, 'Cultic models of the female: Rites of Dionysus and Demeter', *Arethusa* 15: *Texts and Contexts* ((Buffalo, NY,) Arethusa, 1982), p. 146. Cf. also Zeitlin, 'The dynamics of misogyny', p. 153.

13 Cf. Tyrrell, *Amazons*, p. 4, and p. 131, n. 10 for a bibliography on this subject.

14 K. J. Dover, *Aristophanic Comedy* (Berkeley, University of California Press, 1972), p. 159.

15 Cf. A. E. Haigh, *The Attic Theatre* (Oxford, Clarendon Press, 1907; 1st ed. 1889), pp. 324–9; H. C. Baldry, *The Greek Tragic Theatre* (London, Chatto and Windus, 1971), p. 31; Robert Flacelière, *La Vie quotidienne en Grèce au siècle de Périclès* (Paris, Hachette, 1959), p. 102.

16 *The Iliad of Homer*, tr. Andrew Lang, Walter Leaf and Ernest Myers (New York, Random House, 'The Modern Library', 1950), with slight changes.

17 Jack Lindsay's translation, in *The Complete Plays of Aristophanes*, ed. by Moses Hadas (New York, Bantam Books, 1962). Such an unexpurgated translation is not to be found in the Loeb edition. On female masturbation in Greek comedy, see Jeffrey Henderson, *The Maculate Muse: Obscene Language in Attic Comedy* (New Haven, Yale University Press, 1975), pp. 221–2.

18 Cf. Strauss, *Socrates and Aristophanes*, p. 202.

19 On the contest between the two choruses as a residual form of *parabasis* and *agon*, see

Gilbert Murray, *Aristophanes* (Oxford, Clarendon Press, 1933), p. 12; and Strauss, *Socrates and Aristophanes*, p. 203.
20 Tr. Lindsay, *Complete Plays*, p. 300.
21 Cf. Henderson, *Maculate Muse*, p. 137.
22 Ibid., p. 1.
23 Ibid., p. 98.
24 Cf. Tyrrell, *Amazons*, p. 42.
25 Foley, 'The "female intruder"', p. 7.
26 Tr. Lindsay, *Complete Plays*, p. 305.

### 4 *The comedy of doors*

1 Cf. A. W. Pickard-Cambridge, *The Theatre of Dionysus in Athens* (Oxford, Clarendon Press, 1946), p. 59; Roy C. Flickinger, *The Greek Theater and its Drama*, 4th ed. (University of Chicago Press, 1936; 1st ed. 1918), p. 228; A. E. Haigh, *The Attic Theatre*, 3rd ed. revised by A. W. Pickard-Cambridge (Oxford, Clarendon Press, 1907; 1st ed. 1889), p. 188.
2 Cf. K. J. Dover, *Aristophanic Comedy* (Berkeley, University of California Press, 1972), p. 23.
3 Haigh, *Attic Theatre*, p. 194; Flickinger, *Greek Theater*, p. 228.
4 Cf. W. Beare, *The Roman Stage*, 3rd ed. (London, Methuen, 1964), p. 285.
5 Cf. Flickinger, *Greek Theater*, p. 233. See also Haigh, *Attic Theatre*, pp. 194–5. *Contra*, see Beare, *Roman Stage*, p. 250, but I do not find his arguments convincing.
6 Vitruvius, 5.6.8. On side-entrances, see Mary Johnston, *Exits and Entrances in Roman Comedy* (New York, W. F. Humphrey Press, 1933) and Beare, *Roman Stage*, Appendix B.
7 R. L. Hunter, *The New Comedy of Greece and Rome* (Cambridge University Press, 1985), p. 90.
8 Plautus, *The Pot of Gold and Other Plays*, tr. E. F. Watling (Harmondsworth, Penguin, 1965), p. 165.
9 Plautus, *The Rope and Other Plays*, tr. E. F. Watling (Harmondsworth, Penguin, 1964).
10 For a discussion of female and male spaces in terms of Hestia and Hermes, see above, p. 14.
11 For a partial summary of the debate, see R. A. Foakes' Introduction to the Arden edition of the play (1961), pp. xxxiv–xxxix.
12 William Shakespeare, *The Complete Works*, ed. by Stanley Wells and Gary Taylor (Oxford, Clarendon Press, 1988): *The Comedy of Errors* 2.1.s.d. Subsequent references to this edition.
13 'The only authority for the text of *The Comedy of Errors* is the First Folio (1623); all later texts are derived from that source' (Note on the Text, *The Riverside Shakespeare*, textual editor G. Blakemore Evans (Boston, Houghton Mifflin, 1974)). The editors of the *Oxford Shakespeare* print 'Enter Adriana within the Phoenix', presumably indicating that she too is invisible to the audience.

## 5 *The woman in the window*

1 Cf. Margarete Bieber, *The History of the Greek and Roman Theater* (Princeton University Press, 1939), pp. 268–9.
2 For an analysis of this vase-painting see ibid., pp. 285–7.
3 E.g. B. B. Rogers, tr., *Aristophanes*, 3 vols. (Cambridge, MA, Harvard University Press, 'Loeb Classical Library', 1924, 1963), vol. 3, in note to scene beginning line 877, and K. J. Dover, *Aristophanic Comedy* (Berkeley, University of California Press, 1972), p. 197.
4 John Orrell, *The Human Stage: English Theatre Design 1567–1640* (Cambridge University Press, 1988), p. 209.
5 Cf. Lewis Mumford, *The City in History* (Harmondsworth, Pelican Books, 1966), p. 433; and Mark Girouard, *Cities and People: A Social and Architectural History* (New Haven and London, Yale University Press, 1985), pp. 119–20.
6 Cf. Richard and Helen Leacroft, *Theatre and Playhouse* (London, Methuen, 1984), pp. 45–6. On the thorny question of reconstructing the ceiling and its decorations see Remo Schiavo, *Guida al Teatro Olimpico* (Vicenza, Accademia Olimpica, 1980), pp. 30, 131–2.
7 Cf. Philip King, *Amos, Hosea, Micah: An Archeological Commentary* (Philadelphia, The Westminster Press, 1988), pp. 100, 146, 148. Cf. also M. E. L. Mallowan, *Nimrud and its Remains*, 2 vols. (London, Collins, 1966), vol. 2, fig. V.
8 William Shakespeare, *The Complete Works*, ed. Stanley Wells and Gary Taylor (Oxford, Clarendon Press, 1988). I am indebted to Barbara Rosen, of Connecticut University, for directing my attention to this interesting quotation.
9 A similar expression appears in Thomas Heywood and Richard Broome, *The Late Lancashire Witches* (1634), sig. B2ᵛ, ed. Laird H. Barber (New York, Garland Publishing, 1979), p. 141.
10 *The Oxford Chekhov*, ed. and tr. Ronald Hingley, 9 vols. (London, Oxford University Press, 1964–80), vol. 2.
11 Dionisio Minaggio, 'The Feather Book', Blacker-Wood Library, Montréal. Cf. Vito Pandolfi, ed., *La Commedia dell'arte*, 6 vols. (Florence, Edizioni Sansoni Antiquariato, 1957–61), vol. 3, p. 64a. Pandolfi and others spell 'Menaggio'.
12 K. M. Lea, *Italian Popular Comedy*, 2 vols. (Oxford, Clarendon Press, 1934), vol. 2, p. 599.
13 Ibid., pp. 606–7.
14 *Ludovico Ariosto's Orlando Furioso*, tr. Sir John Harington (1591), ed. Robert McNulty (Oxford, Clarendon Press, 1972), 'An advertisement to the reader', p. 17.
15 The complicated question of the influence of the *dell'arte* tradition on the Elizabethan theatre is examined in detail by Lea, *Italian Popular Comedy*.
16 For selections from Coryat, see Ben Jonson, *Volpone*, ed. Philip Brockbank (London, Ernest Benn, 1968), pp. 161–5.
17 The stage-direction 'Juliet appears aloft as at a window' is by Rowe and does not appear in Q2–4, F, Q1. Cf. G. Blakemore Evans, ed., *Romeo and Juliet* (Cambridge University Press, 1984), p. 92. But the scene is sufficiently described in Romeo's words.
18 Ben Jonson, *Volpone*, ed. by Philip Brockbank, The New Mermaid edition (London, Ernest Benn, 1968).
19 Cf. Lea, *Italian Popular Comedy*, p. 359.
20 Locks and thresholds are inextricably linked: 'All locks are an invitation to thieves. A

lock is a psychological threshold' (Gaston Bachelard, *The Poetics of Space* (1958), tr. Maria Jolas (Boston, Beacon Press, 1969), p. 81).

21 Thomas Middleton, *Women Beware Women*, ed. J. R. Mulryne, The Revel Plays (London, Methuen, 1975).

22 Christopher Ricks, 'The tragedies of Webster, Tourneur and Middleton: Symbols, imagery and conventions', in *English Drama to 1710*, ed. C. Ricks (London, Sphere Books, 1971), p. 321. In this essay Ricks provides a thorough analysis of the window scenes in Middleton's play. Jean Chothia kindly called my attention to this essay.

### 6 *The useless precaution*

1 Cf. Jacques Truchet and Alain Couprie, 'Inventoire thématique général du théâtre de Molière', in Jacques Truchet, ed., *Thématique de Molière* (Paris, SEDES, 1985), 'Lieux scéniques'.

2 *Oeuvres de Molière*, ed. Bertrand Guégan, 7 vols. (Paris, Payot, 1925–9). All translations are mine.

3 A traditional street-setting is clearly used up to scene 10, but the painting and duping scenes seem to demand an indoor setting. For an hypothesis of how this could have been handled in Molière's theatre without disrupting the continuous action, see Roger W. Herzel, 'The décor of Molière's stage: The testimony of Brissart and Chauveau', *PMLA* 93 (1978), p. 944.

4 See Paul Imbs, *Trésor de la langue française*, 15 vols. (Paris, Gallimard, 1971–92); Salvatore Battaglia, *Grande dizionario della lingua italiana*, ed. G. Barbieri Squarotti, 19 vols. (Unione Tipografico-Editrice Torinese, 1961–1992).

5 Cf. Lemprière, *Classical Dictionary*, *s.v.*

6 In many respects Molière was an anti-feminist, satirizing women's aspirations to learning and to emancipation from household duties, e.g. in *Les Femmes savantes*. For an informed discussion of Molière's views in the context of seventeenth-century French feminism, see Francis Baumal, *Le Féminisme au temps de Molière* (Paris, La Renaissance du Livre, n.d.).

7 On the theme of the forced marriage in Molière, cf. Jean-François Couvelaire, 'Mariage forcé et mariage contrarié dans le théâtre de Molière', in Truchet, ed., *Thématique de Molière*, pp. 117–52.

8 W. G. Moore, *Molière: A New Criticism* (Oxford, Clarendon Press, 1949), p. 105.

9 Cf. Gaston Hall, *Comedy in Context: Essays on Molière* (Jackson, University Press of Mississippi, 1984), pp. 140–1, for the interesting theory that this is a parody of the idea of auricular conception in baroque devotional art.

10 Cf. Gérard Sablayrolles, Introduction to Molière, *L'École des femmes* (Paris, Larousse, 1970), p. 25; Hall, *Comedy in Context*, pp. 88, 90.

11 Cf. Hall, *Comedy in Context*, pp. 77, 80.

12 Cf. Mikhail Bulgakov, *The Life of Monsieur de Molière*, tr. Mirra Ginsburg (Oxford University Press, 1988), p. 159; see also Léon Thoorens, *Le Dossier Molière* (Verviers, Éditions Gérard, 1964).

13 *Hamlet* 2.2.384. This broader perspective justifies the Ghost's use of 'incestuous' at 1.5.43.

14 Cf. Bertrand Guégan's 'Notes' to his edition of *Oeuvres de Molière*, vol. 3 (1927), p. 351, n. 4: the story appears also in Ser Giovanni's *Il Pecorone* and was also dramatized in 1661 by Dorimond as *L'École de cocus ou La Précaution inutile*. See also Hall, *Comedy in Context*, p. 44.

15 Paul Scarron, 'The Useless Precaution', *The Comical Romance and Other Tales*, tr. Tom Brown and John Savage, 2 vols. (London, Lawrence and Bullen, 1892), vol. 2, p. 156.

16 Paul Scarron, 'La Précaution inutile', *Oeuvres*, 10 vols. (Amsterdam, Wetstein & Smith, 1737), vol. 3: 'Les nouvelles', p. 65.

17 Cf. Hall, *Comedy in Context*, pp. 138–9.

18 Cf. Ibid., p. 139.

19 Herzel, 'The décor of Molière's stage', p. 932.

20 The first three acts of *Le Tartuffe* were acted in Versailles in 1664 causing a great uproar. The full version was first performed in public only in 1669 and published that same year. Cf. Guégan's Notes to *Oeuvres de Molière*, vol. 4 (1928), pp. 319–24.

21 Cf. Guégan's Notes to *Oeuvres de Molière*, vol. 5 (1929), p. 335.

22 Cf. Moore, *A New Criticism*, p. 118.

23 Brissart's derivative frontispiece, based on Chauveau's, is reproduced by Herzel, 'The décor of Molière's stage', p. 939.

24 For this illustration see *Oeuvres*, ed. Guégan, vol. 4, p. 104.

25 Cf. Notes to *Oeuvres*, ed. Guégan, vol. 4, p. 323.

26 For a discussion of the sources and structure of the *dépit amoureux* scenes, see Hall, *Comedy in Context*, pp. 3–18.

27 (Louis) Béjart; for the list of actors of the 1669 production, according to the contemporary Robinet, see Notes to *Oeuvres*, ed. Guégan, vol. 4, p. 322. But according to W. D. Howarth, *Molière: A Playwright and his Audience* (Cambridge University Press, 1982), p. 162, and others, the role was played by Hubert.

### 7 Inside the drawing room

1 On the environment as one of the three determinants of human behaviour in the literary theory of Hippolyte Taine, see Tom F. Driver, *Romantic Quest and Modern Query: A History of Modern Theater* (New York, Delta, 1970), p. 99. See also Raymond Williams, 'Social environment and theatrical environment: The case of English naturalism', in Marie Axton and Raymond Williams, eds., *English Drama: Forms and Development*, Essays in Honour of Muriel Clara Bradbrook (Cambridge University Press, 1977), p. 205.

2 For a different view of Ibsen's use of the Aristotelian unities, see John Orr, *Tragic Drama and Modern Society: Studies in the Social and Literary Theory of Drama from 1870 to the Present* (Totowa, NJ, Barnes & Noble, 1981), p. 8.

3 Brian Johnston, '*A Doll House*; or, The fortunate fall', in Yvonne Shafer, ed., *Approaches to Teaching Ibsen's* A Doll House (New York, Modern Language Association of America, 1985), p. 117.

4 Frederick J. Marker and Lise-Lone Marker, *Ibsen's Lively Art: A Performance Study of the Major Plays* (Cambridge University Press, 1989), p. 75.

5 Quoted in James W. McFarlane, ed., *The Oxford Ibsen*, 8 vols. (London, Oxford University Press, 1960–72), vol. 7, Introduction, p. 12.

6 McFarlane, Introduction, p. 13.

7 Henrik Ibsen, *A Doll's House and Other Plays*, tr. Peter Watts (Harmondsworth, Penguin, 1965), Act 3, p. 224. The translation in *The Oxford Ibsen*, ed. McFarlane, vol. 5, seems cumbersome and awkward in comparison. In his comparative survey of the English translations of the play, van Laan complains of McFarlane's 'clumsy and unlikely turns of phrase'. Cf. Thomas van Laan, 'English translations of *A Doll House*, in *Approaches*, ed. Shafer, p. 12.

8 The controversy over the translation of *Et dukkehjem*, whether it should be *A Doll's House* or *A Doll House*, seems to be mainly a question of British *versus* American usage. Cf. also Yvonne Shafer, Introduction, p. xiv.

9 Ronald Gray, *Ibsen: A Dissenting View* (Cambridge University Press, 1977), p. 57, quoted by Declan Kiberd, *Men and Feminism in Modern Literature* (London, Macmillan, 1985), p. 70.

10 Though seemingly unobtrusive, this recurring word carries with it strong supernatural, anti-positivist connotations, much more so than the modern English 'wonder'. Peter Watts 'miracle' is not inappropriate. Cf. van Laan, 'English translations', pp. 8, 14.

11 Johnston, '*A Doll's house*' p. 115, points out that the Norwegian word '*skyld*' means both. Compare the German '*Schuld*'.

12 Arthur Ganz, 'Miracle and vine leaves: An Ibsen play rewrought', *PMLA* 94 (1979), pp. 9–21, seems to miss the metaphysical dimension of the miracle, interpreting it as 'a noble act of self-abnegating sacrifice' (p. 19).

13 Johnston, '*A Doll House*', p. 114, notes the pagan flavour of the Norwegian '*jol*'. But despite the pagan origins of the holiday and the obvious lack of any reference to its religious significance, there is more to the use of Christmas as a constitutive element of the play than the prettiness of the yule-tree and the presents.

14 Quoted in Frederick and Lise-Lone Marker, 'The first Nora: Notes on the world première of *A Doll's House*', in Daniel Haakonsen, ed., *Contemporary Approaches to Ibsen* (Oslo, Universitetsforlaget, 1971), p. 88.

15 George Bernard Shaw, *The Quintessence of Ibsenism*, in James W. McFarlane, ed., *Henrik Ibsen*, Penguin Critical Anthologies (Harmondsworth, Penguin, n.d.), p. 129.

16 Cf. Gail Finney, *Women in Modern Drama: Freud, Feminism and European Theater at the Turn of the Century* (Ithaca, Cornell University Press, 1989), pp. 149–50.

17 *Hedda Gabler*, tr. Jens Arup, in *The Oxford Ibsen*, ed. McFarlane, vol. 7 (1966), Act 2, p. 21. All quotations from *Hedda Gabler* are from this translation. I have cross-checked problematic passages with Rolf Fjelde's translation (New York, New American Library, 1965), Una Ellis-Fermor's translations of *Three Plays* (Harmondsworth, Penguin, 1950), and Julius Elias and Paul Schlenter's translation in Henrik Ibsen, *Sämtliche Werke*, 5 vols. (Berlin, S. Fischer, n.d.), vol. 5.

18 George Lukács, 'The sociology of modern drama', tr. Lee Baxandall, in Eric Bentley, ed., *The Theory of the Modern Stage* (Harmondsworth, Penguin, 1968), p. 434.

## 8 *Preferring insecurity*

1 Chekhov's interest in 'transition' and 'transformation' has been recognized, for example, by Maurice Valency, *The Breaking String* (London, Oxford University Press, 1966), pp. 271 ff., and John Orr, *Tragic Drama and Modern Society* (Totowa, NJ, Barnes

& Noble, 1981), p. 78. But this transition is seen mainly in terms of the historical, pre-revolutionary context of the plays rather than in the dramatic terms of the plays themselves.

2 Marc Slonim, *From Chekhov to the Revolution* (New York, Oxford University Press, 1962), p. 76.

3 Ronald Hingley, ed. and tr., *The Oxford Chekhov*, 9 vols. (London, Oxford University Press, 1964–80), translates 'the troubles' (vol. 3 (1964), p. 171), but Constance Garnett, *The Plays of Anton Tchekov* (New York, Modern Library, n.d.), p. 88, is surely right in using the more decisive 'calamity'.

4 *The Oxford Chekhov*, ed. and tr. Hingley, vol. 2 (1967).

5 Cf. Stephen Kern, *The Culture of Time and Space: 1880–1918* (Cambridge, MA, Harvard University Press, 1983), p. 149, on Joyce and Proust, and on the perspectivism of Nietzsche and Ortega y Gasset.

6 On Chekhov's use of the *Hamlet* material see my '"The play is the thing" in *Amleto e nel Gabbiano*', in Ferrucio Marotti and Cesare Molinari, eds., *Biblioteca Teatrale* 13–15: *La Scena di Amleto* (Roma, Bulzoni, 1989), pp. 69–83; 'Chekhov's reading of *Hamlet*', *Reading Plays: Interpretation and Reception*, eds. Hanna Scolnicov and Peter Holland (Cambridge University Press, 1991), pp. 192–205, and bibliography there.

7 Cf., e.g., Valency, *Breaking String*, pp. 269–71.

8 *The Oxford Chekhov*, vol. 3 (1964), p. 173.

9 Appendix to *Cherry Orchard*, *The Oxford Chekhov*, vol. 3, p. 318.

10 Letter of 22 August 1903, *The Oxford Chekhov*, vol. 3, p. 319.

11 Leonid Andreyev, 'Chekhov as Panpsychologist', *Letters About the Theater – Letter Two* (1914), in *The Russian Symbolist Theater: An Anthology of Plays and Critical Texts*, ed. and tr. Michael Green (Ann Arbor, Ardis, 1986), p. 364.

12 Andreyev, 'Panpsychologist', p. 363.

13 Stefan Zweig, *The World of Yesterday* (*Die Welt von Gestern*), The Hallam Edition (London, Cassell, 1953), p. 193.

14 Cf. Laurence Senelick, 'Chekhov's drama, Maeterlinck, and the Russian Symbolists', in *Chekhov's Great Plays*, ed. Jean-Pierre Barricelli (New York University Press, 1981), pp. 174–5.

15 Andrei Bely, 'The Cherry Orchard', *Vesy* 1904, no. 2, in *The Russian Symbolist Theater*, ed. and tr. Green, p. 133.

16 Valency, *Breaking String*, p. 282.

17 Letter to Olga Knipper, 29 September 1903, in *The Oxford Chekhov*, vol. 3, p. 320.

18 *The Oxford Chekhov*, vol. 3, p. 84.

19 Ronald Hingley, *A New Life of Anton Chekhov* (London, Oxford University Press, 1976), p. 277.

20 Cf. p. 14, above.

### 9 Constructed rooms

1 Quoted by Martin Esslin, *The Peopled Wound* (Garden City, NY, Doubleday, 1970), p. 33.

2 Interview with Kenneth Tynan, in Esslin, ibid., p. 28.

3 See above, p. 7.

4 Interview with John Sherwood, in Esslin, *Peopled Wound*, p. 31.

5 Cf. Harold Pinter, *Complete Works: One* (New York, Grove Press, 1976), pp. 102, 108.

6 Cf. Guido Almansi and Simon Henderson, *Harold Pinter* (London, Methuen, 1983), pp. 60, 75.

7 Cf. 'A designer's approach: An interview with John Bury', in John Lahr and Anthea Lahr, eds., *A Casebook on Harold Pinter's* The Homecoming (London, Davis-Poynter, 1973), p. 27; Rolf Fjelde, 'Plotting Pinter's progress', in the same volume, p. 100.

8 Esslin, *Peopled Wound*, p. 142.

9 Arnold Hinchliffe, *Harold Pinter* (New York, St Martin's Press, 1967), p. 152, points out that 'This is the first family Pinter has put on the stage.'

10 Harold Pinter, *The Homecoming* (London, Methuen, 1965).

11 On this farcical scene, see above p. 38.

12 Christopher Hudgins, 'Intended audience response: *The Homecoming*', in *Harold Pinter: Critical Approaches*, ed. Steven H. Gale (London, Associated University Presses, 1986), p. 115, criticizes such a reading as 'a failure on the part of the audience to play the role Pinter dictates for it'.

13 Cf. chapter 7, p. 168, n. 1.

14 For an analysis of Ruth's conduct in terms of a territorial struggle, see Irving Wardle, 'The territorial struggle' (1951), in *Harold Pinter*, ed. Michael Scott (London, Macmillan, 1986), p. 170.

15 Bert O. States, 'Pinter's *Homecoming*: The shock of nonrecognition', in *Pinter: A Collection of Essays*, ed. Arthur Ganz (Englewood Cliffs, NJ, Prentice-Hall, 1972), p. 151.

16 Cf. Almansi and Henderson, *Harold Pinter*, p. 19.

17 Esslin, *Peopled Wound*, pp. 156–7.

18 Cf. Fjelde, 'Plotting Pinter's progress', pp. 105–6.

19 William Baker and Stephen Ely Tabachnick, *Harold Pinter* (Edinburgh, Oliver and Boyd, 1973), chapter 7. The slip on p. 111, '"Ruth" gives everything away, for "Ruth" is the name of King David's non-Jewish Moabite mistress', is symptomatic of a certain lack of critical rigour in this book's argumentation.

20 George E. Wellwarth, 'A revisionist approach', in *Harold Pinter: A Casebook*, ed. Lois Gordon (New York, Garland Publishing, 1990), p. 98.

21 Almansi and Henderson, *Harold Pinter*, p. 77.

22 *Complete Works: Two* (New York, Grove Press, 1977), p. 183.

23 Harold Pinter, *Old Times* (London, Methuen, 1971).

24 Cf. Tetsuo Kishi, '"They don't make them like that any more": Intertextuality in *Old Times*', in *Reading Plays*, eds. Scolnicov and Holland, pp. 227–35.

25 Cf. above, chapter 2, pp. 14 ff.

26 Quoted by Esslin, *Peopled Wound*, p. 187 n.

27 See Pinter's speech to the Seventh National Student Drama Festival in Bristol, *Sunday Times*, London, 4 March, 1962, quoted in Esslin, *Peopled Wound*, p. 38.

28 *Schwitters; Exhibition Catalogue* (London, Marlborough Fine Art Ltd., 1963). Cf. also *Kurt Schwitters: 1887–1948*, Sprengel Museum Hanover (Propyläen, 1986), pp. 248–61; and Ernst Nündel, *Schwitters* (Hamburg, Rowohlt Taschenbuch, 1981). I am indebted

to Elaine Shaffer, of the University of East Anglia, for drawing my attention to the work of Schwitters and Lissitzky.

29 Herbert Read, Introduction to Sophie Lissitzky-Küppers, *El Lissitzky: Life, Letters, Texts*, tr. Helene Aldwinckle (London, Thames and Hudson, 1968), p. 8.

30 Cf. Almansi and Henderson, *Harold Pinter*, pp. 14–15.

### 10 *Abstract spaces*

1 Martin Heidegger, 'Building dwelling thinking', in *Poetry, Language, Thought*, tr. Albert Hofstadter (New York, Harper & Row, 1971), p. 156.

2 Cf. Samuel Beckett, *Waiting for Godot* (London, Faber and Faber, 1965), pp. 14–15.

3 Cf. John Fuegi, 'The uncertainty principle and Pinter's modern drama', in *Critical Approaches*, ed. Gale, pp. 205–6.

4 Cf. Samuel Beckett, *Endgame* (New York, Grove Press, 1958), pp. 29–31.

5 Cf. Shari Benstock, 'The transformational grammar of gender', in *Women in Beckett*, ed. Linda Ben-Zvi (Urbana, University of Illinois Press, 1990), p. 183.

6 Samuel Beckett, *Not I* (London, Faber and Faber, 1973), no pagination.

7 Cf. Peter Gidal, 'Beckett and Sexuality', in *Women in Beckett*, ed. Ben-Zvi, p. 187.

8 Ann Wilson, '"Her lips moving": The castrated voice of *Not I*', in *Women in Beckett*, ed. Ben-Zvi, p. 195.

9 In Peter Handke, *Kaspar and Other Plays*, tr. Michael Roloff (New York, Farrar, Straus and Giroux, 1969).

10 Peter Handke, *Kaspar* (Frankfurt am Main, Suhrkampf Verlag, 1967).

11 Cf., for example, G.-A. Goldschmidt, *Peter Handke* (Paris, Éditions de Seuil, 1988), p. 36 and n.

12 Cf. June Schlueter, *The Plays and Novels of Peter Handke* (Pittsburgh, University of Pittsburgh Press, 1981), p. 47.

13 Christopher Innes, *Modern German Drama* (Cambridge University Press, 1979). pp. 244–5. Quoted in Schlueter, p. 49.

14 Nicholas Hern, *Peter Handke: Theatre and Anti-theatre* (London, Oswald Wolf, 1971), p. 63.

### Coda *The child's space*

1 Maureen Duffy, *Rites*, in *Plays by Women*, ed. Michelene Wandor, vol. 2 (London, Methuen, 1983), p. 27.

2 Pam Gems, Afterword to *Dusa, Fish, Stas and Vi*, in *Plays by Women*, ed. Wandor, vol. 1 (1982), p. 71.

3 Caryl Churchill, *Top Girls*, in *The Plays of the Seventies*, eds. Roger Cornish and Violet Ketels (London, Methuen, 1986), p. 553.

4 Charlotte Keatley, *My Mother Said I Never Should* (London, Methuen, 1989), p. 10.

# Index

Printed in the United States
35051LVS00003B/214

9 780521 616089